A GREEN VITRUVIUS

PRINCIPLES AND PRACTICE OF SUSTAINABLE ARCHITECTURAL DESIGN

Vivienne Brophy and J Owen Lewis

SECOND EDITION

earthscan

publishing for a sustainable future

London • Washington, DC

A Green Vitruvius – Principles and Practice of Sustainable Architectural Design

This edition was first published in 2011 by Earthscan

The first edition was published in 1999 by James & James (Science Publishers), and was prepared within the THERMIE programme of the European Commission Energy Directorate, in a project involving the UCD Energy Research Group, University College Dublin (Co-ordinators), the Architects' Council of Europe (ACE), Softech, Turin and the Finnish Association of Architects (SAFA), Helsinki.

This second edition was fully revised and extended by Vivienne Brophy, University College Dublin and J Owen Lewis (now with the Sustainable Energy Authority of Ireland), with assistance from Ray McNally, Rory Walsh and Donal Finn. Graphic design by Sinead Kenny

Earthscan Ltd, Dunstan House, 14a St Cross Street, London EC1N 8XA, UK
Earthscan LLC, 1616 P Street, NW, Washington, DC 20036, USA

Earthscan publishes in association with the International Institute for Environment and Development

For more information on Earthscan publications, see www.earthscan.co.uk or write to earthinfo@earthscan.co.uk

ISBN: 978-1-84971-311-5 hardback
      978-1-84971-191-3 paperback

Cover Image: GSW Headquarters, Berlin. Architect: Sauerbruch Hutton. Source: Christof Gessner.

A catalogue record for this book is available from the British Library

Library of Congress Cataloging-in-Publication Data
Brophy, Vivienne.
  A green vitruvius : principles and practice of sustainable architectural design / Vivienne Brophy and J. Owen Lewis.
      p. cm.
  Includes bibliographical references and index.
    ISBN 978-1-84971-311-5 (hb) -- ISBN 978-1-84971-191-3 (pb) 1. Architectural design--Technological innovations. 2. Architecture and society. 3. Buildings--Repair and reconstruction--Standards. I. Lewis, J. Owen. II. Title.
  NA2542.35.B78 2011
  720'.47--dc22
                                                    2011003267

Printed and bound in the UK
by Ashford Colour Press Ltd.
The paper used is FSC certified.

CONTENTS

THE GREEN BUILDING 1

    The Imperative to Green Design 1

    Architectural Quality, Quality of Service 2

SECTION 1: PROCESS 3

    Introduction 3

    Inception 5

    Design 11

    Tender 16

    Construction 17

    Operation 19

    Refurbishment 20

SECTION 2: ISSUES 21

    Introduction 21

    Comfort 22

    Health 32

    Environment 35

    Objectives 39

SECTION 3: STRATEGIES 43

    Introduction 43

    Urban and Neighbourhood 43

    Site Selection and Analysis 51

    Site Planning 53

    Building Form 58

    Building Envelope 61

    Finishes 73

    Services, Equipment and Controls 78

    Renovation 86

SECTION 4: ELEMENTS 91

    Components 91

    Materials 109

SECTION 5: EVALUATION 123

    Introduction 123

    Design Evaluation Tools 124

    Building Performance Simulation Tools 127

    Environmental Rating Systems 130

    Life Cycle Cost 136

REFERENCES 139

INDEX 143

FOREWORD

While climate change mitigation may be the main driver for demands from the European Union, national governments and even clients for radically higher standards of building performance, green design offers several other advantages. The continuing financial savings which energy-efficient design will achieve can be of real importance in daily life. Well-insulated and efficiently-ventilated buildings will provide more comfortable and more productive environments.

The other reason for architects to promote green design is that of architectural quality. Buildings with more natural and fewer artificial inputs are very often better. Daylit buildings are, in general, more enjoyable than artificially lit ones; natural ventilation, if clean air is available from a quiet external environment, is more acceptable than mechanical; the fewer heat emitters, the better; and so on. Mies van der Rohe said that 'Less is more'; these days, a better way of putting it may be, as Alexandros Tombazis says: 'Less is beautiful'. Classic design elegance is found in the complete, simple solution.

A Green Vitruvius is intended as a single-point general reference for architects wishing to design and realise sustainable buildings. This book offers advice in the areas of energy and water inputs, materials, indoor air quality and wastes. The rational use of energy in buildings involves maximising renewable energy inputs, while minimising fossil fuel inputs, as well as general energy conservation. Materials are discussed with regard to energy embodied, toxicity in use and optimising the use of renewable resources; however further research is needed on various environmental aspects of building, and this book remains a product of its time.

Originally published within a European Commission THERMIE programme project co-ordinated by the UCD Energy Research Group and with the collaboration of Softech, Suomen Arkkitehtiliitto for SAFA, and the Architects' Council of Europe (ACE), the work of the contributors to that edition (O Cofaigh et al, 1999) is warmly acknowledged: Eoin O Cofaigh, Eileen Fitzgerald, Ann McNicholl, Robert Alcock, J Owen Lewis, Vesa Peltonen, and Antonella Marucco.

The practising architect has competency in a myriad of areas: building planning, aesthetics, construction technology, programming, building regulations. It is not easy to reconcile conflicting demands of budget, programme, site and timescale; and to optimise a respect for context, spatial organisation, functionality of layout, soundness of construction, spatial and proportional quality, and inclusive design. No one aspect of the architectural solution can be perfected at the expense of all others. Green design is one of many considerations. We recognise the reality of information overload, and have concentrated not on the 'why', but on the 'how' of green design.

Green design is place-sensitive. One of its attractions in a globalising world is the potential to make place-specific architecture by responding to the clues of a specific climate and site, and, where possible, using sustainable local materials. Most, but not all the advice in this book will be of direct use to everyone. We have striven to balance the weight of advice relevant to practitioners across a variety of climatic conditions.

The information is organised in four independent parts. The reader may wish to seek particular advice at a given moment and not read from start to finish. The sections structure advice in accordance with the design and construction process, the issues to be considered in green design, the strategies to be adopted and the elements of green design. A fifth section advises on design evaluation. We have sought to minimise repetition at the cost of a greater number of cross-references.

2000 years ago the Roman architect Marcus Vitruvius Pollio wrote the ten books on architecture still referred to in every European architect's education. His work has been translated into many languages and has engendered many imitations, some by way of title such as *Vitruvius Britannicus* or *An American Vitruvius*, others by way of content such as LB Alberti's *De Architettura* or Palladio's *Quottro Libri*. The concept of the architectural pattern book offering design principles as well as solutions is universally familiar. This book is intended as a green pattern book for today.

The reference to green is not without its own resonance. To the Vitruvian triad of commodity, firmness and delight, with Eoin O Cofaigh we postulate the addition of a fourth ideal: restituitas or restitution, restoration, reinstatement: where the act of building enhances its immediate and the global environment in an ecological, as well as visual sense.

Vivienne Brophy and J Owen Lewis

THE GREEN BUILDING

THE IMPERATIVE TO GREEN DESIGN

In past centuries, the relative lack of resources to construct and maintain buildings meant energy-conservative and locally sourced inputs were the norm. From Imperial Rome until the nineteenth century only the wealthy could afford thermal baths or orangeries. Since the industrial revolution, but particularly in the past 100 years, the twin phenomena of more widely-diffused wealth and relatively cheaper energy have resulted in widespread increases in energy use. The cost of maintaining a high-efficiency artificial light source is one thousandth of that which a tallow candle represented 120 years ago. Such reductions in proportional cost, and greater affordability, apply not only to energy but to materials produced or transported using energy – which includes all building materials. As a result, the cost of building and running buildings has fallen many times over, and for some decades it appeared unnecessary to consider every design issue from an energy-cost viewpoint.

In 1973 the first oil crisis prompted governments to seek secure sources of energy and reduce dependency on imported fuel. As the decade wore on, such measures became less urgent. By 1979, the time of the second oil crisis, society had again forgotten about the need to conserve energy. But in the intervening decades it has become evident that reduction of dependency on oil is not the main imperative to green design. It is now impossible to ignore the global environmental crisis, whether this be the destruction of the ozone layer by chlorofluorcarbons, the loss of wildlife habitat and diversity through pollution, desertification and deforestation, or the threat of climate change associated with greenhouse gases including increasing levels of carbon dioxide caused by emissions from building heating and cooling, and other inputs. The architectural profession has been aware of this imperative for some years now: the 1993 'Chicago Declaration' by the Union Internationale des Architectes (UIA) is a clear statement of intent in this regard, as is much of the content of 'Europe and Architecture Tomorrow' published in 1995 by the Architects' Council of Europe.

Sustainable design integrates consideration of resource and energy efficiency, healthy buildings and materials, ecologically and socially sensitive land use and an aesthetic that inspires, affirms and enables (UIA, 1993).

All analyses indicate that to control greenhouse gas emissions efficiently and cost-effectively, there must be increased emphasis on environmental performance and energy efficiency in all buildings. A sustainability ethos in building will require the consideration of environmental implications associated with design, construction and operation of buildings and neighbourhoods; and greater emphasis on the improvement of existing buildings. Most buildings are used for several decades, and many survive for centuries. As the community's principal physical asset, getting good value requires that the building's full life cycle be considered, avoiding short-sighted attempts to merely minimise initial cost. A strategy on sustainable development will seek to prolong the life of existing structures, and indeed to prolong the utilisation of the materials with which they were originally constructed. Adaptation is usually preferable to new building, and upgrading of energy performance usually represents a more efficient deployment of resources. Technically, the aspiration that future new buildings will overall make net positive energy contributions (instead of requiring energy inputs) is entirely viable.

While radically reduced consumption of energy in use is still the most important factor in sustainability, strategies to substantially reduce environmental impact are also needed in other areas of building design, construction, and use. These include waste production, building materials and systems, and consumption of natural resources including vegetation, soil and particularly water.

THE IMPERATIVE TO GREEN DESIGN

ARCHITECTURAL QUALITY, QUALITY OF SERVICE

ARCHITECTURAL QUALITY, QUALITY OF SERVICE

There are many facets to architectural quality. The architectural profession promotes competition among architects on the basis of quality of architectural design and quality of service provided to the client. These two issues, building and service, are part of one process.

Quality of architecture at the scale of the fixture or fitting involves suitability for use, durability in performance, and visual delight. Suitability for use involves ergonomic considerations, especially for those who are not ablebodied or strong, and correct selection of materials, related to the functions they will support. Durability of performance involves proper length of life, taking all costs into account including the environmental. Delight derives from elegance, style and the contribution to the building's architecture made by even the smallest details.

At the scale of the building, too, quality of architecture involves suitability, firmness and durability, and delight. Suitability for use: rooms which are the correct size and scale for individual or group use; a place to sleep which is quiet, warm or cool as appropriate for the time of year, with fresh air and somewhere secure to rest; an office which is bright, practical, and which allows us to do good work; a suitable place for ritual or social interaction; a place which can adapt over time to changing functions and needs; and a place which is ecologically sound, with a healthy built environment. Durability in performance: buildings must be dry, economic in energy consumption and maintenance, last for a satisfactory life span, and function without defect. Delight: elegance of proportion, a joy in good craftsmanship, an awareness of the possibilities of colour, light and shade, form and outline, and cultural appropriateness and significance through respect for the past and for regional identity, and through belief in the cultural legitimacy of the present (ACE, 1995).

This book is about one aspect of architectural quality: green design.

Over and above design is the issue of quality of service to the client. Good management within the construction project of quality, cost and time is indispensable:

The promoter's interests are: procurement of the desired accommodation at the appropriate level of quality, within an agreed time scale and as rapidly as possible; for an agreed budget and as cheaply as possible; and, for commercial owners – developers – the highest rate of investment return, in a trouble-free design and construction process where the outcome is in line with requirements and predictions (ACE, 1995).

Not all clients may yet want the sort of service needed to achieve environmentally friendly architecture, however, ACE says that it is necessary for architects to ensure that all aspects of sustainability are taken into account in the development of the living environment (Kerstein, 2004).

Owner-occupiers are generally receptive to discussion of life cycle costing and are conscious of the benefits to the building user of environmentally aware design. However, clients building for immediate disposal may believe that low initial cost is the key issue, and the most such clients may want is to comply with regulations. It is difficult to make green architecture in the face of client indifference. For this reason a part of this book deals with management issues which touch on green design: the architect-client contract, initial and life cycle cost, working with consultants and construction contract administration.

Sustainable design methods offer the architect the opportunity to re-integrate design skills which have diverged in the past century with damaging consequences. In this regard, the synthesis which the architect can make from the varied inputs of colleagues, consultants and clients is invaluable. This provides the architectural profession with a challenge and an opportunity.

SECTION 1: PROCESS

INTRODUCTION

Every experienced architect is familiar with the different stages of their national design and construction process. As processes may vary from country to country, in this publication the structure adopted reflects ACE and European standardisation discussions.

INCEPTION
- Briefing
- Initial studies

DESIGN
- Concept
- Preliminary
- Developed
- Detailed

TENDER

CONSTRUCTION
- Supervision
- Commissioning

OPERATION
- Operational support
- Maintenance support

REFURBISHMENT

The management of this process is not the architect's exclusive responsibility. In varying measures, at all stages from pre-project, through the project and the detail design to construction and acceptance, the architect may be exclusively responsible, have shared responsibility, or merely play a partial role. However, there is always an architect-client contract, there is a project brief and the architect must work with specialist consultants, whether professional engineers or contractors with design responsibility. National building regulations are inescapable. No matter what the precise extent of the architect's responsibility on cost estimation, the definition of quality includes reasonable value for money.

The input of the architect and the other project team members – client, engineering, cost and other technical specialists, contractors and subcontractors – differs greatly from stage to stage. To significantly improve the performance of buildings, and particularly larger buildings, it is necessary to combine passive strategies, active systems and innovative technologies; this requires an integrated building design process in which multiple disciplines and design issues are brought together in a manner that permits synergistic benefits to be realized. A whole-of-system approach, considering interconnections between the building form, envelope components and their systems, will require project team members to integrate their roles and responsibilities and act collaboratively. The role of the architect is of considerable importance in the realisation of sustainable development. The architect, as usual leader of the design team, has a professional duty to incorporate sustainable strategies and to inform the client and design team of these issues. The opportunity to influence the environmental performance of the completed building varies with the stages: the potential for improvement is greatest at the initial stages, and as the project reaches building permit or building regulations approval is reduced and less cost-effective.

Any list of key issues will be arbitrary. We might have chosen three, or six, or twenty. The most important issues vary with climate, and hence with project location. Key issues also vary with building size and complexity, and with building use, and hence the demand for heating, cooling, ventilation or daylight. A summary list should be treated with caution. However, the design process balances many different issues, and somehow the architect must manage to deal intuitively with all those issues, especially at the early stages. So a table of key strategies at different stages is provided.

INCEPTION
Briefing
Initial studies

DESIGN
Concept
Preliminary
Developed
Detailed

TENDER

CONSTRUCTION
Supervision
Commissioning

OPERATION
Operational support
Maintenance support

REFURBISHMENT

TABLE 1.1 GREEN STRATEGIES AT DIFFERENT STAGES OF THE PROCESS

Stage	Issues
INCEPTION Briefing	• Identify green design as an issue to be considered • Agree environmental performance targets for the building • Favour brownfield over greenfield and locate beside existing settlement with proximity to transport and services if possible
INCEPTION Initial Studies	• Record site biodiversity and ecological quality • Analyse site for sunlight, shelter and available shading • Research building type and analyse good practice examples • Consider what is achievable within cost constraints
DESIGN Concept	• Locate buildings with reference to passive strategies, including solar and daylight access • Discuss passive heating, cooling and ventilation options • Consider thermal mass to dampen temperature fluctuations • Consider water supply and waste handling methods • Investigate locally available materials • Make iterative studies of design concepts to assess performance
DESIGN Preliminary	• Optimise proportion and distribution of external envelope openings with heating, cooling and daylighting in mind • Apply appropriate room heights for heating, cooling and daylighting design • Utilise appropriate thermal mass for building use and heating pattern: intermittent or continuous • Specify design criteria for services • Calculate predicted building energy performance and assess against targets
DESIGN Developed	• Finalise layout (plans, sections, elevations) for statutory approvals: implications for daylight/ventilation/passive and active systems • Select materials and construction methods having regard to thermal mass and life cycle issues • Undertake simulation to confirm performance of energy design strategies
DESIGN Detailed	• Detail for thermal performance, daylight, and controlled ventilation • Specify glazed and opaque elements for energy performance • Analyse life cycle performance of components, materials and finishes • Consider environmental performance in selection of heating and cooling systems and controls • Specify electrical lighting equipment and controls for lowest consumption • Specify sanitary fittings for low water consumption and waste disposal • Develop specifications for good workmanship and site management
TENDER	• Explain the requirements of green design to tendering contractors • Specify more demanding construction practices and tolerances • Include for construction performance testing and innovative system checking
CONSTRUCTION Supervision	• Protect and ensure no damage inflicted by site works on the natural landscape • Ensure acceptable methods of site waste separation, re-use and recycling • Ensure that contractor does not substitute materials or components without architect's approval • Check quality of workmanship – ensure integrity of insulation, minimal thermal bridging and air leakage
CONSTRUCTION Commissioning	• Undertake performance testing of building envelope • Ensure that components and systems meet performance specifications • Make sure client and users understand passive and active systems and controls • Provide operation and maintenance manuals
OPERATION Operational support	• Monitor building systems for actual as against projected performance • Undertake whole building environmental assessment • Undertake post occupancy user evaluation study
OPERATION Maintenance support	• Consider indoor air quality and healthy building environment • Use green finishes materials where these were originally applied • Use environmentally-acceptable cleaning and sanitation products
REFURBISHMENT	• Undertake energy audit prior to commencing refurbishment project • Survey the potential for upgrading of active services • Survey the potential for upgrading of envelope

INCEPTION

THE CLIENT-ARCHITECT RELATIONSHIP

The scope of services to be provided

In some Member States, the content of the client-architect contract is regulated by law, with the scope of the architect's appointment, fees to be charged and conditions of the architect's appointment prescribed by the State. Elsewhere, these matters are negotiated individually.

Fees for green design

Certain marketing advantages may accrue to providing what have often been seen as the 'special services' of green design at no extra cost to the client. Leaving this aside, there are conflicting viewpoints about the ethical acceptability of charging special fees for green design services. Many architects feel that professional duty indicates that they should undertake sustainable design work as part of their standard service. No building designed at this time which ignores environmental issues can be said to be good architecture.

On the other hand, extra work is inevitably involved in a service which results in improved environmental performance, reduced energy consumption and lower life-cycle financial cost. Many architects are of the view that such work merits compensation by way of an appropriate extra fee. While many materials and component suppliers provide sustainability-related information on their products as a matter of course, a good deal of time can be spent assessing environmental performance of materials. Also, contractors may need time-consuming reassurance about innovative aspects of the work, and much time may be needed for particularly thorough site inspections.

Table 1.2 GREEN TASKS WHICH MIGHT BE IDENTIFIED IN THE CLIENT-ARCHITECT CONTRACT	
Stage	**Tasks**
Initial studies	• Instigation of integrated interdisciplinary design process • Advice to client and team on sustainability issues (environmental and life cycle cost, goal setting for the project) • Interview consultants for competence in sustainability • Analysis of site microclimate and topographical modelling
Concept and preliminary design	• Calculation of environmental performance objectives for heating, cooling and lighting • Research sustainable systems, materials and components • Advice to consultants on environmental issues and holistic design • Study of alternative methods of complying with building regulations, particularly with regard to building envelope, heating, cooling and ventilation standards, water supply and consumption and waste treatment and disposal.
Developed design	• Simulation of building to assess heating, lighting and ventilation strategies • Study of room interiors to optimise comfort – thermal, visual and acoustical • Detail of building facades to optimise energy performance • Analysis of life cycle impact of components, materials and finishes
Tender	• Pre-qualification examination of contractors in relation to environmental performance requirements, testing and evaluation • Advice to contractors on site protection and waste disposal
Commissioning, operation and maintenance support	• Supervision and evaluation of performance testing of building envelope • Provision of client operational manuals with life cycle costing advice • Advice to client and users on use of passive and active environmental features in the building • Evaluation of monitored data • Post occupancy user evaluation
Refurbishment	• Comparative life cycle cost analyses of new build as against refurbishment costs • Environmental audit of existing buildings • Advice on upgrading building envelope and services

Finally, it is correct that particular expertise in any professional area, whether green design or any other, be appropriately rewarded.

Every architect will individually decide this, having regard to the individual circumstances of fee negotiation, personal and client commitment, degree of expertise available and so on. At the same time, it will never be possible to isolate fully time spent in sustainable design research and studies and recover all the extra cost involved. Where they have not done so already, national professional organisations should consider incorporating 'green design clauses' in their standard client-architect contracts.

CONSULTANTS

Scope of input

The choice of consultants is important, especially at the outset of the project. They should be competent, firstly to understand the issues involved and, secondly to give the architect the best advice. In a green design process the focus of specialist consultants will often be different. In the green building, consultants first optimise the use of passive environmental control measures, having regard to life cycle as well as initial cost. Only then should they advance active systems. By increasing the passive contribution, active systems can often be much smaller, and of a radically different nature, than those in a conventional building.

A second way in which the nature of some specialist inputs is different in green design is in precision of estimating. Conventional engineering, particularly in space heating, cooling or artificial lighting systems, works to constant pre-determined design standards. The primacy of passive measures means that some degree of tolerance, or lack of fixed conditions, is to be accepted. Studies show, moreover, that building users tolerate wider environmental variation when they themselves can influence the situation, for example by opening a window or turning on a light, and significant cost and energy savings can be achieved by even small shifts in design temperatures.

Appointing consultants

In selecting consultants, the architect should specify from the outset that sustainability is a fundamental consideration in the project, and identify the consultant's level of understanding in this regard. The goal of the design process is to integrate specialist areas to achieve optimum performance of the total building, not to achieve optimum performance of the separate parts; and performance is to be considered over the project life cycle, through design, use and decommissioning.

Consultants' fees are often calculated as a proportion of the cost of the specialist work. Where mechanical and electrical engineering services are concerned, this might for commercial reasons tend to increase the scope of heating, cooling, lighting and ventilation installations. The cost of the services installations is regularly as high as 30–35% of total project cost. It may be useful to agree a different fee basis, and calculate the fee as a proportion of the total cost. This has the advantage of allowing for advice even where there may be no conventional service installations. Daylighting studies, calculation of alternative heat losses and gains and of ventilation rates, and modelling of total building performance are all indispensable to environmentally aware design, and engineers are often better equipped than architects to carry out the numerical, as opposed to intuitive, studies, necessary in any moderately complex building. An added refinement to the total building percentage fee is to pay a fee premium inversely related to the energy costs during the 12 months after handover, measured on a $kWh/m^2/yr$ index. Alternatively, the fee can be calculated on an hourly basis, or be fixed. A fixed fee can act as an incentive to minimise the scope and complexity of specialist measures to be installed.

Early consultant appointment, site visits and multi-disciplinary project meetings can contribute enormously to project success.

Table 1.3 KEY AREAS FOR GREEN SPECIALIST ADVICE AND INPUT

Building structure	• Re-use of demolition spoil and use of as-found materials • Selection of sustainable structural systems • Life cycle analysis of components and materials • Long-life, loose fit design (good load bearing capacity, generous floor to ceiling heights) • Relationship between mass and thermal performance
Envelope design and construction	• Evaluation of relationship of openable area to lighting and thermal performance • Construction detailing for optimal performance • Sustainable materials and finishes and their impact on indoor air quality • Building envelope performance testing – thermal bridging and air permeability
Lighting services	Maximisation of available daylight use: • Daylighting studies including daylight factor analysis, daylighting simulations • Selection and location of lighting components: use of task lighting, choice of high efficiency fittings • Lighting management: controls to integrate natural and artificial light,
Electrical power	Minimisation of electricity consumption: • Isolation of electrical circuits at night-time, optimised cable sizing • Specification of low-energy lifts • Consideration of combined heat and power systems to maximise total energy efficiency • Evaluation of electrical energy consumption
Heating engineering	Maximisation of passive heating techniques: • Building planning and façade design to maximise useful solar gain • Evaluation of passive solar gains and assessment of overheating potential • Comparative U-value calculations to ensure optimised thermal performance • Modelling of heat flows through the building in different temperature situations at different times of the year • Maximum efficiency of active heating measures: • Selection of heating method and fuel • Selection of high efficiency heat emitters, plant size optimisation • Optimisation of controls including Building Energy Management Systems (BEMS) • Input on life cycle costing calculations
Cooling engineering	Maximisation of passive cooling techniques: • Thermal mass and ventilation to promote passive cooling • Modelling of temperature changes to predict internal in relation to ambient temperatures • Façade and shading system design and modelling of shading and daylight/solar gain • Design of active systems to minimise energy consumption
Water services	Minimisation of water consumption: • Selection of components for water conservation and the re-use of grey water • Design of self-contained waste treatment systems • Design of landscape to minimise surface water run-off
Ventilation	• Energy efficient passive and active ventilation systems • Building modelling to evaluate and optimise ventilation
Cost estimating	• Comparative life cycle cost studies, for individual components and alternative systems, to incorporate initial cost, cost in use, cost of demolition and re-use including recycling • Environmental cost accounting
Landscaping	• Assessment of ecological issues • Soft landscaping for life cycle winter solar access (height of vegetation, shading, light reflection, sunlight penetration) and shelter (prevailing wind directions and intensity, modelling of earth berms) • Passive cooling techniques for urban areas • Indigenous vegetation: conservation and propagation • Waste treatment plants e.g. reed beds

Briefing Stage: Scope of architect's services

- *To develop the brief for the project, with and on behalf of the client, and with the involvement of the design team members and specialist consultants. This task involves research of the client's requirements with regard to project quality, timescale and cost.*

- *The brief includes all information and requirements produced through dialogue between the client and the design team, on the site; schedules of accommodation; room and building functional, environmental and spatial performance; project cost and timescale; post-construction testing; post-handover evaluation and maintenance; and the budget.*

BRIEFING STAGE

Work at the briefing stage is very important in sensitising client and consultants to green design issues.

The process of assembling a brief with the client is mutually informative. Briefs change as the client's intentions for building size, performance, cost and project timescale emerge. With sustainable design, unless the client is better informed than the architect, the architect must advise on the potential of good design to improve environmental performance. So, the process of constructing the brief becomes one of sharing information in the light of the potential for a sustainable building. Explanation of a long-life, loose-fit, low-energy strategy at this stage will help the client come to terms with much of what is involved.

There may be a choice of site available. Input regarding sustainability issues can help determine site choice. See advice on greenfield as against brownfield sites, access to public transport, solar access, overshadowing, shelter, and quality of land.

Where the client is not an expert in green issues, it is necessary to discuss the appointment of design team members with appropriate experience or specialist consultants; and also the extent to which the client may accept or welcome alternative performance criteria for the sake of a better building. These would include, for example, a variable internal environment and higher initial costs.

Initial and life cycle cost

A major issue with which green design must engage is that of initial as against life-cycle building cost. The construction cost of good design is often no greater than that for poor design. On the other hand it is true that increased spending on higher quality components is often worthwhile. Thicker insulation materials, high performance glazing, passive infrared detector lighting switches, weather compensating controls on heating systems and photoelectric cell controls on artificial lighting are more expensive initially than conventional components. However, in many cases these cost differentials are falling, and higher initial costs can be recouped quite quickly by savings in operational costs.

For the owner-occupier, the decision is easier than for, for example, the tenant undertaking a fit-out; but until external environmental costs are in some way factored into direct costs, the decision may still be difficult. Many building owners intending to sell or lease will find a four-year payback time acceptable as this can be factored into a sale or letting price without total loss. Depending on the length of lease, tenants may find payback times of up to 10 years worthy of consideration. Far-sighted owner occupiers may consider payback times of up to 25 years. The public benefits of good design can endure for centuries, as the historic centres of so many European cities attest.

Table 1.4 ISSUES AT BRIEFING STAGE

General	• Identify green design as an issue for consideration • Discuss capital against life cycle costs
Consultants	• Advise on appointment of design team. If client is appointing, do they have 'green' expertise? Do they need to be supplemented by specialist consultants e.g. daylighting or energy consultants? • Recommend bringing consultants on board at an early stage and discuss payment for services • Ensure that the scope of appointments includes the requisite environmental advice
Heating	• Explain the possibility of passive measures, their contribution to performance and implications of their use: e.g. there may be fluctuations in temperature • Explain the need for site microclimatic data • Identify a use profile of the building, occupant numbers and activities at different times of the day and week • Assess if the client or building occupants will be actively involved in the management of passive environmental control systems on a day-to-day basis; e.g. opening and closing windows and shutters • Assess how the client feels about sunspaces, draught lobbies and about zoning the plan • Assess if the client is prepared to pay for and use programmable controls, passive infra-red switching or active systems • Assess if the client will consider a CHP installation, district heating
Cooling	• Discuss client acceptance of passive cooling measures if these are judged useful • Clarify acceptance of temperatures above comfort levels, say, five days per year? Or never? • Identify the precision of environmental control required by client
Lighting	• Discuss daylight maximisation as a desirable goal • Assess if client prepared to pay for and use programmable controls, passive infra-red switching or active systems
Ventilation	• Discuss occupant operation of manually operated ventilation • Discuss feasibility of passive stack ventilation • Assess requirement for mechanically assisted ventilation • Identify the possibilities of waste heat recovery
Water	• Assess if the client will consider water-saving sanitary fittings – cisterns, controls and taps • Discuss the levels of water re-use possible – 'green', 'grey', and 'black' water • Discuss disposing of surface water run-off on site, and advise on the need for treating run-off from car parks
Waste	• Discuss the issue of construction waste – sorting, reuse, recycle • Discuss the provision of space for composting of domestic refuse • What provision might be made for recycling? Extra storage space needed?
Site Works	• Discuss the ecology of the site and the necessity for an assessment to identify existing vegetation to be conserved and discuss how this might affect the design • Discuss the provision of sheltered and secure bicycle storage on site.
Materials	• Discuss life cycle assessment of materials and how this may impact on selection • Discuss the selection of finishes, especially internal wall and floor finishes, which will impact indoor air quality • Discuss external envelope finishes, especially window and glazing, in connection with improved thermal performance and maintenance requirements • Discuss the requirement to assess quality of construction
Cost	• Assess the extent to which the client is concerned with life-cycle issues - investigate the client's intention for the building: short or long-term investment • Explain life cycle costing and try to obtain agreement that a measure of life-cycle costing may be factored into all design and specification decisions
Timescale	• Assess if client is aware that sufficient time will be required by the design team to evaluate design strategies, simulate performance, assess materials and components, specify innovative components and systems etc
Contractor	• Discuss importance of the selection of an experienced contractor and how green design will impact on the construction process

Analysis, studies and consultations of budgetary, administrative, town planning and technical character, so as to assimilate the legal, financial and technical constraints necessary for the setting up of the project based on the client's brief.

The documents and services to be provided include:

- *research and analysis*
- *planning studies*
- *examination of the site to take account of the chosen approach*
- *analysis of administrative constraints*
- *feasibility of the brief on the site.*

INITIAL STUDIES

Early studies explore the broad alternative design possibilities for the project, having investigated planning and other regulatory constraints (such as regulations on pollution, construction, noise, waste), and weigh-up cost and time considerations. Site surveys should be to hand, to include not only topographical information but also information about site environmental quality and potential. All the design team should be involved in this work.

Where planning constraints on site density, waste treatment, or car parking seem likely to adversely affect the design, identify these issues and raise them with the Planning Authority.

Depending on the nature of the project, preliminary studies may involve alternative site development strategies, in which case issues of insolation, overshadowing of buildings and of adjoining sites and shelter come into play. At a larger scale, or where a refurbishment or extension project is concerned, alternative dispositions of layout may allow varying scope for future energy-conscious design: organising the plan to place rooms requiring heat on south-facing facades and so on. In either case the issues raised will need to be evaluated in greater detail at the later stages.

The Initial Studies will generally be accompanied by a report. It may be useful to incorporate a section to specifically identify green issues. Headings which may be useful would include: site selection, including land quality, access to transport and local services; site analysis, including overshadowing, solar access, shelter and potential for other renewable energy.

Table 1.5 ISSUES AT INITIAL STUDIES STAGE	
Site selection and analysis	• Examine a number of alternative sites if this option is available and favour brownfield sites over greenfield, with existing transport and services
	• Obtain environmental information about the site and evaluate possible passive strategies to optimise building performance
	• Evaluate existing buildings and examine potential for their reuse
	• Record the ecology of the site and assess the impact which alternative building forms may have
	• Evaluate the site for renewable energy potential
	• Incorporate green issues into the feasibility studies reports

DESIGN

CONCEPT DESIGN STAGE

Decisions at this early stage in the design are of the utmost importance, when the project first acquires a provisional direction. Alternative floor plans are explored; there is a site planning and/or a building organisation strategy and a concept for the sections through the building and materials are given some thought - although it is quite likely that none of these matters are yet fixed. Costs are broadly computed.

To achieve holistic design quality, the architect makes decisions based on informed intuition, which synthesise experience, training and imagination and are based on an interdisciplinary input from design team members and external consultants. Intuition, of course, is subsequently explored and tested and evaluated rigorously.

Concept Design Stage: Scope of architect's services

Initiation and graphic presentation of alternative architectural solutions, enabling the client to understand the possible solutions and take decisions about their further development, involving:

- *developing the initial concept and proposing one or several general solutions for the overall forms translating the main elements of the brief;*

- *defining the general technical solutions envisaged;*

- *indicating the approximate timetable for carrying out the proposals;*

- *examining the compatibility of the proposals with the overall provisional budget;*

- *solutions which will facilitate subsequent proposals for adaptation of the programme and preparation of complementary technical studies.*

The documents and services to be provided include:

- *an analysis of the brief;*

- *a summary of the thinking behind the proposed solutions;*

- *models and drawings to show a preliminary architectural solution in sketch form.*

Table 1.6 ISSUES AT CONCEPT DESIGN STAGE	
Site planning	Protection and use of pre-existing site characteristics: • Orientate the building to optimise defined heating or cooling load – optimise insolation, south facing slope; cooling load – optimise ventilation and daylight, solar shading • Shelter the building to reduce heat loss through infiltration and radiation • Protect and design landscape for screening and absorbing noise and pollution • Minimise hard landscaping for water run-off and conservation of vegetation
Building form	• Consider the benefit of compact form to reduce heat loss • Provide for floor height and depth to optimise daylight, to enable passive ventilation and appropriate solar access. • Consider providing daylight through roof glazing and atria
Building envelope	• Evaluate broad proportions of fenestration, with effects on daylighting, ventilation and solar ingress while mindful of overheating possibilities on east, west and south facades
Materials	• Assess environmental impact of structural system and external envelope

To develop the general form of the project, in plan, section and elevation, based on the preferred solution and derived from the chosen design approach, involving:

- *defining the general composition on plan;*

- *confirming the compatibility of the chosen solution with the requirements of brief and site, and with the various regulations applicable;*

- *examining the functional relationships between the different elements of the brief and the spaces provided;*

- *defining the passive and active environmental strategies*

- *establishing the building's appearance, its broad dimensions and the types of materials, which, when taken together, facilitate a summary estimate of construction cost.*

- *consultations with Public Authorities;*

- *co-ordinating the work of any technical specialists.*

The documents and services to be provided include:

- *a report explaining the general concept;*

- *floor plans at 1:100 [1:200 for large projects] with significant details at 1:50;*

- *elevations and sections at 1:100 [1:200 for large projects];*

- *site and landscaping plans at 1:200 [1:500 for large projects];*

- *description of types of materials;*

- *summary of environmental evaluation studies;*

- *general timetable for the execution of the project;*

- *summary estimate of provisional costs;*

- *explanation of the technical principles applied;*

- *consultation with administrative authorities and technical consultants.*

PRELIMINARY DESIGN STAGE

At preliminary design stage the provisional direction previously sketched is amended and developed through models, plans, sections and elevations. Earlier decisions are confirmed or modified. The building acquires a definitive form, layout, type of construction and method of servicing. Materials are proposed. The initial investigations of comfort and environment should now be confirmed by simplified evaluation tools and numerical studies. Following approvals from administrative authorities, it becomes increasingly difficult to make major changes.

Table 1.7 ISSUES AT PRELIMINARY DESIGN STAGE

Site planning and external landscaping	• Consider layout and orientation of building groups in relation to insolation and overshadowing • Consider size and location of hard surfaces, in relation to desired sunlight and shelter • Use earth berms and shelter planting to create protected and sheltered areas
Building form	• Form and layout should optimise appropriate solar collection and daylight use • Shallow plans optimise daylight and natural ventilation strategies and reduce the amount of energy required, particularly in commercial buildings • Form and layout should minimise heat loss • Reduce surface to volume ratio • Locate rooms according to heating, cooling, daylight and natural ventilation use • Passive solar spaces should face within 15° of due south • Create buffer spaces by locating cool rooms on northern and exposed facades, and unheated conservatories on the south • Use thermal mass to absorb and store thermal energy • Use simplified tools to assess options
Building envelope	• Consider proportions of glazing for daylight distribution and passive heating and cooling appropriate to each façade • Consider glazing ratios and balance with overall U-values, balance thermal and daylighting requirements • Control glare and overheating, particularly on east and west facades, and consider shading devices • Insulate as far as practicable and cost effective, provide night insulation • Detail for complete insulation with minimal thermal bridging and air infiltration • Evaluate thermal performance
Materials	• Consider use of structural thermal inertia to dampen internal temperature fluctuations • Evaluate environmental impact of materials – embodied energy, impact on habitats, toxic emissions and ease of recycling or re-use
Consultants	• Include design team and specialist consultants in early design decisions • Review environmental principles, indicate how environmental strategies will be developed at detailed design stage and how proposals will be evaluated
Systems	• Provide outline illustration of environmental performance particularly through plan and section diagrams for passive and active energy flows: heating season – day and night; cooling season – day and night and energy flow • Consider energy efficient and innovative heating, cooling and lighting systems
Cost	• Consider factoring environmental and life cycle cost in initial estimates • Include for tight specification of building envelope, components and systems to deliver better performance, improved environmental quality, and/or lower life cycle energy and environmental cost
Administrative authorities	• Consult about innovative propositions for fresh water supply, rainwater disposal or reuse, grey and black water disposal • Discuss advantageous tariffs for low consumption with utilities • If the building generates electricity (photovoltaic, wind) discuss buy-back with the utility as necessary

Developed Design Stage: Scope of architect's services

To obtain legal authorisation for construction and, to this end, to undertake whatever detailed design is necessary, with the integration of the work of specialist consultants where required. Beyond this stage, as changes may involve repeated consultations with statutory authorities, relatively little revision will be possible to the form and many of the technical specifications. The project takes account of all applicable regulations and integrates the technical and architectural factors needed to relate the building to the site.

The documents and services to be provided include:

- *a descriptive report on the general characteristics of the project;*
- *plans of all floor levels, sections and elevations at scale 1:50 [1:100 for major projects];*
- *a preliminary energy and environmental audit;*
- *an updating of the programme;*
- *a summary estimate of costs of the works, detailed by construction element;*
- *procedural documents such as construction permits.*

DEVELOPED DESIGN STAGE

Applications for building permit require definitive presentation of the design.

Glazing proportions will need to be analysed, using sketch design evaluation tools such as the LT Method (refer EVALUATION).

For Building Regulations approval the principal green design issues will be calculations for energy performance, including sometimes, embodied energy and material analysis. Some countries accept commercial energy calculation methods. Elsewhere, prescribed calculation methods will have to be followed.

When developing the structural design consider low energy and long life issues; e.g. greater cover to reinforcement, protection of structural steel. Long life design is particularly important for pre-stressed concrete, which is difficult to demolish for recycling or re-use using present technology.

The building's adaptability to future, unpredictable uses involves both structure and services. A load-bearing capacity greater than indicated in the engineering codes applicable to the function being accommodated might be useful. For example, it might be that the floor-loading capacity and hence the structural system employed for a residential building would differ from that required in an office (higher load-bearing capacity, larger spans) and the design should consider such flexibility of function. The loose functional fit afforded by a framed structure may make such a system preferable to one of load-bearing walls. Design for changed future services, flexibility and renewal. The services consultant prepares information on the building services systems. Building energy performance is often calculated by the architect, or in more complex buildings the services consultant. Calculation criteria and outputs should be made in accordance with national or regional requirements, the most widely used being kWh/m2/yr.

Results can be compared to normalised performance indicators for that building type in the given climate, providing a good projection of building performance and an indication of relative achievement. An early check on the environmental impacts of the building will also be undertaken at this stage.

Table 1.8 ISSUES AT DEVELOPED DESIGN STAGE

Site planning	• Confirm earlier decisions on site: building siting and positioning for insolation, daylight and shelter; form for over-shadowing; layout and extent of hard and soft landscaping • Consider disposal of surface water within the site • Consider treatment of polluted water from vehicle hard standings • Consider harvesting renewable energy on site
Building form	• Confirm floor to ceiling heights to maximise daylight and natural ventilation and avoid overheating • Confirm façade proportions, and provision and design of external shading if necessary • Consider passive ventilation strategies and window design • Confirm previous decisions on selection of sustainable materials
Consultants	• Consider long life and loose fit building structure and the adaptability of structure and services for different building use • Review long-term adequacy of load-bearing capacity • Ensure accessibility to ductwork, pipes and wires, with removable covers, demountable trunking • Size conduit drops in walls for ease of change
Systems	• Develop design of building services systems from the principles previously enunciated • Calculate building energy performance and check environmental impact

DETAILED DESIGN STAGE

Detail design, particularly of the external envelope; technical specification of building components and workmanship; and coordination of the engineering consultants, particularly mechanical and electrical services but also structural, have considerable implications for green design at this stage.

Detail the external envelope for best performance. (The most sustainable material for glazing frames is softwood timber; however, in a long-life building, thermally broken composite frames may also be an appropriate choice.)

Select roof and floor finishes for long life: the proportional extra cost of better sheet materials is more than offset by longer service life.

When designing mechanical services in detail, specify components for good energy performance over a long life, and simulate design performance.

Specify sanitary fittings to minimise water consumption in use.

Mechanical ventilation systems increasingly include heat recovery. In residential buildings, proprietary components achieve 80–90% heat recovery. These require ducts of typically 100 mm diameter to and from living and circulation spaces to a central collection point, frequently in the roof space, from where air is drawn in or expelled to the outside.

Passive infra-red light switching and compact fluorescent lighting devices and increasingly LEDs are cost-effective with short payback periods. Use task lighting where possible and design for lower ambient lighting levels.

Locally produced masonry: clay bricks, concrete blocks, and tiles reduce the environmental impact of transporting heavy materials. (refer ELEMENTS; Materials)

Detailed Design Stage: Scope of the architect's services

To develop the design and construction details for the project including:

- *Detailing the external building envelope for best performance;*
- *Evaluating all components and materials;*
- *Preparing technical specification of building components, materials and workmanship;*
- *Co-ordinating the design team input to detailed design;*
- *Reviewing mechanical systems, electrical components and sanitary fittings.*

Table 1.9 ISSUES AT DETAILED DESIGN STAGE	
Site planning	• Specify rainwater soak-aways • Locate and design alternative wastewater treatment systems
Building envelope	• Select high performance building components and materials, especially frames and glazing • Specify innovative, efficient passive ventilation components with heat recovery • Insulate beyond building regulation requirements if cost effective • Detail to avoid thermal bridging and air infiltration
Materials	• Specify for long life, low embodied energy and a healty indoor environment • Source materials, and particularly heavy components, locally • Monitor consultants to ensure strategy agreed at earlier stages is implemented
Systems	• Specify mechanical services components for good energy performance over long life: gas-fired condensing boilers, best available thermostatic radiator valves, weather compensating heating system controls, underfloor low pressure hot water central heating, mechanical ventilation systems to include heat recovery components, low energy lift installations, passive infrared light switching and compact fluorescent lighting, dual flushing WC cisterns, photoelectric cell operated urinals and washbasins, energy and resource efficient domestic appliances • Minimise inefficiencies in systems

TENDER

Green design requirements should be made explicit in all tender documents. If the architect requires sustainable performance, this should be made clear because of the need for properly competitive bids and to ensure that the requirements are fully taken into account by the tenderers.

It is important to undertake a preliminary selection process in which the main contracter is required to provide evidence of previous experience in delivering sustainable building projects. It is essential that the requirement for more demanding construction practices and testing procedures for building and system performance is evident and that it is understood that the specification of components and materials must be followed.

This is of particular importance where a main contractor is providing a package deal: objective performance criteria for selection of components and design of systems should be provided. Such instructions would include:

- structural system: long service life, high load-bearing capacity, low embodied energy and sustainable materials where possible;
- completion elements: window and door glazing and frame types;
- finishes: floor and wall finishes for long service life, to be specified;
- wall, floor and ceiling materials within minimal toxic out-gassing.

Apart from design elements to be priced by contractors on a design-and-build or package-deal basis, the conventional site arrangements can be influenced by sustainable design. Limiting working space is important in conserving pre-existing vegetation. Specification clauses requiring contractors to protect and subsequently avoid all such areas, with drawings indicating the relevant areas, can improve levels of site protection. Clauses requiring the retention and reuse on site of all topsoil will conserve this resource.

Some sub-contractors, particularly specialist mechanical, ventilation and sanitary engineering contractors, will be required to provide detailed design services as part of their works. Particular components should be specified by type or name where necessary. These would include:

- mechanical services: energy-efficient heating systems, emitters, and controls;
- electrical services: energy-efficient switching, light fittings and controls;
- sanitary engineering: water-saving fittings and equipment.

These issues should be considered in addition to normal good construction practice.

Table 1.10	ISSUES AT TENDER STAGE
Site planning	• Agree contractors' vehicle access routes and working space to protect pre-existing natural features and vegetation • Specify to conserve ecology and re-use top soil • Provide directives on the use of as-found material; on construction waste minimisation, handling and disposal; and on the use of environmentally-friendly cleaning materials. • Give directions on materials handling and storage to minimise material spoil
Contractors	• Make green design requirements explicit in all tender documents, especially in specialist packages for design and construct works • Review contractor's experience with green design projects • Outline the requirement for more demanding construction practices and testing building and system performance procedures • Ensure that specification of components and materials is adhered to and state that no substitution is acceptable unless provided in tender documents

CONSTRUCTION

SUPERVISION

On site, the main contractor deals with his or her own employees, and with a host of specialists. Many issues come into play: construction quality, adherence to tight programmes, and efficient control of labour and material costs, having regard to site safety and unpredictable weather.

Environmentally-conscious construction management and the correct execution of certain items of work can considerably improve building performance. Measured studies of buildings constructed to an identical design show significant variations in energy consumption which, while partly attributable to different building users, also arise from the standard of construction. The main areas of concern in the external envelope include:

- quality of external envelope construction to minimise heat loss;
- correct installation of insulation, to achieve completeness and minimize thermal bridging;
- sealing of opes, opening elements and around pipes;
- correct installation of vapour control membranes to reduce infiltration and avoid interstitial condensation.

Building envelope performance testing will be undertaken by the contractor or specialist when the building is practically complete and would consist of, at least, an air permeability test and thermographic survey. Remedial measures will have to be undertaken if stated requirements are not met.

The architect checks that the specified components and materials are provided. Substitution by the contractor of less acceptable components may lead to a poorer performance of glazed units, insulation, or paint. For such materials, as well as for mechanical and electrical components, check delivery invoices when in doubt.

The architect also ensures that instructions on respecting and protecting existing landscape or other site features are followed.

Toxic waste, including asbestos insulation, and asbestos-cement sheeting, should be disposed of off-site in an approved waste storage facility.

Construction Stage: Scope of architect's services

At construction stage, the architect checks general conformity with the designs of the works being executed. Any instructions needed for the contractors to coordinate and correctly execute the works are provided.

The documents and services to be provided include:

- *preparation of contract documents, including the contract, drawings, specifications and any guarantees;*
- *programming separate contractors where applicable;*
- *monitoring the construction work in accordance with the project timetable, applicable rules and standards, and the contract documents, with regard to building dimensions, quality, standards and appearance;*
- *issuing instructions for executing the works;*
- *arranging and recording of site and progress meetings;*
- *reviewing building envelope performance tests;*
- *making periodic valuations of the works.*

Table 1.11 ISSUES AT SUPERVISION STAGE	
Check proper site procedure	• Gathering and storage on site of topsoil for subsequent re-use • Adequate protection of existing landscape, water, vegetation and other site features • Correct handling and storage of materials • Use of any as-found elements such as hardcore or earth • Storage and system for recycling of component and material packaging • Correct disposal of toxic waste • Use of environmentally-friendly cleaning agents
Check construction standards	• Correct specification of components and materials on site • Correct health and safety procedures in place e.g. cutting, spraying • Quality of external envelope construction • Weather-tightness of opening elements • Sealing of openings around pipes penetrating the external envelope. • Correct installation of insulation to ensure completeness and minimise thermal bridging • Correct installation of vapour control membranes to reduce infiltration and avoid interstitial condensation • Procedures for testing building envelope performance

The contractor should undertake straightforward housekeeping measures to minimise construction waste, and store materials packaging for recycling. Correct handling and storage of materials will reduce waste.

COMMISSIONING

Prior to acceptance of the building for the client, the architect inspects the building for final completion in accordance with the drawings and specifications. Hand-over can involve provision of as-constructed drawings and specifications, performance test reports, advice on system and component operation, maintenance and repair, guidance on performance of services installations, and a Safety File with advice on safe maintenance and repair.

Whether the design features are passive or active, the client will best optimise building performance by having the working of the building thoroughly explained and illustrated. Advice on environmentally-conscious maintenance of the building will also be valuable.

Table 1.12 COMMISSIONING: ADVICE ON BUILDING OPERATION AND MAINTENANCE	
Correct building maintenance	• Maintain and renew floor and wall finishes selected for health and environmental performance • Provide for regular cleaning of windows, luminaires, light shelves and shading systems • Maintain sanitary components to minimise water consumption. • Maintain internal and external planting • Use sustainable, non-toxic, biodegradable cleaning agents • Apply paint and thin film coatings in properly ventilated spaces • Undertake annual inspection of active systems to check continued efficiency of boilers, cooling equipment, radiator valves, infrared switching, heating and cooling controls
Operating energy management systems	Provide guidance manuals for client and building occupants so that they understand passive and active user systems' operation to: • maximise the use of daylight and minimise use of artificial lighting • prevent overheating in summer: moveable shading, night-time cooling • optimise ventilation system, both passive and mechanically assisted: natural ventilation user input, fans, optimise balance of ventilation, heating and cooling demand • maximise heat gain in the heating season: control of night-time ventilation, operate blinds to maximise insolation, close internal doors to retain captured heat, open shutters to promote desired ventilation • optimise mechanical system controls such as programme time clocks, operate weather compensating controls, set thermostatic radiator valves, seasonal manipulation of flow temperature in heating system. • Operate electrical installations: correct replacement of light fittings, discuss switching on lighting and power, lighting sensors, power zoning. • Avoid peak electricity costs

OPERATION

OPERATIONAL AND MAINTENANCE SUPPORT

After commissioning and practical completion, an evaluation of the performance of the completed building and the quality of the indoor environment is desirable. The extent of such evaluation will obviously vary with the targets set for the building, the expectations of the client, the complexity of the building and the available budget.

Energy consumption data can be collected by reference to utility bills over a full heating and cooling year, which can be compared with best practice data locally available.

Monitoring of spaces with simple data loggers can detail comfort conditions, and a Building Management System can provide fuller performance information in complex buildings.

Environmental assessment may be undertaken by the use of an assessment methodology, such as BREEAM or LEED (refer EVALUATION).

It is important to assess the quality of the indoor environment and the satisfaction of building occupants in relation to thermal, visual and acoustical comfort, particularly in working environments; post-occupancy evaluation methods are well established.

This can also provide useful information for the design team in their review of the achievement of the brief requirements, and should inform future designs.

Operation and Maintenance: Scope of architect's services

It is desirable that a performance evaluation of the completed building is undertaken and a maintenance programme to ensure long term environmental quality is developed including:

- *Monitoring building systems for actual performance;*
- *Undertaking whole building environmental assessment;*
- *Undertaking post occupancy user evaluation study;*
- *Providing a maintenance schedule for systems to optimise performance;*
- *Providing guidance on maintenance of finishes.*

Table 1.13   OPERATION: EVALUATION OF ENVIRONMENTAL PERFORMANCE AND USER COMFORT

- Be aware that a two year drying out period may be necessary, depending on climatic conditions and building construction, before defects can be assessed. Check for air infiltration as a result of drying out and shrinkage leading to poor air tightness

- It is also essential that a period for adjusting active systems is provided to match system operation to user requirements

- Investigate energy consumption through an entire heating and cooling season, by reference to utilities' invoices for electricity, gas, other. These can be totalled over a year and consumption in kWh/m^2 readily derived. This can be compared with reference figures for an assessment of the overall performance of the building

- Monitor space comfort by simple data loggers linked to a computerised data collection system, to establish the effectiveness of heating or cooling installations and help determine whether active installations are over or under utilised.

- Undertake post occupancy user surveys to assess user satisfaction in relation to thermal, visual and acoustic comfort. Questionnaires can be helpful in this regard.

- Check water consumption, by monthly and yearly meter readings and calculate daily consumption in litres per head calculated from the number of building users. Data may be checked by reference to established benchmarks to establish the level of performance

- Assess waste production and review waste management procedures

- Evaluate the building's total environmental impact with an appropriate building environmental assessment methodology; e.g. BREEAM, LEED, GBTool etc, undertaken by trained assessor

REFURBISHMENT

Refurbishment Stage: Scope of architect's services

The scope of refurbishment projects can vary from redecoration to part-renewal of primary structure with the attendant alterations and renewals. Services equipment for heating, lighting, ventilation and cooling become more efficient, and external envelope elements such as windows, doors, shading devices and opaque elements have potential for improved performance. The following table provides a list of works which might be usefully addressed in projects of significant scope.

In general, it is more sustainable to refurbish and re-use existing buildings than to demolish and build anew. Refurbishment involves the consumption of fewer materials and less energy for demolition and transportation. It is also usually more labour-intensive than new build. This is apart altogether from the cultural benefit of keeping familiar buildings and landmarks, and the learning possibilities of working with old buildings, many of which have lasted for many years employing sustainable materials and techniques.

With the challenge of achieving greater energy efficiency and reduced greenhouse gas emissions associated with buildings, the refurbishment of existing buildings has become even more important. Topical issues include stronger building energy regulation, providing cost optimal energy efficiency retrofitting guidance linked to general maintenance and retrofit, defining requirements for system performance and integrating renewable technologies.

Current building regulations can pose a problem in refurbishment works. In most Member States, building regulation requirements are expressed in performance terms: 'reasonable thermal insulation', 'adequate structural performance', and often are only required when large extensions are being undertaken. Associated guidance is conceived in terms of new build and does not always take into account the reality of load-bearing capacity, thermal insulation performance, or other characteristics of existing generously-dimensioned building stock. It may not allow previously applicable lower standards to be maintained without extensive and often visually intrusive upgrading, even though the most sustainable act would be to conserve and refurbish the old building and not to demolish and construct afresh.

An energy audit of the building will be essential prior to determining the brief for the refurbishment work. Such an audit can be carried out by the architect, but specialists will have much to contribute by way of strategies for sustainable refurbishment which can often be startlingly cost-effective. These audits, coupled with an assessment of energy performance of the refurbished building, may provide useful indications of the potential for improvement.

Table 1.14 ISSUES IN REFURBISHMENT	
Before developing the brief	• Undertake an energy audit of the building

Identify the building's potential for environmental improvement and consider the following	• Increase daylighting through roof or façade
	• Introduce passive climate control devices: reduce overheating through reduction of internal gains or the use of external shading devices, louvres or blinds in conjunction with façade refurbishment
	• Reduce heating demand through installation of draught lobbies and by upgrading the building envelope. Control infiltration by applying draught stripping and sealing around opes
	• Upgrade of thermal insulation, reduce thermal bridging and improve air tightness
	• If windows or external door sets are to be replaced specify the most appropriate, best performing models available
	• Install secondary glazing to create small sunspaces, pre-heat ventilation air, and reduce transmission of external noise
	• Increase natural ventilation by installing opening sections to windows and roof lights
	• Improve indoor air quality by substituting natural for synthetic finishes: linoleum, water based paints etc. Replace poor floor and wall finishes with high performance natural materials
	• Optimise performance of active systems through better controls: time clocks, thermostats, building energy management systems, and more efficient fittings: lights, heat emitters
	• Improve controls on active service systems. The following will often be cost-effective:
	   - solid state programmable controllers for heating and cooling
	   - automatic switching systems for lighting
	   - individual thermostatic room and /or radiator control
	   - weather compensating controls
	• Integrate energy producing components such as roof-mounted solar water heaters and photovoltaic cells

SECTION 2: ISSUES

INTRODUCTION

Defining the design parameters which need to be considered in green building design is not easy, particularly if this is to be of use to the architect at the early, conceptual stages.

In developing a green building the designer should take into account not only the comfort and health of the occupants but also the effect of the building on the local and global environment.

1. OCCUPANT COMFORT

Comfort is affected by many factors, such as the activity, clothing, age and gender of the individual, and aspects of the internal environment such as air temperature, surface temperature, humidity, air movement, noise, light and odours.

2. OCCUPANT HEALTH

A poor internal environment has implications for the health of the occupants:

- it may contain toxic or allergenic substances
- it may be stressful or unsafe
- it may facilitate the transmission of communicable diseases

3. ENVIRONMENTAL IMPACT OF THE BUILDING

The processes of constructing and operating a building affect the environment. Effects on the local area have always been recognized but now it is also appreciated that buildings contribute to larger impacts, such as resource depletion and climate change.

A green building should integrate consideration of environmental impact and occupant health and comfort. While the principal physical parameters which define comfort are known and generally accepted, those which determine the quality of the internal environment in respect of occupant health, and the impact of the constructing and operating a building on the external environment, are still uncertain to some extent.

The relationship between the comfort of the body, the making of a building and the impact on the wider environment, and visa versa, is the subject of this publication.

INTRODUCTION

COMFORT
Thermal comfort
Visual comfort
Indoor air quality
Acoustic quality
Objectives

HEALTH
Indoor air quality
Materials
Daylight
Noise
Objectives

ENVIRONMENT
Energy
Materials
Water
Waste
Noise

OBJECTIVES

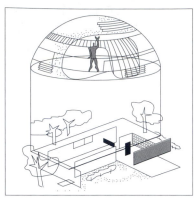

Theoretical approach to balanced shelter

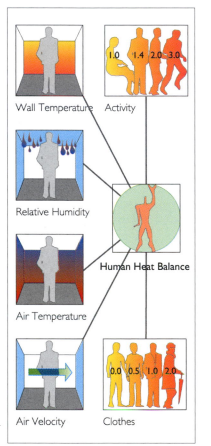

Wall Temperature   Activity

Relative Humidity

Human Heat Balance

Air Temperature

Air Velocity   Clothes

The parameters that effect thermal comfort

Units:
The unit of metabolic energy is the 'met'

1 met = 58 W/m²

where the surface area of the human body is approx. 1.8m². The unit of thermal resistance due to clothes is the 'clo'

1 clo = 0.155 m²K/W

Units of metabolic energy

COMFORT

The building modifies the external, natural environment by moderating the climate and providing protection and shelter, and designers need to understand how the external climate, the building fabric and the human body interact. Comfort is subjective and depends on age, gender, culture and who is paying the bill. In practice designers aim to provide conditions that are acceptable to a majority of users.

Conventional comfort standards, such as those in ASHRAE Standard 55-2010 and ISO 7730, are based on studies carried out in climate laboratories. Field studies suggest that laboratory-based predictions may not be entirely reliable, because they do not allow for people's adaptive responses (taking off a jacket or closing blinds, for example) or their need for some variety in their environment *(Roaf and Hancock, 1992)*. Consequently, optimum temperatures prescribed in standards may result in overestimated heating and cooling requirements, and a more flexible approach may be appropriate to less heavily engineered interiors.

THERMAL COMFORT

Thermal comfort can be defined as a sense of well-being with respect to temperature. It depends on achieving a balance between the heat being produced by the body and the loss of heat to the surroundings.

The internal temperature of the human body is maintained at a constant level. The body has no means of storing heat and any heat generated by it has to be dissipated. The actual balance depends on seven parameters. Three (metabolism, clothing and skin temperature) relate to the individual. The other four (air temperature, relative humidity, surface temperature of the elements in the room and air speed) are linked to the surrounding environment. While the parameters may be applied in a general way, design will also need to take into account the fact that specific local conditions (sun streaming into a window, body weight, subjective factors and adaptation) are all important and will affect perception of comfort.

Metabolism is the sum of the chemical reactions that occur in the body to keep body temperature balanced at 36.7°C and to compensate for heat lost to the surroundings. Production of metabolic energy (heat) depends on the level of physical activity. Clothing impedes the exchange of heat between the surface of the skin and the surrounding atmosphere. Skin temperature is a function of metabolism, clothing and room temperature. Unlike internal body temperature, it is not constant.

Air/room temperature affects heat loss from the human body by convection and evaporation.

Relative humidity is the amount of moisture in the air as a percentage of the maximum moisture it could contain at that temperature and pressure. It affects heat loss by allowing greater or lesser degrees of evaporation. Except in extreme situations, the influence of relative humidity on the sensation of thermal comfort is relatively small. In temperate regions, for instance, raising the relative humidity from 20% to 60% allows the temperature to be decreased by less than 1°C while having little or no effect on thermal comfort.

Mean radiant temperature is the average surface temperature of the elements enclosing a space. It influences both the heat lost by radiation from the body and the heat lost, by conduction, when the body is in contact with surfaces. Poorly-insulated buildings have cold internal surfaces and higher air temperatures are needed to compensate. An increase in mean radiant temperature means that comfort conditions can be achieved at lower air temperatures, and a reduction of 1°C in air temperature may save up to 10% of energy consumption. So insulation saves energy, not only by reducing actual building heat loss, but also by reducing design air temperatures.

Air speed does not decrease the temperature but causes a cooling sensation through heat loss by convection and increased evaporation. Within buildings, air speeds are generally less than 0.2m/s.

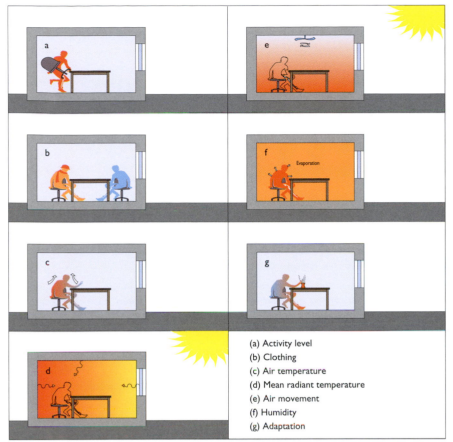

(a) Activity level
(b) Clothing
(c) Air temperature
(d) Mean radiant temperature
(e) Air movement
(f) Humidity
(g) Adaptation

Designing for thermal comfort

It is common practice to design to internationally accepted fixed design temperatures, but research shows that people are not passive in relation to their thermal environment. Where appropriate they will look for comfortable conditions (shade or sunshine, wind or shelter), and change their position, activity and clothing to make themselves more comfortable.

In field studies the range of temperatures which people report as comfortable is wider than might be expected. People accustomed to high temperatures report them to be acceptable, suggesting a degree of acclimatisation which alters the level of thermal acceptability, and the necessity to rigidly conform to international design temperatures. Allowance for adaptation by both people and buildings, means that definitions of comfort, too, can be broadened. Intelligent building design will provide mass to reduce temperature swings; adjustable elements such as blinds, shutters and ventilation to respond to changing conditions; and active heating or cooling systems, to maintain the desired temperature or at least ameliorate the outdoor climate.

ACTIVITY	W/m²	met
Resting		
Sleeping	40	0.7
Reclining	45	0.8
Seated, quiet	60	1.0
Standing, relaxed	70	1.2
Walking (on the level)		
0.89 m/s	115	2.0
1.34 m/s	150	2.6
1.79 m/s	220	3.8
Office Activities		
Reading, seated	55	1.0
Writing	60	1.0
Typing	65	1.1
Filing, seated	70	1.2
Filing, standing	80	1.4
Walking about	100	1.7
Lifting, packing	120	2.1
Driving / Flying		
Car	60-115	1.0-2.0
Aircraft, routine	70	1.2
Aircraft, instrument landing	105	1.8
Aircraft, combat	140	2.4
Heavy vehicle	185	3.2
Miscellaneous Occupational Activities		
Cooking	95-115	1.6-2.0
House cleaning	115-200	2.0-3.4
Seated, limb movement	130	2.2
Machine work		
sawing (light table)	105	1.8
light (electrical industry)	115-140	2.0-2.4
heavy	235	4.0
Handling 50kg bags	235	4.0
Pick and shovel work	235-280	4.0-4.8
Miscellaneous Leisure Activities		
Dancing, social	140-255	2.4-4.4
Calisthenics / exercise	175-235	3.0-4.0
Tennis, singles	210-270	3.6-4.0
Basketball	290-440	5.0-7.6
Wrestling, competitive	410-505	7.0-8.7

Typical metabolic heat generation for various activities

CLOTHING	THERMAL RESISTANCE	
	m²K/W	clo
Nude	0	0
Shorts	0.015	0.1
Typical tropical clothing ensemble: briefs, shorts, open-neck shirt with short sleeves, light socks and sandals	0.045	0.3
Light summer ensemble: briefs, long light-weight trousers, open-neck shirt with short sleeves, light socks and shoes	0.08	0.5
Light working ensemble: Light underwear, cotton work shirt with long sleeves, work trousers, woollen socks and shoes	0.11	0.7
Typical indoor winter ensemble: Underwear, shirt with long sleeves, trousers, jacket or sweater with long sleeves, heavy socks and shoes	0.16	1.0
Heavy traditional European business suit: cotton underwear with long legs and sleeves, shirt, suit including trousers, jacket and waistcoat, woollen socks and heavy shoes	0.23	1.5

Thermal insulation provided by various combinations of clothing

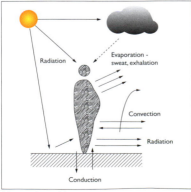

Heat gain and loss processes

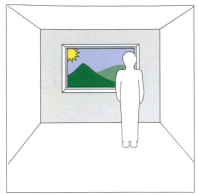

Windows offer distinct advantages

Luminance (candelas/m²) is the light flux leaving a surface and reaching the eye of the observer.

Illuminance (Lux) is the light striking unit area of a specified surface.

Lux is the SI unit of illuminance produced on a 1m² surface by a luminous flux of one lumen universally distributed over that surface.

Daylight factor (%) is Illuminance at a specified point indoors, expressed as a percentage of the simultaneous horizontal illuminance outdoors under an unobscured sky.

Definitions of light

	Average	Minimum
Hospital ward	5.0%	1.0%
Office	5.0%	2.0%
Classroom	5.0%	2.0%
Living room	1.5%	0.5%
Bedroom	1.0%	0.3%
Kitchen	2.0%	0.6%

Recommended daylight factors (CIBSE)

Luminance ratio

background of visual task : environment
3 : 1

background of visual task : peripheral field
10 : 1

light source : adjoining fields
20 : 1

interior in general
40:1

Recommended luminance ratios

VISUAL COMFORT

Poor lighting can cause eyestrain, fatigue, headaches, irritability, mistakes and accidents. Comfortable lighting conditions in a space are dependent on quantity, distribution and quality of light. The source of light may be natural or artificial or a combination of both, but windows have distinct advantages. In schools, hospital wards and factories the absence of a view out produces psychological discomfort. In offices the psychological benefits of windows have been found to be even greater than the physical benefits of which the occupants themselves were aware.

Almost all spaces need artificial lighting after dark. Some spaces and activities will need it during daylight hours. Where this is the case, the light spectrum of the artificial light should be as close as possible to that of natural light.

Quantity
Recommended lighting levels for particular tasks are well defined and if specified and implemented in accordance with standards are unlikely to cause problems for occupants. Establish the lighting requirements for the specific occupants and activities planned for the building through reference to tables of recommended illuminances for different activities such as the CIBSE-UK Guides or equivalent sources.

Distribution
Distribution of light in a space is often more important than quantity. The perception of brightness is influenced by the evenness of lighting levels. Where there is too great a difference between the daylight levels beside windows and at a distance from them, people in the area which is relatively darker tend to switch on lights, even though the daylight illuminance in their part of the room may be functionally adequate. The perception of the distribution of light can be defined in terms of either contrast or glare. Contrast is the difference between the appearance of an object against that of its immediate background. For comfort, there are limits to the amount of contrast which can be allowed between different parts of a visual field. Contrast can be defined in terms of luminance, illuminance or reflectivity compared between adjacent surfaces. The amount and distribution of light (and hence the amount of contrast) in a room is influenced by the reflectivity of the surfaces.

Glare is excessive contrast, usually caused by the introduction of an intense light source into the visual field, causing a feeling of discomfort and fatigue. The result may be anything from mildly distracting to visually blinding for the occupant. Glare can be caused directly, indirectly or by reflection.

Direct glare results when a light source with high luminance enters directly into the field of view. It can be experienced with interior light sources, sun or sky. Indirect glare occurs when the luminance of surfaces is too high. Reflected glare is caused by reflection from light sources on polished surfaces.

Quality
Visual quality is harder to define, but includes direction, colour and variation over time. Daylight provides excellent quality in terms of direction and both colour appearance and colour rendering. People enjoy daylight and sunlight, and the views that come with them. They tend to accept greater variation in light intensity in naturally lit spaces than they are prepared to tolerate from artificial lighting systems.

INDOOR AIR QUALITY

Compared with the other parameters of comfort, this is the one about which there is the most uncertainty. Provided that the outdoor air is of acceptable quality the traditional problems of stuffiness and odour can usually be resolved by ensuring adequate air change rates, efficient air distribution and control of interior pollution sources. Where clean outdoor air is not available, or the building's particular use makes heavy demands on the ventilation system, other steps may have to be taken (refer HEALTH; Indoor Air Quality).

ACOUSTIC QUALITY

Although acoustic quality is not a primary issue in sustainable design, 'green' design strategies should take acoustic consequences into account. For example, natural ventilation may imply open windows or ventilation openings between interior spaces; obtrusive noise or loss of acoustic privacy are not acceptable by-products. If carpeting or other absorbent floor finishes are omitted to allow the structure to act as a thermal store, other measures may have to be taken to reduce the transmission of impact noise and provide enough sound absorption in occupied spaces.

Standard environmental parameters include acceptable and recommended noise levels.

Sources of noise discomfort include:

- external: traffic noise or loss of acoustic privacy from open windows (may conflict with natural ventilation requirements);

- internal: loud or disruptive noises generated by activities within the building;

- building construction and finishes: impact noise from hard surfaces (possibly resulting from use of structure as a thermal store);

- building services: noise created by building services (e.g. mechanical ventilation).

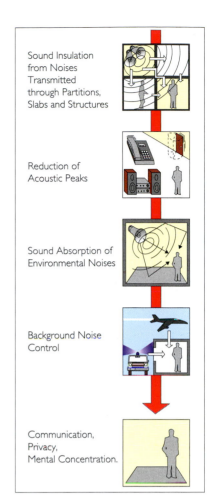

Sources of noise discomfort

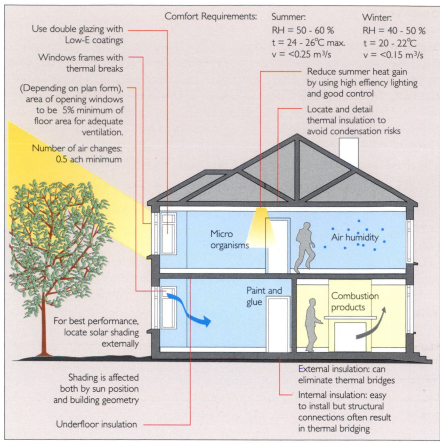

Comfort Requirements:

	Summer:	Winter:
	RH = 50 - 60 %	RH = 40 - 50 %
	t = 24 - 26°C max.	t = 20 - 22°C
	v = <0.25 m³/s	v = <0.15 m³/s

Use double glazing with Low-E coatings

Windows frames with thermal breaks

(Depending on plan form), area of opening windows to be 5% minimum of floor area for adequate ventilation.

Number of air changes: 0.5 ach minimum

Reduce summer heat gain by using high effiency lighting and good control

Locate and detail thermal insulation to avoid condensation risks

Micro organisms

Air humidity

Paint and glue

Combustion products

For best performance, locate solar shading externally

Shading is affected both by sun position and building geometry

Underfloor insulation

External insulation: can eliminate thermal bridges

Internal insulation: easy to install but structural connections often result in thermal bridging

Thermal comfort and indoor air quality in the home

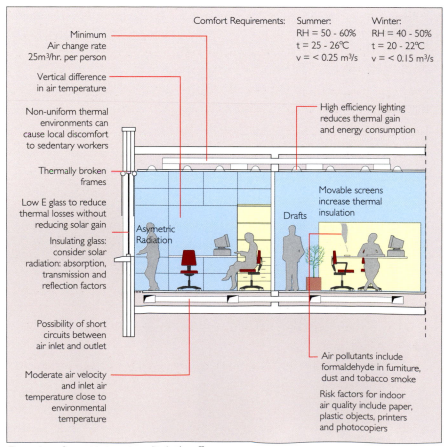

Comfort Requirements:

	Summer:	Winter:
	RH = 50 - 60%	RH = 40 - 50%
	t = 25 - 26°C	t = 20 - 22°C
	v = < 0.25 m³/s	v = < 0.15 m³/s

Minimum Air change rate 25m³/hr. per person

Vertical difference in air temperature

Non-uniform thermal environments can cause local discomfort to sedentary workers

Thermally broken frames

Low E glass to reduce thermal losses without reducing solar gain

Insulating glass: consider solar radiation: absorption, transmission and reflection factors

Possibility of short circuits between air inlet and outlet

Moderate air velocity and inlet air temperature close to environmental temperature

High efficiency lighting reduces thermal gain and energy consumption

Movable screens increase thermal insulation

Asymetric Radiation

Drafts

Air pollutants include formaldehyde in furniture, dust and tobacco smoke

Risk factors for indoor air quality include paper, plastic objects, printers and photocopiers

Thermal comfort and indoor air quality in the office

OBJECTIVES

Shelter occupants from the elements

Gathering information on climate is part of the development of any healthy building strategy. It enables designers to evaluate a site so as to anticipate adverse weather conditions or natural hazards which could affect the building.

- Buildings should be planned and located in relation to topography and microclimatic conditions.
- The building should be designed and constructed to keep out moisture (rising, penetrating, condensation).
- Structures and roofs should resist high wind speeds and snow-loads.
- The envelope should prevent excessive air infiltration.
- In cold climates, envelopes and service pipes should be protected against frost damage.
- Specific measures should be taken to reduce risk of local flooding.
- Tall buildings should be provided with lightning conductors.

Maintain a comfortable thermal environment

Thermal comfort is the state in which no significant strain is imposed on the thermo-regulatory mechanism of the body. Maintaining an indoor thermal equilibrium should therefore prevent undue raising or lowering of body temperature, while at the same time assisting physiological functions to proceed.

- The ambient temperature should provide thermal comfort to occupants. (20–22°C winter, 24–26°C summer are reasonable starting points, but allow for activity and adaptive behaviour.)
- Optimal temperature should be achieved at knee height (0.5m from the floor).
- Mean radiant temperature should be less than 3°C below assumed optimum indoor air temperature.
- There should not be any excessive air movement in rooms (acceptable levels 0.1–0.15 m/s for winter; 0.25 m/s for summer).
- Relative humidity should be kept at an acceptable level (40%–70% at northern latitudes; 50–60% in summer and 40–50% in winter in Mediterranean climates).
- Heating systems should be easy to control.
- An average ratio of window to wall of 30% for the building as a whole makes a good starting point for design. Then adjust to account for climate, orientation and building use. In warm climates consider limiting window area to about one tenth of floor area.
- Shading devices such as venetian blinds, shutters and screens, deflectors, or photo-, thermo- or electro-chromic glasses can be used to control sunlight penetration.
- Light-coloured paint on external walls will reflect solar radiation.
- Green belts, trees, climbing plants, as well as water reservoirs, can be used to reduce temperatures of walls and roofs in warm conditions.
- In warm climates buildings should be oriented to take advantage of prevailing summer winds.
- Natural night ventilation is effective in reducing air temperatures during hot weather.

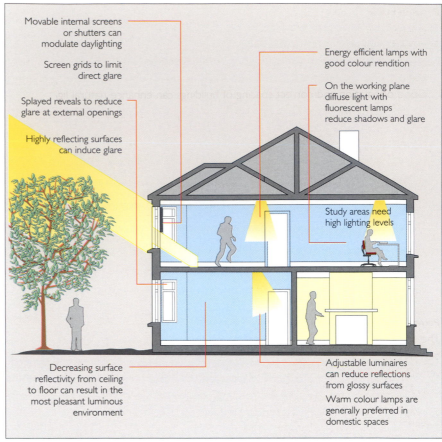

Movable internal screens
or shutters can
modulate daylighting

Screen grids to limit
direct glare

Splayed reveals to reduce
glare at external openings

Highly reflecting surfaces
can induce glare

Energy efficient lamps with
good colour rendition

On the working plane
diffuse light with
fluorescent lamps
reduce shadows and glare

Study areas need
high lighting levels

Decreasing surface
reflectivity from ceiling
to floor can result in the
most pleasant luminous
environment

Adjustable luminaires
can reduce reflections
from glossy surfaces

Warm colour lamps are
generally preferred in
domestic spaces

Visual comfort in the home

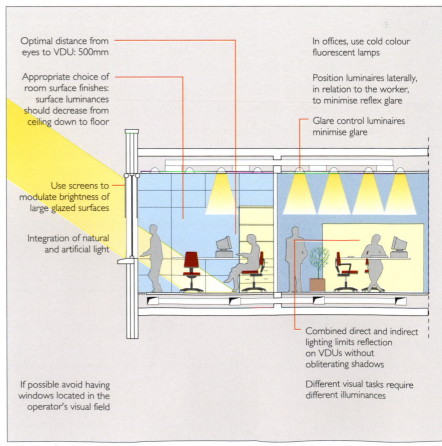

Optimal distance from
eyes to VDU: 500mm

Appropriate choice of
room surface finishes:
surface luminances
should decrease from
ceiling down to floor

Use screens to
modulate brightness of
large glazed surfaces

Integration of natural
and artificial light

If possible avoid having
windows located in the
operator's visual field

In offices, use cold colour
fluorescent lamps

Position luminaires laterally,
in relation to the worker,
to minimise reflex glare

Glare control luminaires
minimise glare

Combined direct and indirect
lighting limits reflection
on VDUs without
obliterating shadows

Different visual tasks require
different illuminances

Visual comfort in the office

Provide visual comfort

The aim of good lighting practice should be to provide lighting which is both qualitatively and quantitatively adequate. In all climates a balance needs to be maintained between natural lighting requirements and the requirement for thermal comfort.

- Good orientation and correct spacing of buildings can enhance natural lighting.
- Glazing ratio and window design should ensure that building interiors receive adequate natural lighting.
- To ensure an appropriate distribution of daylight, aim to have some sky visible from most places within the room.
- The spectrum of daytime artificial lighting should resemble that of daylight.
- Natural and artificial lighting should both meet physiological and health requirements: optimum intensity, similar brightness, protection against glare, avoidance of shadows, adequate contrast.
- Wherever feasible rooms should have rooflights or windows, giving occupants some visual contact with the outdoor environment.

Provide sufficient ventilation

The importance of adequate ventilation in maintaining good indoor air quality is becoming more widely recognised, not least because of the tendency towards lower ventilation levels as a result of changing construction styles and techniques and/or deliberate action to reduce heat losses.

- Ventilation rates should comply with air quality standards and sanitary recommendation; average 8 l/s per person (offices).
- Air filtration alone may provide an acceptable level of air exchange. However, all buildings should have provision for additional controlled ventilation, designed to be effective and easy to use.
- The openable area of windows should extend close to ceilings to allow hot air in the upper part of the room to escape.
- Windows should incorporate controllable 'trickle ventilation' features such as two-position casement fasteners.
- Windows should allow for easily operated and controllable ventilation.
- Air inlets and outlets to mechanical systems should be situated to avoid acoustic nuisance to neighbouring properties.
- If air-conditioning is unavoidable, it should be designed to facilitate regular cleaning and maintenance.

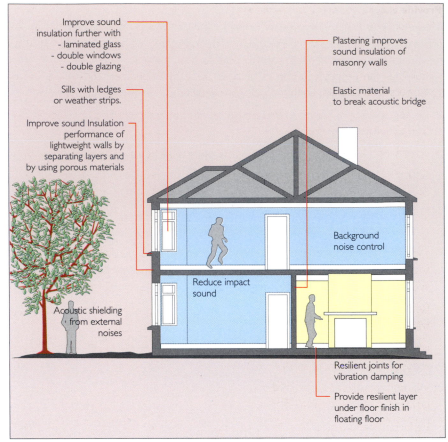

Improve sound insulation further with
- laminated glass
- double windows
- double glazing

Sills with ledges or weather strips.

Improve sound Insulation performance of lightweight walls by separating layers and by using porous materials

Acoustic shielding from external noises

Plastering improves sound insulation of masonry walls

Elastic material to break acoustic bridge

Background noise control

Reduce impact sound

Resilient joints for vibration damping

Provide resilient layer under floor finish in floating floor

Acoustic comfort in the home

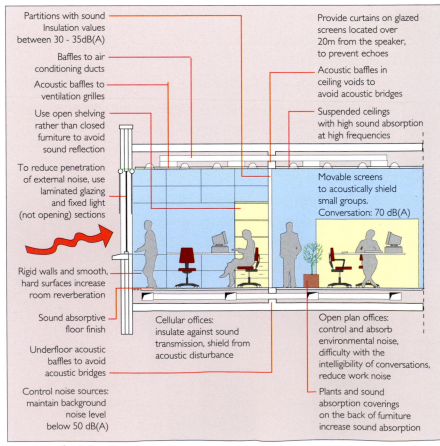

Partitions with sound Insulation values between 30 - 35dB(A)

Baffles to air conditioning ducts

Acoustic baffles to ventilation grilles

Use open shelving rather than closed furniture to avoid sound reflection

To reduce penetration of external noise, use laminated glazing and fixed light (not opening) sections

Rigid walls and smooth, hard surfaces increase room reverberation

Sound absorptive floor finish

Underfloor acoustic baffles to avoid acoustic bridges

Control noise sources: maintain background noise level below 50 dB(A)

Provide curtains on glazed screens located over 20m from the speaker, to prevent echoes

Acoustic baffles in ceiling voids to avoid acoustic bridges

Suspended ceilings with high sound absorption at high frequencies

Movable screens to acoustically shield small groups.
Conversation: 70 dB(A)

Cellular offices: insulate against sound transmission, shield from acoustic disturbance

Open plan offices: control and absorb environmental noise, difficulty with the intelligibility of conversations, reduce work noise

Plants and sound absorption coverings on the back of furniture increase sound absorption

Acoustic comfort in the office

Provide acceptable acoustic conditions

Many human activities – concentrated intellectual work, conversation, music and sleep, for example – demand controlled noise levels and/or acoustic privacy.

- Buildings can be protected from outdoor noise by orientation and by the use of barriers such as walls, earth mounds or vegetation.

- Noise-generating activities or equipment within the building should be located as far as possible in unoccupied spaces.

- Spaces with shared walls and floors should preferably be of similar use.

- Reduction of sound transmission is best achieved by increasing the mass of structural building elements. This is particularly effective at lower frequencies.

- Air-borne sound transmission is minimised by eliminating gaps in the external envelope and in internal partitions.

- Window openings are one of the main sources of noise infiltration. Depending on the environment, they may be sealed or incorporate insulated glazing components such as laminated glass. Ventilation grilles should be provided with sound baffles.

- Resilient layers under floating floors and suspended ceilings reduce impact noise transmission in apartment buildings.

- Indirect sound transmission through cavity walls should be reduced by sound-absorbing materials in the cavity.

- Where excessive interior noise pollution is expected, specify sound-absorbant building components and materials.

- Reduce noise transmission in office environments, by incorporating high level baffles, which reflect sound back into the space.

- Drain-pipes should not be carried in ducts next to living rooms or bedrooms.

- Lift and other motors should be mounted on resilient supports.

- Ventilation fans should be as large as possible so as to run at the lowest possible speed.

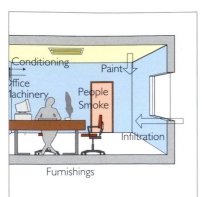

Principal sources of pollutants in an office building

- Asbestos fibre

- Formaldehyde vaopur

- Volatile Organic Compounds (VOCs)

- Tobacco smoke

- Radon gas

Common indoor air contaminants

- Impact on environment

- Habitat destruction

- Release of toxins to air and water

- Toxic waste production

- Impact on health of occupants

- Create indoor pollutants

- Cause indoor pollutants

Issues to be addressed in the specification of materials

- Natural origin

- No off-gassing constituents

- Good thermal properties

- Hygroscopic

- Diffusible

- Absorptive

- No electrical charge

- Resistant to microfauna

Materials and health-positive properties

HEALTH

Conditions inside a building clearly affect not only the comfort but also the health of the occupants and users. Poor air quality, toxic materials, lack of daylight or excessive noise can have lasting consequences for health.

INDOOR AIR QUALITY

More than most environmental issues, indoor air pollution has a direct impact on health and, by implication, on productivity. Health effects ascribed to indoor air pollution include allergies and asthma, infectious disease, cancer and other genetic damage. Widespread, chronic, low-level effects in particular buildings are referred to as 'sick building syndrome' (SBS). Indoor air quality is determined by air quality outside the building, pollutant emissions within the building and the ventilation rate, as well as by the efficiency of filtration and standard of maintenance of mechanical systems, and so on.

Most people spend approximately 90% of their lives inside buildings and the impact of constant exposure to low level emissions from the wide variety of materials commonly found in buildings today is unknown. Many of these pollutants originate in the building itself. With an increase in the use of organic solvents, interior finishes emitting volatile organic compounds (VOCs), cleaning agents, and office appliances, indoor air pollution has become a serious concern.

Making buildings more airtight to conserve energy does not have to affect indoor air quality. There will be less infiltration and incidental ventilation; however, controlled ventilation should provide adequate clean fresh air. Poor ventilation rates will create unhealthy conditions, and along with increased indoor pollutant sources may cause real problems. According to Baker the phenomenon of sick building syndrome is observed almost exclusively in mechanically ventilated buildings *(Baker, 1995)*. What is certain, however, is that in poorly ventilated spaces mould spores and house dust mites thrive, and VOCs reach higher concentrations. It is also well established that where mechanical systems are installed, a healthy indoor environment will only be achieved if systems are correctly installed, fully commissioned and properly maintained.

These factors increase the need for care in the specification of materials and in the design of ventilation systems.

Three main approaches are used to control indoor air pollutants:
- removing the source of pollution from the building;
- controlling pollutant emissions at source;
- expelling the pollutants from the building through ventilation measures.

MATERIALS

A number of toxic chemicals and materials are used in common building materials, finishes and consumer goods. Some of these products pollute indoor air or water supplies; others cause damage by contact or ingestion. These can affect the workers who make them or install them in a new building, the building's users, and/or the workers who demolish or refurbish the building at the end of its useful life.

Lead and asbestos are well-established health hazards. Some synthetics such as polyvinyl chloride (PVC) can also lead to hazardous emissions in use. Paints, preservatives and adhesives are common sources of toxic emissions. For information about the impact of different categories of materials on health and the environment (refer ELEMENTS; Materials)

DAYLIGHT

The integration of effective daylight design in buildings not only improves energy efficiency but also contributes to the health and well-being of the occupants. Daylight, another form of renewable energy, displaces the use of electric lighting in buildings thus reducing energy consumption and polluting emissions. Poor daylight availability in indoor spaces can also directly affect the well-being of the occupant. Full spectrum light is known to be conducive to good health (*Lockley, 2008*). But daylight also stimulates the human physiology and helps to regulate our circadian rhythm, our 24-hour biochemical, physiological and behavioural cycles (*Sharon, 2009*). With people spending ever-longer periods of time indoors, exposure to full spectrum natural light becomes important. Research has demonstrated benefits to children attending schools designed with above average levels of natural light (*Küller, 1992; HMG, 1999*). Even view is important and is known to lead to better recovery times for patients in care (*Ulrich, 1984*).

NOISE

Exposure to excessive noise levels can produce stress-related illnesses and hearing loss. Sources of noise nuisance are listed in COMFORT; Acoustic Quality.

OBJECTIVES

Protect against outdoor air pollutants
The interior environment has a continuous but variable influx of air pollutants from the outdoor air. Included in this category are suspended particulates, sulphur oxides, nitrogen oxides, hydrocarbons, carbon oxides and lead.

- Where possible, site buildings away from roads and other sources of pollution.
- Provide internal and external planting to absorb pollutants and reduce dust.
- Avoid gaps in the external envelope which allow unplanned infiltration of external air.
- Where outdoor air is of unacceptable quality provide sealed windows and mechanical ventilation.
- Locate the intake of any mechanical ventilation system to avoid sources of airborne contaminants.

Control pollutants from processes within the building
The occupants and activities within a building are sources of emissions. Common pollutants include carbon and nitrogen oxides, odours, tobacco smoke, water vapour, airborne pathogens and toxic emissions from appliances and machinery.

- Most cases of carbon monoxide (CO) poisoning are caused by incomplete combustion of heating and cooking fuels. Appliances and flues must be properly maintained and ventilation adequate.
- Provide local extract ventilation for smoking areas, and for spaces housing emission-generating appliances or equipment.
- Provide adequate natural ventilation to rooms to dilute airborne micro-organism concentrations.
- Allow direct sunlight to enter all rooms, where possible.
- Provide sufficient natural and artificial lighting to enable inspection and cleaning.

Protect against radioactive emissions
In ordinary circumstances the largest contribution to radon exposure arises from inhaling decayed radon products in indoor air.

- When high levels of radon are suspected, radiological monitoring should be undertaken.

Clakamas High School, Portland. Architect: Boora Architects. Source: Michael Mathers

Clapham Manor Primary School, London. Architect: dRMM. Source: Photo © Jonas Lencer

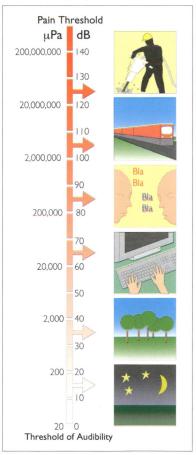

Noise Levels

- Increase ventilation rates in buildings both under the floor and within rooms.
- Provide a barrier between the ground and the living space, or seal floors and walls to reduce radon emissions.

Specify non-toxic building materials, finishes and equipment
- Require manufacturers or suppliers to indicate the content of any materials or components it is proposed to incorporate in the building and select the least injurious.
- Minimise the use of VOC-emitting finishes which will be exposed to the indoor air.
- Design for easy access to services so as to facilitate proper maintenance of any air-conditioning or mechanical ventilation equipment.
- Seal or remove, after evaluating condition, any asbestos-containing materials in existing buildings, provided that this will not create more hazard from dust and fibre release than would occur by leaving it in place.
- In existing buildings replacement of lead piping and lead-lined water tanks should be considered where chemical attack from water represents a problem.

Design for adequate daylight
- Rooms in which occupants spend any substantial part of their day should be provided with windows/rooflights if the function of the space permits.

Protect against excessive noise and vibration
Actions to avoid excessive noise or vibration are listed in COMFORT; Objectives above.

ENVIRONMENT

The range of impacts of buildings on the environment is diverse. Problems which result from construction-related processes, such as global warming, ozone depletion, loss of natural habitat and biodiversity, soil erosion and release of toxic pollutants are now well known. It is useful to think of the proposed building as a new, living, healthy entity. The building is an integral part of the site. The two diagrams illustrate the linear, open systems of conventional buildings and the closed, cyclical, sustainable systems which represent the alternative.

A building is a physical structure composed of different elements and also a kind of 'living machine'; a place where people go about their lives, appliances use electricity, temperature is regulated, and so on. There are two main headings under which the environmental impact of the building must be analysed:

1. As a physical structure, a building is dead, the mere 'sum of its parts'. These parts are individually extracted, manufactured, assembled, maintained, demolished, and finally reused or disposed of. Each part has a set of effects associated with these processes, and the total environmental impact of the building is the sum of these effects.

2. As a 'living machine' the cost to the environment is that of running the building during its lifetime: the inputs that will be required, such as energy and water, and the outputs, such as CO_2 and wastes.

To establish the true environmental impact of a building, the analysis may be carried out in a way that reflects the relative importance of different building elements and processes, and the priorities for reducing environmental impacts. This is called life cycle analysis. The information required to carry out this task comprehensively for a whole building is substantial, and so detailed as to render the task impractical to undertake in most circumstances. It is possible, however, to analyse selected building elements or components. While the idea of cradle-to-cradle analysis may be out of reach for all but the specialist, understanding the concept will help rationalise choices.

Although various factors exert their influence upon the different stages of a building's lifetime, it is during planning and construction that almost all of them are fundamentally fixed. Decisions at this time determine the extent of resource and energy consumption during future stages, such as maintenance, renovation, conversion and restructuring. Issues which need to be considered fall into five main categories:

- energy consumption
- material use
- water use
- waste management
- noise control

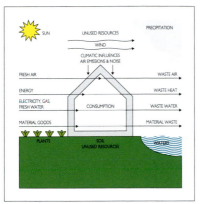

Wasteful use of resources in a conventional building

Cyclical use of resources in a sustainable building. Source: GAIA Vista Architects

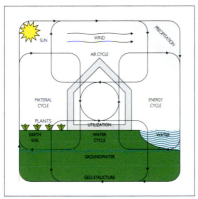

Cradle to cradle. Cradle to Cradle® is a registered trademark of MBDC.

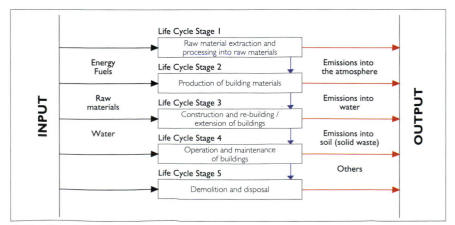

Building life cycle flow chart

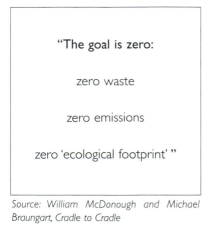

"The goal is zero:

zero waste

zero emissions

zero 'ecological footprint' "

Source: William McDonough and Michael Braungart, Cradle to Cradle

Embodied energy

Typical values in MJ/kg	
Kiln dried sawn softwood	3.4
Kiln dried sawn hardwood	2.0
Air dried sawn hardwood	0.5
Hardboard	24.2
Particleboard	8.0
MDF	11.3
Plywood	10.4
Glulam	11
LVL	11
Plastics	90
PVC	80
Synthetic rubber	110
Acrylic paint	61.5
Stabilised earth	0.7
Local quarried stone	5.9
Gypsum plasters	2.9
Plaster board	4.4
Fibre cement	4.8
Cement	5.6
In-situ concrete	1.9
Clay bricks	2.5
Concrete blocks	1.5
Glass	12.7
Aluminium	170
Copper	100
Galvanised steel	38
Recycled aluminium	17

Note: Figures quoted can vary by a factor of 10.

Embodied energy of building materials

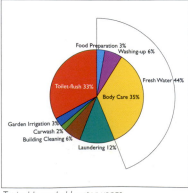

Typical household water usage

ENERGY

The use of energy in conventional buildings impacts on the environment through the consumption of non-renewable resources and by contributing to global pollution through greenhouse gas emissions. Energy saving is without doubt, the quickest, most effective, and best value means of reducing greenhouse gas emissions and offers a major contribution to combating climate change (*EC, 2005*).

Energy use in the building sector consumes about 40% of EU and US final energy. Efficiencies in the building sector have the potential to achieve the EC targets of 20% reduction in energy consumption and CO_2 emissions by 2020, with cost effective savings potential estimated at around 11% of total EU final energy consumption (*EC, 2008a*). The European Directive on the Energy Performance of Buildings (*2002/91/EC*) (EPBD) requires mandatory building energy assessment and certification for all buildings when sold or let. In order to prepare an energy performance certificate an assessment of the building's energy-related characteristics and systems must be undertaken. This generally includes as a minimum, an analysis of

• the form and area of the building envelope and its thermal, solar and daylight properties and air permeability

• space heating installation and hot water supply and their efficiencies, responsiveness and controls

• ventilation, cooling and air conditioning systems and controls

• fixed lighting

• fuels and renewable energy sources.

The EPBD Recast (*2010/31/EU*), adopted by the European Parliament and the Council of the European Union in 2010, strengthens the energy performance requirements and has a goal that by the end of 2020 all new buildings will be nearly zero energy (*EU, 2010*).

In designing to be energy efficient the focus should be on ensuring that

• Passive design principles are implemented so that building energy requirements are minimised

• Renewable energy sources are deployed to provide for the reduced energy needs

• Where conventional systems are employed, the most efficient and least polluting types are specified.

In a typical building today, the amount of energy consumed in use (and where that energy is sourced) is still the single most important consideration from an environmental perspective. The impact of this operational energy outweighs the impact of other assessment criteria in environmental and life cycle assessment; however, as future buildings become much more energy efficient other assessment criteria become significant. The UK Building Research Establishment has noted that in some new, well-insulated buildings, the energy embodied in their fabric could amount to as much as 50% of the energy used to operate them over a 25 year period. Current common energy performance calculation methodologies employ simple, easy-to-use methodologies (in order to make energy certification cheap and the results acceptably consistent) but mandatory calculation tools will have to develop so as to accommodate stricter building standards, more complex and innovative solutions, operational energy, life cycle environmental and cost analysis, indoor environmental quality, and broader environmental issues.

MATERIALS

Criteria for the selection of materials and components include cost, aesthetics, performance and availability. Environmentally-responsible specification of building materials and components, and of the manner in which they are assembled, means that consideration of embodied energy and local and global environmental impacts must be added. Effects on the building interior and the broader environmental impacts of various categories of materials are covered in HEALTH; Materials above.

The choice of materials and components has an important role in determining energy performance. The embodied energy in a concrete structure may be high, but if it is designed to enhance passive solar heating and cooling, it can easily produce an equal reduction in energy consumption over a few years of use. Other components, such as low-emissivity windows and efficient heating and lighting installations, are so important to energy efficiency as to greatly outweigh any increased impact from their manufacture and disposal.

WATER

The careless use of water causes a variety of environmental problems. This covers both the supply of water for use in buildings and handling of surface and waste water in built-up areas.

The EU Water Framework Directive 2000 establishes a legal framework for the protection and restoration of clean water in Europe to ensure its long-term sustainable use. The directive addresses inland surface waters, transitional waters, coastal waters and groundwater and establishes several innovative principles for water management, including public participation in planning and the integration of economic approaches with the recovery of the cost of water services.

Under many building codes all water used in buildings must be of potable quality. This water is drawn from the natural environment, often reducing groundwater levels and water levels in streams, lakes and marshlands. Its treatment requires the construction and operation of water treatment plants, with all the use of materials and energy that that implies.

After use, waste water must be routed through sewers to be treated again, or treated on site, before being released, more or less purified, back into the natural environment. In addition, impervious urban surfaces speed up rainwater run-off, reducing natural evaporation, causing soil erosion in landscaped areas and the banks of natural waterways. More construction – drains, culverts, embankments – is needed to prevent flooding. Under storm conditions surface water is often mixed with untreated or partially treated sewage in overflow systems, discharging pollutants into the environment.

The design team can influence the manner in which building owners, users and contractors protect clean water as follows:
- Employ water conservation measures, equipment and appliances
- Ensure protection of ground water sources
- Ensure safe disposal of waste water.

WASTE

Household and commercial refuse, street litter, construction debris, industrial process and other wastes together with sewage sludge present environmental problems. Even though existing waste handling systems in most European countries tend to minimise local impacts, eventual disposal has significant effects, including contamination of land, air

Impervious surfaces. Source: D'Arcy Norman.

Damaged natural habitat. Source: Beth Shotton

Building construction waste. Source: Alan Stanton

Landfill waste. Source: D'Arcy Norman

and water sources, at the regional and global scale. The EC Waste Framework Directive of 2008 *(Directive, 2008/98/EC) (EU, 2008b)* sets the basic concepts and definitions related to waste management and lays down waste management principles such as the "polluter pays principle" or the "waste hierarchy" and provides the overarching legislation framework for the following:

Collection

Transport

Recovery

Disposal.

The design team can influence the manner in which building owners, users and contractors contribute to sustainable practices by

- Reviewing waste production from conception to operation of building.

- Designing to minimise waste in the building fabric, reducing off-cuts and spoiled material on site.

- Planning safe and adequate storage for different categories of waste, preliminary to recycling or to safe and efficient disposal. Minimise the use of skips and other convenient general waste 'magnets'.

- Informing the contractor of his or her responsibilities on site during the construction phase. The development of a waste management strategy should address the reduction through careful handling of materials and sorting of waste for re-use or re-cycling.

In Sweden it has been calculated that the construction of a ten-storey building generates waste equivalent to one full storey. However, the development of more sustainable practices for construction and demolition wastes is heavily dependent on the existence of handling facilities and of a market for recycled materials.

NOISE

The increase in high-density schemes together with mechanisation and urbanisation means that noise is a serious problem in most human settlements throughout the world. The effects are local rather than global, but do have a significant impact on the quality of life in affected areas.

OBJECTIVES

USE RENEWABLE ENERGY SOURCES

Renewable energy sources can be integrated into the building façade, or sited appropriately in most new or existing buildings. This leads to a reduction of fossil fuel consumption for heating, cooling, and electrical supply, minimising the environmental impact of buildings and contributing to the reduction of CO_2 emissions.

- Minimise the energy demand of buildings for heating, cooling and lighting purposes, by making use of passive solar systems and technologies (atria, sun spaces, solar walls, solar chimneys, ventilated roofs and walls, daylighting, etc.).
- Use air solar systems for providing preheated ventilation to the indoor environment.
- Use of water solar systems and collectors for sanitary hot water requirements and low temperature space heating.
- Integrate photovoltaic panels within roofs and southern-oriented façades, appropriate in size and peak power for electricity production and energy load management.
- Facilitate the use of local district heating with biomass.

SPECIFY LOW ENERGY SYSTEMS AND APPLIANCES

Design should incorporate energy conscious solutions at both building and district level. The successful application and implementation of innovative measures in energy technologies requires cooperation with energy suppliers at the building concept stage, in anticipation of smarter utility grids.

- Time shifting of electricity peaks should be introduced wherever practicable, achieved through suitable thermal properties of the building and better control technologies.
- Equipment specification should include load management systems with control devices that optimise the electricity tariff.
- Heating and cooling systems should incorporate building energy management systems (BEMS).
- Electric lighting should use energy-efficient lamps and ballasts, and appropriate automatic lighting control systems.
- Radiant systems can reduce the energy needed to heat large spaces with highly intermittent use.
- Low temperature local district heating/cooling systems can be integrated with waste energy from other sources or renewable energies.
- Ventilation systems should incorporate heat exchange and recovery from exhaust air extractors.

USE MATERIALS WISELY

Building design should consider the cradle-to-cradle approach in the specification of materials to minimise resource use and emissions generation and facilitate re-use and recycling.

- Include environmental assessment in the review of appropriate materials and components.
- Design for durability of materials and components.
- Design for flexibility, allowing for change in building use over time.
- Design for ease of refurbishment - façades and internal partitioning should permit removal and replacement without structural disturbance.

- Incorporate a methodology for dismantling buildings and re-using or recycling building components through ease of separation into constituent elements at the end of their life.
- Design should facilitate ease of maintenance of components and systems
- Require contractor to use eco-friendly cleaning materials during construction and at final clean-up.

PROVIDE SUFFICIENT CLEAN WATER

57% of the world's population get their drinking water from a piped connection that provides running water in their homes and a further 30% are provided with safe water sources *(World Health Organisation, 2010)*. The critical issue in supply is the qualitative aspect. Toxic products can pollute water supplies, making them unfit for consumption. Control measures at this level are of paramount importance to public health and to the safety of our environment.

- In new developments water supply, water distribution, waste water disposal, drainage and sewerage should form an integral part of a master development plan.
- Piped water supplies need to be protected against contamination from harmful bacteria or chemicals in the ground.
- External or internal water storage tanks should always be covered to discourage algae growth due to exposure to sunlight and to prevent the entry of rodents, while facilitating regular cleaning operations.
- Materials used for water services should not represent a source of bacterial or chemical contamination to supplies.

PROVIDE FOR WATER CONSERVATION AND RE-USE

Design should minimise the consumption of water, and reduce the environmental impact of new and existing settlements, by using water-saving technologies and other measures.

- Develop a water conservation strategy for the building.
- Install water meters to facilitate measurement and control of water use.
- Incorporate water saving technologies for WCs, showers and other water-using appliances.
- The principle of grey/black water usage should be included at an early design stage.
- Site planning and building design should incorporate provisions for storage of rainwater and treatment of grey/black water where appropriate and permitted.
- Landscapes should be designed for minimum irrigation.

PROVIDE SANITARY MEANS OF WASTE AND SURFACE WATER DISPOSAL

Adequate water disposal contributes to health and environmental improvement. Inadequate surface-water drainage can cause periodic flooding of roads, wells and housing, creating safety and environmental hazards.

- Develop a waste water management strategy for the building.
- Identify if on-site treatment systems are viable options.
- Design and construction of drainage systems should conform to health principles. Ensure that effluent does not leak into surrounding ground, contaminating water supplies.
- Plumbing should be easily accessible for maintenance, and avoid back-pressure that might lead to contamination of the water supply system.

- Materials for plumbing systems should be selected for strength, durability, low embodied energy and the ability to resist the corrosive action of wastes.

PROVIDE FOR REUSE AND RECYCLING OF CONSTRUCTION AND DOMESTIC WASTE

Careful design and site management can reduce construction wastes. Facilities for storage, collection and disposal of domestic waste after the building is occupied are essential. Methods of disposal depend largely upon the availability of suitable sites, cost of transport, socio-economic factors and local conditions.

Construction waste:

- Design for standard sizes to reduce on-site cutting and require the contractor to use off-cuts to feasible maximum.
- Enforce specification requirements for handling, storage and protection of materials.
- Require contractors to plan careful estimating and ordering of materials.
- Specify separation, storage and collection or re-use of recyclable materials, including packaging.

Domestic waste:

- Facilities for handling waste should provide adequate space for on-site treatment, combined with convenience for the occupier and waste collector and high standards of hygiene, safety and amenity.
- Provide spaces for individual storage containers for each dwelling in residential developments.
- Provide adequate and accessible containers for recycling in work areas in commercial developments.
- Provide designated access routes to all containers for the waste collector, without passing through any part of the building.
- Consider the refuse shelter as a properly designed integral part of the building complex.

Control outdoor noise:

- Industrial buildings should be insulated to prevent noise transmission at source.
- Urban main streets should be widened with protective belts of greenery to separate different zones.
- Vehicular traffic should be prohibited or reduced in residential areas, particularly at night.
- Avoid paving and other hard surfaces where possible so as to minimise ground reflection. Use vegetation and grass areas to absorb noise.

SECTION 3: STRATEGIES

INTRODUCTION

Optimised performance and environmental quality of a building is best based on passive design principles and achieved through the development of form, envelope and systems of the building. With modern architectural science, the availability of innovative technologies and materials and sophisticated computer software to simulate and evaluate performance, the envelope can become an interactive environmental mediator rather than a mere separator as in the past. Research and demonstration projects have shown that the successful delivery of an holistic sustainable building demands an inclusive design decision-making process, through which the interconnections between building siting, form and envelope and engineering systems are considered and pursued in integrated design strategies, to achieve cost optimal solutions and quality architecture.

It is essential to be familiar with a wide range of passive and active strategies which may act as a map to guide your design choices; firstly introducing passive design strategies to reduce demand for energy, water and materials, and secondly, providing for the reduced energy needs to be met from renewable sources while integrating energy saving, efficient technologies and control systems.

Climatic conditions, urban or rural location, site features, building function, availability of materials and components: all impact the selection of design strategies. The following section lays out many strategies that may be employed as the design process develops in a series of processing cycles, evolving towards design solutions to facilitate the development of an optimal solution.

URBAN AND NEIGHBOURHOOD

URBAN FABRIC

Urban form is the result of the complex interaction of interdependent pressures and influences: climatic, economic, social, political, strategic, aesthetic, technical and regulatory. Many planning decisions have a pervasive and long-lasting impact on social cohesion and the quality of life of the individual, as well as on the global environment.

On an urban scale the issues of conservation of fossil fuel and energy resources, and the need for more environmentally friendly energy sources are magnified. However, energy efficiency is not a goal in itself, but part of an integrated search for sustainable development which recognises the local, regional and global impact of cities on air, land, water, vegetation, wildlife and the human population.

The architect rarely has the power to make decisions about the location of the project within the urban fabric. In many cases the site, whether urban, suburban, brownfield or greenfield, will have been selected before the architect becomes involved in the project.

The role of the architect in masterplanning varies across cultural and jurisdictional boundaries, and has distinct cultural differences between States, but in general architects have more influence on the shaping of the designed environment in the more historically urbanised countries. Specialised education for architects in these countries prepares the profession for active roles in city design and planning, and in particular, preparing the design context for other architects who work more conventionally on individual buildings.

At the scale of the city block, architects are more often involved in the planning process,

INTRODUCTION

URBAN AND NEIGHBOURHOOD
Urban fabric
Microclimate
Land use
Density
Transportation
Green space
Water and waste
Energy

SITE SELECTION AND ANALYSIS
Site selection
Site analysis

SITE PLANNING
Microclimate
Density
Transportation
Green space
Water and waste
Energy

BUILDING FORM

BUILDING ENVELOPE
Opaque/solid elements
Translucent elements
Transparent elements
Energy production elements
Sunspaces
Atria

FINISHES
Building energy performance
Daylighting
Indoor air quality

SERVICES, EQUIPMENT AND CONTROLS
Heating
Cooling
Ventilation
Lighting

RENOVATION
To retrofit or not?
Building envelope
Hazards
Construction and completion

and the design decisions they make have significant consequences for sustainability. In many countries, such as The Netherlands or Spain, the making of the plan for the city block is highly structured and regulated, while in others the architect has more scope for design intervention.

Urban fabric of Athens

At this scale, many of the decisions about the neighbourhood, the block and the building, as well as the shared lives of the occupants of the blocks, are made, sometimes without consciousness of the impact of these decisions. Orientation/daylight, three dimensional aspects of form, mix of uses, transport (public transport access, parking, cycling provision) and accessibility, efficient building typology, green/landscaped areas, shared open space, play space, refuse/recycling facilities, allowance for adaptability; all of these can be profoundly influenced for better or worse by masterplanning decisions of architects. The list is non-exhaustive, and design decisions have economic, social and indeed political impacts beyond the limits of the urban block itself.

The fact that place-specific urban block design is a requirement for most urban form in Europe offers an opportunity to architects, working with the other design professionals. While it is arguable that the spatial design training of the architect uniquely qualifies this profession to conceptualise and formulate spatial design proposals, other professionals including engineers, landscape architects and planners are increasingly part of the multi-disciplinary team of designers of the built environment. Increasing emphasis is being placed on the working methods of the integrated design team for large scale urban design work, as more joined-up thinking generally leads to better outcomes. A recent development is the rising numbers of architects seeking specialist training in urban design and urbanism, and a consequent re-appraisal of the context of the individual building design.

MICROCLIMATE

The urban climate differs from that of the surrounding territory, and there is a strong relationship between urban forms and spaces and strategic energy-efficient urban design. At block and neighbourhood scale, design decisions can improve local microclimate through creating shelter from excessive exposure to sun or wind, for example, or ameliorating the negative effects of urban conditions such as noise and atmospheric or visual pollution. Different layouts result in differing microclimates, providing greater or lesser comfort.

Temperature

Large towns tend to be considerably warmer than the surrounding countryside. Typically, daily mean temperatures are 1–2°C higher; more on a still summer evening. This is caused by several factors which together constitute 'the heat island' effect.

- Heat is given off by buildings, transport systems and industry
- Dense surface materials in ground and buildings store and conduct heat more effectively than do soil or vegetation.
- Buildings impede wind flow, reducing its potential cooling effect.
- Impervious surfaces, which induce fast water run-off, reduce evaporation, so there is less cooling effect.

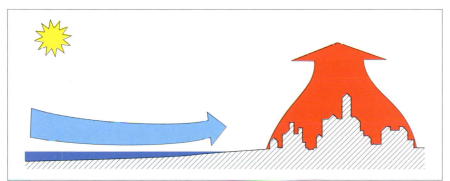

The 'heat island' effect

Wind

Because of the obstacles to wind flow presented by buildings and other structures, air movement in towns tends to be slower on average but more turbulent than in the countryside. It has been calculated that wind velocity within a town is typically half of what it is over open water.

Sunlight

It is obvious that buildings and other urban structures obstruct direct sunlight to some degree. Whether this is a benefit or disadvantage depends on other parameters of the microclimate. Depending on latitude, exposure to or protection from summer sun can be the more important.

Air quality

Pollutants from traffic, heating systems and industrial processes absorb and scatter sunlight, weakening direct solar radiation but increasing diffuse radiation on cloudless days. Air quality has implications for solar energy applications and for natural ventilation. In addition, pollutants contribute to the faster decay of building materials. Air quality, especially concentrations of CO, CO_2, SO_2, NO_x and particulates, also affects human health. It is estimated that there are ten times more particulates in city air than in the countryside *(Hough, 1995)*. The findings of a recent study conducted in Athens, Greece to investigate adverse effects of long-term air pollution exposure suggest that air pollution is a contributing factor in the occurrence of rhinitis and lung function impairment in mail carriers *(Karakatsani et al, 2010)*.

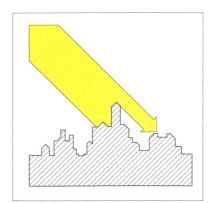

Urban fabric traps solar gain

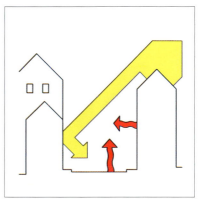

Dense materials store and radiate heat

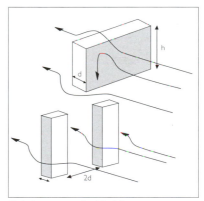

Turbulence around tall buildings

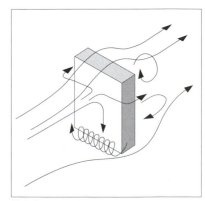

Turbulence and buildings

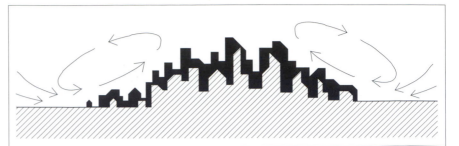

Air movement in towns is more turbulent than in the countryside

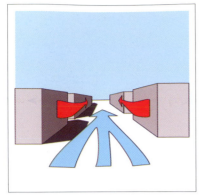

Prevailing wind funneled through a city street

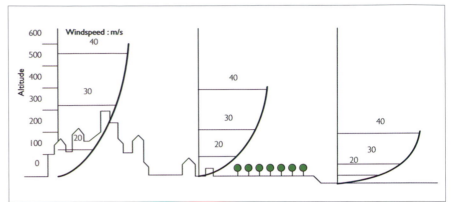

Wind speed at a given height is lower in towns than over open land

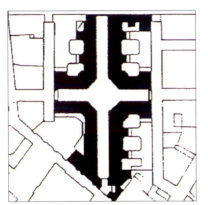

Site plan of the galleria in Milano, Architect: Mengoni

Air pollution has to be considered in two ways: firstly, the effect of pollutants on building design and performance and on the occupants' health; and secondly, the need to ensure that the buildings do not contribute themselves to more air pollution.

- Take account of prevailing winds in street layouts and orientations. Lay out buildings to shelter public spaces, unless cooling or dispersion of atmospheric pollutants is needed.

- In cool climates choose favourable solar orientations for streets and open spaces. Where possible, prevent surrounding vegetation or structures from overshadowing solar collection areas in the heating season. In warm climates, on the other hand, existing shade can be exploited.

- Remember the effects of surface materials at ground level. Stone, brick, concrete and similar materials with high thermal capacity form a heat store which can contribute to high air temperatures. Water can have a cooling effect through evaporation, as can vegetation through shading and evapo-transpiration.

Warm climate street layout providing solar shading. Source: Derry O'Connell

Cool climate open space provides shelter and sunshine. Source: Jeff Wilcox

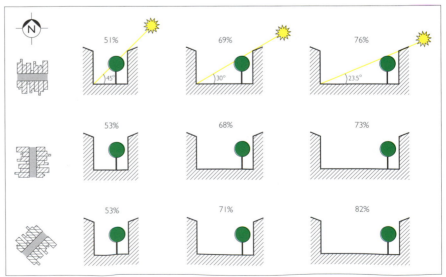

Solar access to buildings related to distance of obstructions

LAND USE

Land use is a highly significant factor in sustainable urban form. During much of the twentieth century, zoning regulations have resulted in the separation of the places where citizens work from the districts in which they live or shop or find recreation. This results in many people travelling greater distances on a daily basis, diminishing the quality of their lives and, in addition, increasing levels of global pollution through emissions from the transport systems they are forced to use.

In the effort to build more sustainable cities these policies are beginning to change. City or neighbourhood centres, multi-purpose buildings and spaces with a mix of civic, office, retail, leisure and residential uses encourage multi-purpose trips. Housing developed within reach of school, work, shops, social and health facilities reduces travel, giving people easier access to jobs, and businesses, easier access to potential customers and workers.

A wide mix of house types should be provided within a given urban area, so that people can find suitably designed and priced accommodation within short commuting distance of work. Such areas can attract a wide range of skills and professions for local employment. Mixed age groups can even-out peak demand for leisure facilities, public transport and other services.

Infill urban sites, already serviced and part of an accessible infrastructure, should be exploited wherever possible. Re-using an existing brownfield site avoids many of the service and infrastructural costs of developing a greenfield site and, in addition, raises environmental and aesthetic quality in its immediate neighbourhood.

DENSITY

It is generally argued that sustainable urban development patterns rely on the intensification and renewal of the existing fabric, and the application of bio-climatic principles to all of the activities carried on there. However, there are arguments for both high and low density.

Higher densities can mean lower energy consumption in buildings, less wastage of greenfield sites, greater use of public transport and increased potential for district and other forms of common heating. It can also have socio-economic benefits. For example, the commercial survival of many services depends on relatively high population densities for their customer base. In most western countries higher density residential developments are being concentrated near public transport nodes. However, while high density areas are associated with more efficient provision of services and accessibility, possible negative impacts such as lack of public space and pollution need to be addressed. Low density may result in higher quality of life, larger houses, the possibility of working from home, and a garden or green space for vegetable growing and composting, but can also mean inefficient use of transport.

Large or high buildings tend not only to use more energy inside, but also to have a more severe impact on the immediate external environment in terms of shade, wind turbulence and rain shadow. Reducing size or density can improve microclimate, but if this increases investment costs profits are reduced, or housing, for example, becomes less affordable. It is important that in maintaining the same densities different building forms are adopted to create better climate conditions externally and internally without affecting cost. This is easier to achieve in large integrated developments with central control than in situations where individual owners are restricted only by planning codes.

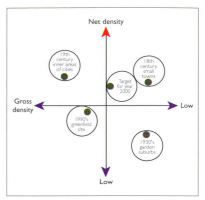

Comparison of different periods of housing in terms of net and gross densities, suggesting a shift from the prevailing 1990s pattern towards the ideal of the eighteenth century town; compact, mixed use developments, surrounded by green areas for recreation, garden farming etc. Source: Barton, Davies and Guise

For neighbourhood developments an average net density per hectare of 100 people [or about 40–50 dwellings] is recommended (Barton, Davies and Guise, 1995) on the basis that:

- It is the necessary density to support a good bus service

- It is the lowest density for viable district heating schemes

- It is the highest density capable of allowing good solar access with appropriate layout and it is the average level that permits a wide variety of dwelling and garden size.

Average net density per hectare for neighbourhood developments

Advantages of medium to high density developments:

- For a certain population size, increasing the density will leave more land for green areas.

- Schemes for food growth and production at a community scale become feasible.

- Reduced travel distances favours cyclists and pedestrians.

- District heating and cooling systems become feasible if local sources of waste heat are available.

Advantages of medium to high density development

Dublin Light rail system. Source: Vincente Navarro flickr.

Dublin bike scheme. Source: Dublin City Council

TRANSPORTATION

Land use, density and urban transportation systems are closely interdependent. Cheap road and rail transport and specialised land-use zoning have encouraged dispersed settlement patterns. These require citizens to make many journeys and also make public transport systems uneconomic. The traditional private car is the most wasteful user of energy and source of emissions today, so sustainable architecture needs to be combined with measures to reduce and restrict its use. Success partly depends on public policies for traffic calming, parking restrictions, road pricing, bus/taxi priority and other factors outside the control of most architects. It is likely that we will see a shift towards electric vehicles in response to public policy in many countries, with important consequences for energy and emissions, but also urban environmental quality.

At block scale, the detailed planning of access to public transport and the provision of convenient pedestrian and cycle pathways which tie into the broader urban systems is critical. Significant development should be within easy walking distance (approximately 400m) of public transport. For cyclists and pedestrians, routes should be continuous, reasonably direct, and free from heavy traffic, noise or pollution. Such systems encourage cycle and pedestrian travel for both functional and recreational purposes.

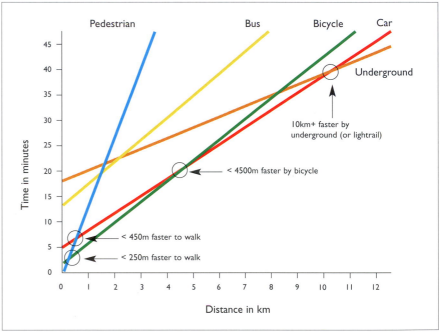

Travel times from door to door for different modes of transport in urban areas. (Based on Peter Newman and Jeffrey Kenworthy, Cities and automobile dependence: an International Sourcebook, Gaver Publishing, 1989)

GREEN SPACE

An important aspect of sustainable urban planning is the provision of green space at a number of scales. Play space, public parks and gardens in urban areas, and multi-purpose open spaces on the perimeter reduce pollution, create wildlife zones, and give access to the countryside for urban dwellers. They also contribute to the social, physical and psychological health of individuals and the community.

The green spaces in a neighbourhood can moderate local microclimate. Vegetation and water modify humidity, air temperature, wind, sunshine, noise and air pollution. They also have a role in the management of surface water and, potentially, of effluent. At the scale of the city, parkland has a significant effect on microclimate. Temperatures can be lower by 5–10°C in urban parks than in densely built areas around them. The effect on pollution is also significant.

A particularly beneficial strategy is to connect green spaces and wildlife habitats by linear or circular green links into a city-wide network. These links can be quite narrow and still facilitate the free movement of pedestrians, cyclists and animals throughout the system. Designers can set industry in parkland, or re-claim brownfield sites for open space. Try to ensure that recreational and pedestrian spaces have some protection from noise, traffic and pollution. However, uncultivated marginal land or the strips of land bordering railways or motorways or on industrial sites can be just as effective as parkland in fostering flora and fauna.

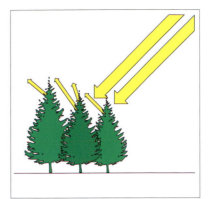

Vegetation modifies air temperatures near the ground

Linear green link Bastille Viaduct, Paris. Source: BE Sophanara

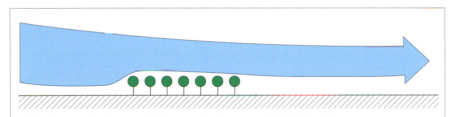

Shelter belts reduce wind speed

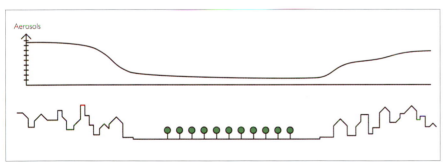

Aerosols

Vegetation absorbs or filters pollutants

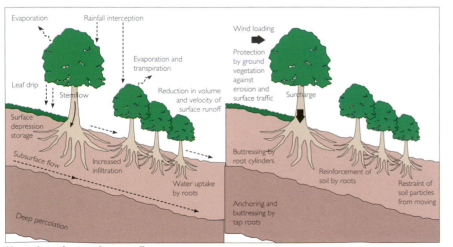

Evaporation · Rainfall interception · Evaporation and transpiration · Leaf drip · Stemflow · Reduction in volume and velocity of surface runoff · Surface depression storage · Subsurface flow · Increased infiltration · Water uptake by roots · Deep percolation

Wind loading · Protection by ground vegetation against erosion and surface traffic · Surcharge · Buttressing by root cylinders · Reinforcement of soil by roots · Restraint of soil particles from moving · Anchoring and buttressing by tap roots

Vegetation reduces surface run-off

Over one day, a single, large tree can transpire 450 litres, diverting 230,000 Kcal of energy away from raising air temperatures, equivalent to five average air-conditioner units running for 19 hours each.

To increase humidity at a site:

- Increase the water retention of surfaces and reduce drainage
- Provide a means of evaporative cooling using fountains, ponds, sprinklers and sprays for example
- Use vegetation in preference to hard landscaping materials where possible
- Use low planting to reduce moisture evaporation from ground

- Vegetation absorbs ozone, sulphur dioxide, carbon dioxide, and other pollutants, reducing the amounts present in the atmosphere
- Soil micro-organisms are particularly effective in contributing to the conversion of carbon monoxide to carbon dioxide
- Plants placed at roadsides release oxygen which combines with nitrogen oxide to form nitrogen dioxide, which is again absorbed by plants

Advantages of vegetation

Water resource. Source: Eric Jusino

Constructed wetlands, Hockerton Housing Project, Nottinghamshire. Source: Hockerton Housing Project Trading Limited

Constructed wetlands, Hockerton Housing Project, Nottinghamshire. Source: Hockerton Housing Project Trading Limited

Composting of organic waste

WATER AND WASTE

Waste handling and water conservation are closely linked. Poor handling of waste can irretrievably compromise the quality of water, with consequences for human and animal populations. Clean water is a resource to be protected at all times.

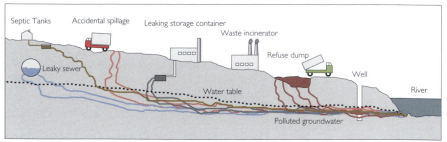
Impact of poor waste handling on water resources

Avoid designing landscape features which use water taken from the public drinking water supply and also any actions which might lead to its contamination.

Policies and designs should:
- minimise the demand for water suitable for drinking;
- minimise the amount of waste water to be handled by mechanical treatment;
- minimise the production of solid wastes, particularly unsorted wastes.

These steps will reduce the capital and running costs of public water supply, drainage and waste handling systems.

Systems which separate surface water from foul water are essential, while those separating grey water from black water are highly desirable. Filter strips of permeable ground cover and holding ponds allow rainwater to percolate back into the soil. Grey water and black water ideally should be handled on site through separation, treatment and composting rather than delivered via public sewers to conventional treatment plants. Reed beds and commercial percolation systems can be utilised for treatment. Constructed wetlands, combined with effluent treatment, can reduce sewage treatment costs by up to 90% compared with conventional mechanical systems

Communal provision at neighbourhood or block scale may make separation, collection and re-use of solid waste more economic. Organic waste can be composted. Combustible waste may be utilized to provide district heating, but the scale of operation must be large enough to warrant a system which prevents the release of other pollutants into the atmosphere.

ENERGY

Energy efficiency at the urban scale is promoted by attention to land-use, density, transportation, water and waste – and also by using the opportunity to support renewable energy sources cost-effectively at the urban scale.

This clearly depends on the particularities of local climate and conditions: renewable energies such as hydro or wind-power, ground water or biomass, active solar or PV may or may not be practical options. However, even at neighbourhood or block scale, opportunities for use of renewable energies and the more efficient use of conventional energy sources (e.g. combined heat and power or district heating) present themselves more often than might be expected (refer ELEMENTS; Components). In developments with a mix of residential and industrial buildings, educational or hospital campuses, these possibilities are well worth investigating. It is also desirable to ensure that large scale new or refurbished projects are assessed to quantify their environmental impact over their lifetime.

SITE SELECTION AND ANALYSIS

In most projects the site has been selected before the architect is appointed. Where this is not the case and the architect has a role in the selection process, the issues discussed in this section can be added to those usually considered when alternative sites are being investigated. The purpose is to transfer down to the level of the individual site the sustainable approach to microclimate, land use, density, transportation, green space, water, waste and energy that the previous section addressed at the urban and block scale. This should result in a choice which offers better conditions for the building user, a more benign effect on the global environment and, very possibly, lower development costs.

SITE SELECTION

Decisions on how to use the site, if indeed it should be built on at all, establish the base on which all later design decisions rest. The site provides the context for, and impacts on, the buildings, but the buildings in turn modify the site, affect neighbouring buildings and existing communities and may alter the local ecosystem.

Site selection checklist

- Is the land suitable for the intended purpose (does it have cultural, historical, archaeological or scientific significance?) and for development?
- Can it be developed without being destroyed?
- Are there better uses for the land, such as agriculture?
- Is public transport available nearby?
- Is there any potential for renewable energies or district heating?
- Does the site have daylight availability and solar access?
- Are there lakes, ponds or streams, or wetlands? Can groundwater be tapped?
- Is the site vulnerable to flooding, contamination risks?
- What is the condition of air, water and soil? What about noise?
- Is there a pre-existing infrastructure of power, water supply, communications, waste handling, and drainage?
- Depending on the intended use, are there appropriate commercial or community services nearby?
- Can existing structures be re-used?
- How might future developments on adjacent land affect the project?

It is important to emphasise that in sustainable site selection the site is considered not in isolation, but rather in its context, with a view to its place in and its contribution to the wider environment.

SITE ANALYSIS

An environmental analysis of the site enables the architect to optimize the opportunities for solar access, daylight penetration and natural ventilation through natural means, minimizing the impact on the site and the surrounding areas. At the macro-scale, the general climate of the region sets the stage with characteristic temperature, humidity, precipitation, cloudiness, wind speed, wind direction and sun path. Normal maxima and minima are used to define the amount of rainwater that must be drained away; the directions of favourable and unfavourable winds; when solar radiation should be invited or avoided and from which direction; and when the temperature moves outside the comfort zone.

At the local scale this climate will be modified by particular conditions. Drainage will affect humidity; industrial smoke or waste gases may reduce solar radiation; topography will affect wind speed.

Site and layout factors influencing microclimate

Outside designer's control:

Area and local climate

Plan shape of the site

Topographical conditions such as form, shape and aspect of the ground

Retained existing buildings

Road access

Services access

Planning constraints such as densities, building heights, tree preservation

Covenants restricting the form or character of development

Within designer's control:

Arrangement of buildings on site, such as orientation and siting

Road pattern and access, garages and stores

Location of open spaces, gardens and courtyards

Design of buildings including form, height, building structure and façades

Strategies for heating, cooling and daylighting

Other site features for consideration:

Tree cover – major and local wind shelter planting

Ground profiling – mounds and banks

Walls and artificial wind breaks and snow barriers

Ground surface -paving, grass and decorative planting

BRE Digest 350 Climate and Site Development Part 3

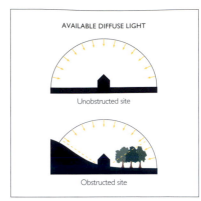

Effect of obstruction on daylight availability

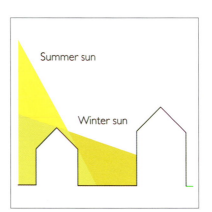

Effect of topography on solar access

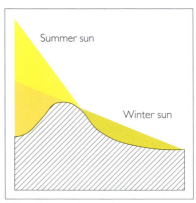

Effect of buildings on solar access

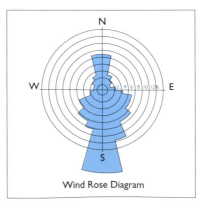

Local wind patterns

At the micro-scale of the site itself available daylight, solar energy, wind speed and temperature are all subject to modification by topography, vegetation and existing buildings, walls and fences. The micro-scale is the scale at which most can be done to manipulate the environment around the building. The objective is to exploit the naturally occurring beneficial features and minimise the negative features which may affect building performance.

Site analysis checklist

- Air temperatures / monthly mean temperatures for day and night
- Daylight: obstructions on or near the site that may affect the availability of light
- Sunlight: note slope and orientation of the site; maximum potential hours of sunlight based on climate data; sun angles based on site latitude; any overshadowing
- Wind: the wind rose for the area will give the directions and frequencies of the prevailing winds, but note the degree of exposure and local effects due to topography
- Topography: obstructions on the site can deflect the wind and provide shelter, but they may create overshadowing
- Structures: detail any structures which can be re-used and soil, stone or timber on the site that can be used for construction, landscaping or shelter
- Vegetation: note the type, size and condition of trees, shrubs, shelter belts, crops, ground cover
- Water: note the level of the water table and the existing pattern of water movement
- Soil: note type and firmness which may affect foundations, drainage and planting
- Air quality and noise levels: note aspects which will impact ventilation options
- Site area: note space availability for on-site waste recycling or digestion, for permaculture, for biomass or food production
- Hazards: record contaminated soil or ground water, radon or electromagnetic radiation sources, water retention
- Views: views from, of, or through the site may deserve preservation or exploitation
- Human and vehicular movement patterns.

In particular note,

Sunlight

- A south facing slope receives more solar radiation than a level site, which is important during winter when the sun angle is low
- North facing slopes over 10% or facing within 45° of north are generally unsuitable for successful passive solar applications.
- Any overshadowing by hills, trees or existing buildings will affect the amount of light available. Define large or nearby obstructions, even those to the north of the site.

Wind

- Wind speeds on the crest of a hill may be 20% greater than on flat ground
- At night time the cold air will tend to move downwards on exposed slopes, while the air is warmer higher up
- A slight wind even on calm days is characteristic of sea-coasts or lake shores
- Deep valleys or long straight avenues can funnel and accelerate wind speeds
- High buildings can create localised high wind speed and turbulence.

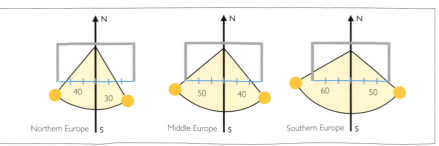

Best orientation for solar gain varies with latitude

SITE PLANNING

Urban and Neighbourhood Scale considered primarily the impact of development on the regional and global environment and on the community in which it sits. At the level of the site these continue to be of concern, but the designer begins to consider also the implications for the owner and for the users of the buildings which are to be built. The value of interdisciplinary team work at this stage cannot be overstated.

Good design should exploit or manipulate site characteristics to reduce energy consumption, optimise conditions for the building and comfort for its occupants, while interacting positively with the wider environment.

Site planning typically involves the evaluation of a number of site characteristics, but some of the natural characteristics of the site and the potential of renewable energies are often ignored. There are a number of critical relationships: those between the buildings themselves; between the buildings and the topography of the site; and the overall harmony of behaviour between buildings, vegetation and natural and artificial land forms. When internal and external spaces are designed with bioclimatic aims, buildings and the space surrounding them react together to regulate the internal and external environment, to enhance and protect the site, local ecosystems and bio-diversity.

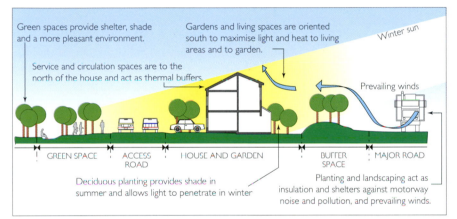

Some site strategies for residential areas

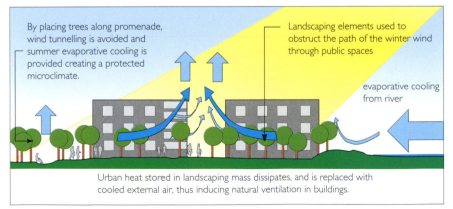

Some site strategies for commercial buildings

MICROCLIMATE

At the level of the individual site we consider microclimate from two viewpoints. We are concerned to modify site microclimate so as to create optimum conditions within the building while consuming the minimum of energy. We also want to design and locate the buildings so as to provide pleasant exterior spaces to be enjoyed by occupants and passers-by.

Plan safe pedestrian routes

Type of open space	Index
Woodland	100
Shrubs	118
Groundcovers	475
Roses	1,075
Rose gardens	1,291
Annuals	6,855
Perennials	1,842
Hedges	1,303
Lawns (overall maintenance)	210

Plants: comparative costs of maintenance. Source: Aaenemerij Plantsoerien vande Gemeete, Dept of Parks, Rotterdam

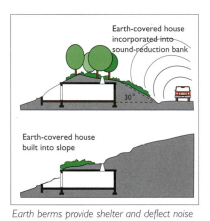
Earth berms provide shelter and deflect noise

Roof garden. Source: Charles Vinz

DENSITY

Site coverage is usually determined by the interaction of financial objectives and local ordinances. Preserve and reinforce what you can of natural landscape and topography or, where this is inappropriate, try to ensure that the new buildings do not compromise conditions in nearby buildings or neighbouring streets and urban spaces. Remember that large buildings, in addition to using more energy in construction and in use, have a more radical effect on the immediate microclimate.

TRANSPORTATION

Pedestrian and cycle routes should generally follow the contours of the site, to a normal maximum gradient of 1:20. In planning these routes take advantage of landmarks, views and existing vegetation, but try to ensure that pathways are sufficiently busy or overlooked that users are safe. Where parking is needed it can be integrated into the overall landscape. Parking areas do not need to have an impervious surface. Perforated blocks allow them to be grass-covered; when not in use for parking, the parking area can form part of the landscaping.

GREEN SPACE

Gardens and other green spaces provide visual and physical release from the enclosure of the building. Where site space is limited, a diversity of options such as balconies, terraces, roof gardens or courtyards can be explored. In residential areas, gardens allow the opportunity to grow food and should ideally be provided in a variety of sizes. In green spaces design will exploit landscape, water and vegetation to modify wind and shelter, light and shade, noise and air quality to provide the best conditions for the users of the building and the site.

Existing trees and vegetation should be protected and used in conjunction with new planting to create a desirable microclimate. Natural, indigenous planting has many advantages, and selecting the right varieties of trees, shrubs and ground cover can greatly reduce maintenance costs.

Avoid planning landscape features which will need irrigation in summer, unless provision is being made for the storage and re-use of rainwater or grey water.

Indigenous Planting

While significantly reducing maintenance costs, indigenous planting also:

- promotes long-term landscape stability and sustainability
- increases biological diversity
- enhances groundwater recharge through increased absorption
- regenerates organic soil layer through decomposition of above-ground growth
- reduces soil erosion with soil-holding root systems
- reduces downstream flooding by virtually eliminating surface water run-off
- preserves and/or restores existing plant and seed banks, maintaining genetic memory
- improves air quality through permanent carbon fixing in the soil
- improves water quality through filtering of dirty water and slowing of surface water velocities and reduces irrigation
- reduces usage of herbicides, pesticides and fertilisers

Earth

- Earth berms will provide shelter and deflect noise
- On a sloped site the building should be terraced rather than the land flattened.

Trees and Shrubs

- Tree and shrub belts can reduce wind velocities by up to 50% for a distance downwind of 10–20 times their height

- Trees in leaf reduce the amount of available light to 10–20% of its unobstructed value; even in winter deciduous trees reduce it by 40 or 50%

- Dense shelter belts of trees and shrubs act as a sound barrier

- Trees and shrubs absorb CO_2 and can remove up to 75% of dust, lead and other particulates from the air

- Trees and shrubs can lower summer temperatures by shading and evapo-transpiration (the loss of water through the soil by evaporation and transpiration of the plants growing on it)

- Trees and shrubs can increase winter temperatures by slowing wind speeds and reducing radiation to the night sky

- Trees with tall trunks and high canopy provide shade from the sun and, at the same time, permit cooling air circulation near ground level

- Shrubs or small trees can be used to shade any air conditioning or heat pump equipment which is located externally. This will improve the performance of the equipment, but, for good airflow and access, plants should not be closer than 900mm to the compressor

- Carefully evaluate existing plants on site to identify those which can play a role in an energy-conserving landscape. Mature trees will require less effort to maintain and will generally be of a larger size and more established than newly planted varieties

- If large trees need to be planted, it is best to select varieties that have a moderate rather than fast growth rate. These are sturdier against storm damage and generally more resistant to insects and disease.

Surface Cover

- Ground-cover planting and/or turf has a cooling effect through evapo-transpiration

- The temperature emitted by ground-cover will be 10–15° cooler than that of heat-absorbent materials such as asphalt or a reflective material such as light coloured gravel or rock

- A heat-absorbent material will continue to radiate heat after sunset

- Vines can be used to provide shading on walls and windows. Trellises placed close to the walls can be used to support growth without touching the walls

- Deciduous vines will allow winter sunlight to penetrate, while providing welcome summer shading. Evergreen vines will shade walls in the summer and reduce the effects of cold winds in the winter.

Water Features

- In southern Europe water features can help moderate microclimate through evaporative cooling of outdoor spaces

- Where possible, try to isolate the space to be cooled from the surroundings, so as to concentrate the benefits of the cooling presence of water in a limited area. The courtyard is a classic form

- The effect of a fountain on relative humidity depends on its design and water flow and surrounding vegetation and planting

- In sustainable landscape design the site's natural drainage patterns can be used to create water features.

WATER AND WASTE

The conservation of water and the disposal of waste have become significant issues in the environmental assessment of buildings, as is underlined by the EU Framework Directives for both water and waste.

At present, most developed sites deal with rainwater run-off from building roofs and impervious ground surfaces by channelling it into drains. These may be hazardous in storm conditions when rainwater mixed with sewage overflows into streams. A natural drainage system mimics nature, eliminates sewage treatment concerns and costs substantially less to build. Surface water can be diverted into filter strips of permeable

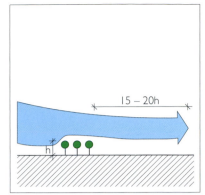

Natural shelter belts: extent of sheltered zone

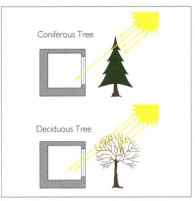

Trees reduce the amount of available light

Trees lower summer temperatures

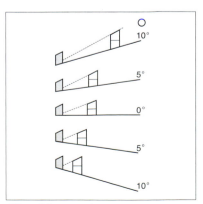

Effect of slope on solar access

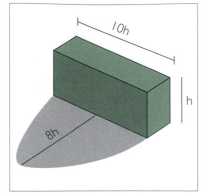

Solid barrier: maximum sheltered zone

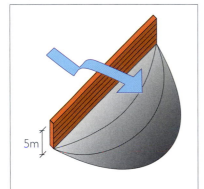

Calculated areas of protection behind a permeable windbreak

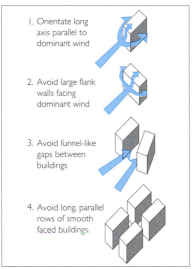

1. Orientate long axis parallel to dominant wind

2. Avoid large flank walls facing dominant wind

3. Avoid funnel-like gaps between buildings

4. Avoid long, parallel rows of smooth faced buildings.

Choose form and arrangement of building clusters to avoid downdraughts and shelter external spaces

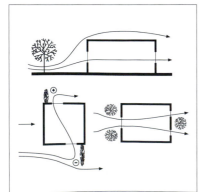

Funnel cool breezes around or through buildings to reduce cooling load

ground cover and holding ponds, following the natural drainage patterns of the site to percolate back into the soil. While these systems can be cost effective for the developer such natural systems need proper design and maintenance plans to function effectively.

Minimise the extent of impervious surfaces such as driveways, parking and paving. This slows run-off, reducing damage to neighbouring land and waterways and the load on the district sewage system. Ensure that as much rainwater as possible finds its way back into the soil in as clean a condition as possible. Consider harvesting rainwater, collecting and storing rainwater for irrigating vegetation, cleaning exterior surfaces and other outdoor uses.

As for foul water, there is a wide range of treatment plants available, including septic tanks, rotating bio-disks, reed beds, and dry toilet systems. Separation of grey water and black water offers the possibility of re-using site-treated greywater for irrigation and other uses.

Grey water from sinks and bathrooms can be treated and stored on site and reused for wc flushing and landscaping. Then only black water remains to be handled by separation, treatment and composting on site or delivered via public sewers to conventional treatment plants.

Disposal routes for treatment systems should be considered under local environmental legislation, the vulnerability of local streams and groundwater aquifers. Carefully evaluate the following:

- Access to existing district sewer systems
- Access to surface water with sufficient assimilative capacity for waste volumes and concentrations
- Water table level
- Permeability of subsoil
- Density of existing neighbourhood development, utilizing the soil as a disposal mechanism through percolation beds
- Sensitivity of the environment.

Provide on-site facilities for separation, storage and recycling of domestic waste. Organic waste can be composted for use in site landscape or, in residential areas, for private gardens.

ENERGY

Creative use of the site to reduce heating and/or cooling loads within the building represents one of the greatest opportunities in site design. The best position for the building is found by assessing the interior demands of the building in relation to data gathered in the course of the detailed site analysis (refer STRATEGIES; Site Selection and Analysis).

Heating

In northern latitudes, where heating load is the dominant factor in many buildings, the 'ideal' orientation for passive solar design is a south-facing principal façade. In residential buildings large glazed areas on the south façade allow the sun to flood into the building in winter-time and openings on the northern façade can be reduced to the minimum. Many studies have shown that for a given site with given houses, simple site replanning and dwelling reorientation can almost halve energy demand per house.

In non-residential buildings at these latitudes the daylight gained through larger glazed areas on the north façade may more than balance the heat losses through them, but overheating must be prevented by shading on south façades. In these buildings glazing on east or west façades is often the cause of overheating and is difficult to shade effectively. In either case it is wise to site the proposed buildings in the zone with the least overshadowing during the most important hours of the heating season. South-facing slopes receive more sun than ground sloping north. Place taller buildings to the north, so they do not overshadow the lower ones. When assessing the potential solar gain, take account of any shade or partial shade from trees, and thermal radiation from adjacent buildings, walls and surfaces.

As stated in earlier sections, site topography will affect wind speed and direction. In many areas of Europe the wind blows predominantly from one direction and design should attempt to deflect or reduce this without reducing solar gain.

Wind speed or direction can be modified by new land forms, structures and vegetation, and the form of individual buildings can be designed to block or divert winds. Using or creating shelter on the site can cut heat loss from buildings through convection and infiltration, improving the comfort of indoor (and outdoor) living spaces.

Cooling

In southern latitudes orient the building and design glazed areas to minimise solar overheating, taking advantage of any existing shade or providing shading devices. But do not forget the need for adequate daylight to minimise internal gains from electric lighting.

In the south, especially with lightweight, low thermal inertia buildings, specific measures may be required to maintain comfort conditions. In the cooling season, it may be useful to direct the prevailing wind flow, using building form, vegetation or topography to funnel cool breezes around or through the building, reducing the cooling load.

When hard surfaces are used, pale colours are more effective in reflecting solar radiation and consequently keeping down surface temperatures, but they may cause glare. For cooling, it is best to minimise the use of heat absorbent materials near buildings or shade them from any direct sunshine.

Use vegetation in the form of trees or vines, and ground cover planting instead of hard surfaces. Both will lower temperatures through shading and evapo-transpiration.

Consider the use of water features to provide evaporative cooling.

Ventilation

External air quality and noise will affect the choice of ventilation strategy and the extent to which opening windows can be used.

Sound is reflected by surrounding objects and hard surfaces. It is reduced by distance and barriers (such as walls, buildings and earth berms), and absorbed to some degree by soft ground surfaces and walls.

Trees can play a double role in this regard. Dense shelter belts act as a sound barrier and, in addition, absorb CO_2 and can remove up to 75% of dust, lead and other particulates from the air.

Daylight

The amount of daylight available in the building will be affected by the placement of the buildings on the site, the amount of overshadowing, the external landscaping and finishes. Pale surfaces on the ground and on neighbouring buildings will increase the amount of light available to the interior.

The location of trees in relation to buildings needs careful consideration, because they reduce light transmission even when leafless in winter. One rule of thumb is to locate only smaller trees (5–10m high, depending on distance) to the south of the building.

Pale surfaces reflect solar radiation. Architect: Sottomayor, Dominguez and Lopez de Asian

Pale surfaces increase daylight to interior, Elizabeth Fry Building, University of East Anglia. Architect and source: John Miller and Partners

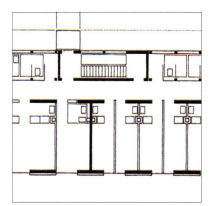

Spaces located in plan in relation to heating and cooling needs. Hostel at Windberg Plan. Architect and source: Herzog and Partner Architects

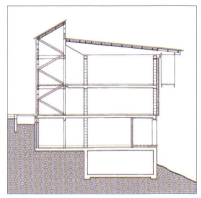

Spaces located in section in relation to heating and cooling needs. Hostel at Windberg section. Architect and source: Herzog and Partner Architects

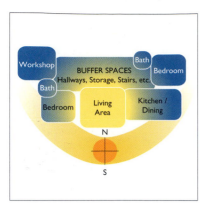

Location of housing indoor spaces

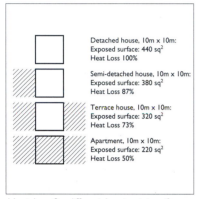

Heat loss for different housing types. Source: Barton, Davies and Guise, 1995

Energy efficient row housing, Ballymun, Dublin. Architect: DTA Architects. Source: John Searle

Apartments use less energy than other housing forms, Clarion Quay, Dublin. Architect: Urban Projects. Source: Ciaran O'Brien

BUILDING FORM

Building plan and form emerge in a complex process. Functional, technical and aesthetic considerations all contribute to a synthesis. Wind, solar availability and direction, shelter and exposure, air quality and noise conditions will inform the relationship of the building to its external environment and effect the form and the design of the envelope. Bioclimatic heating, cooling, daylighting and energy strategies should be meshed at an early stage with the architect's other priorities. Simply making the building the right shape and the correct orientation can reduce the energy consumption by as much as 20–35% at no extra cost.

Getting the form and spatial organisation right first time is important. Changes once the building is built are difficult if not impossible, and both financially and environmentally costly.

Zone and orient spaces, both in plan and in section, in relation to their heating, cooling, lighting and ventilation needs so as to minimise the total energy demand of the building. Where possible, locate spaces requiring continuous heat on southern façades so that they can benefit from solar gain; buffer them to the north with spaces which do not need it. Rooms needing only intermittent heating can occupy less favourable orientations. For optimal performance of passive solar heating, daylighting and natural cooling, the heat gaining spaces should all face within 15° of due south.

Conversely, spaces needing cooling should be located on northern façades. Spaces where daylight is important clearly need to be located near to the walls or roof of the building. For natural ventilation the depth and section of the building are critical.

Meeting these objectives for every space, while also satisfying the normal functional demands of any building, is not easy, and heavily influences its form.

In terms of heating and cooling the optimum shape of a building is one which loses the minimum amount of heat in the heating season and gains the minimum amount in the cooling season. This of course will vary according to the climatic zone in which the building is located.

A building elongated along the east-west axis exposes the longer south side to maximum heat gain in the winter months, and the shorter east and west sides to maximum heat gain in summer. At European latitudes the south façade of a building receives at least three times the solar radiation in winter as the east and west. In summer the situation is reversed. In both in summer and winter, the north side receives very little radiation. Consequently a building elongated along the east-west axis, the extent of elongation dependent on climate, is held to be the most efficient shape in all climates for minimising heating requirements in winter and cooling in summer.

In all climates, attached units like row houses or terraced houses are the most efficient because only two walls are external, and the opportunity for cross-ventilation is available. For a given floor area, apartments use less energy than terraced houses; terraced less than semi-detached; and semi-detached, less than detached houses.

Two formal elements often used in conventional buildings, the sunspace and the atrium, can play a useful role in passive solar design.

Familiar in the form of the traditional domestic conservatory, glazed balcony or loggia, the sunspace has, over time, proven to be a practical and versatile element of passive solar heating. Employing a combination of both direct and indirect gain approaches, it can be incorporated into the design of a new building, or can be a valuable addition to an existing one.

The atrium has the potential to transform both functionally and climatically what might have been seen as an anonymous street or a drab, lifeless courtyard into a sheltered, functional amenity, an asset to any development. For this reason, the covering of open spaces between buildings with glazed roofing has become a common feature, but exploitation of the potential to reduce heating, cooling and lighting demands tends to be overlooked. A correctly designed atrium will improve indoor comfort and reduce payback time.

Most European buildings, of course, have both a heating and cooling season, so must provide for some degree of adjustment to meet changing conditions. In addition, on many sites the microclimate conditions create their own conflicts, such as severe wind exposure on the southern façade for example. Furthermore, constricted sites, difficult boundary conditions or local regulations may place further restrictions on the designer's ability to achieve optimum response to climate.

Finally, energy considerations alone can never determine building form. Design for flexibility and 'loose fit' to encourage re-use in the future, but remember also that in terms of environmental impact the expression 'less is beautiful' is a useful guide.

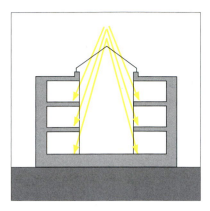

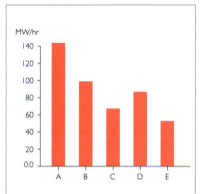

Annual heating energy consumption for a building with an atrium: A - No atrium; B - Atrium present, but no ventilation coupling with the building; C - Ventilation pre-heating, D - Ventilating air expelled into atrium, raising its temperature; E - Recirculation of air between building and atrium. Source: Baker, 1995

Northern Latitudes

Where heating is the dominant requirement the following strategies can be effective:

- low surface to volume ratio;

- maximising solar gain;

- reduction of the surface area facing north, or exposed to prevailing winds

- insulation of building envelope;

- control of ventilation and infiltration;

- use of draught lobbies to separate heated spaces from unheated spaces and from the outside;

- location of entrance doors away from corners and from prevailing winds;

- use of 'buffer spaces' on northern or exposed façades, and unheated conservatories or 'sunspaces' on the south. The less the temperature difference between internal and outdoor temperatures, the lower the rate of heat loss through the envelope;

- use of atria and courtyards to act as thermal buffer space and introduce daylight into deep plans;

- use of thermal mass to store heat produced by solar gain and release it as interior temperatures fall.

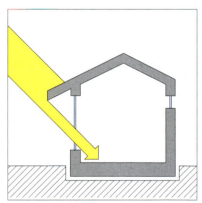

Horizontal overhangs shade the building envelope

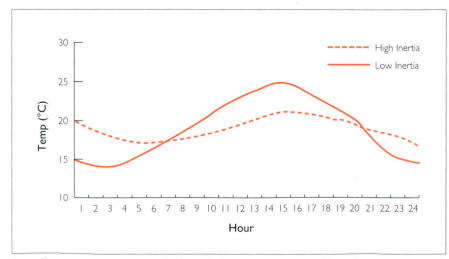

Internal temperatures on a hot day in buildings of high and low thermal inertia. Thermal mass can help in both hot and cold climates

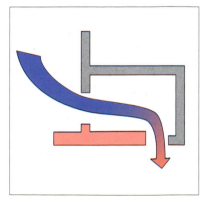

Locate openings to catch prevailing winds

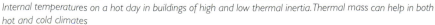

Southern Latitudes

Where cooling is the dominant need the following strategies may apply:

- low surface to volume ratio;

- reduction of the surface area facing south;

- provision of overhangs, arcades, shutters and canopies to shade building envelope

- insulation of building envelope, particularly the roof;

- control of ventilation and infiltration when exterior air temperatures are high;

- provision of solar chimneys to encourage stack ventilation where outdoor temperatures are sufficiently cool;

- location of openings on shaded side of building or so as to catch prevailing winds;

- use of 'buffer spaces' on southern façades;

- use of thermal mass to store heat produced by solar gain thus reducing overheating in interior spaces;

- use of courtyards to form reservoirs of cool air close to building and introduce daylight to deep building plans;

- use of water features for evaporative cooling.

BUILDING ENVELOPE

In sustainable architecture the link between building performance and the design of the envelope is critical. Any well-built building enclosure is expected to keep out wind, damp and rain, to let in light and air, to conserve heat and to provide security and privacy. In a sustainable building we may also expect it to mediate the effects of climate on the users and the energy systems of the building, collect and store heat, redirect light, control air movement and generate power.

A better envelope may sometimes be more expensive to build, but if it improves the balance between heat gain and heat loss, reduces the size of heating plant, eliminates the need for perimeter heating, or cuts fuel bills, the extra cost may be balanced by savings in the operation of the building. A life cycle cost analysis should be used.

Apart from any ventilation openings they may contain, the opaque areas of walls, floors and roofs are static elements. The functions include thermal functions such as heating and cooling through shelter and insulation and by reduction of temperature swings through use of thermal mass; as well as acoustic and energy production functions.

The glazed elements of the building may be more dynamic to respond to short- and long-term changes in interior and exterior conditions. They have more complex functions such as daylighting, as well as providing views and communication with the outside; heating through controlled use of solar gain and cooling by shading and ventilation.

Legislation on energy performance in buildings has led to more focus on the performance of the building envelope and the optimization of heat transfer between inside and outside, and also decentralized energy production via the building envelope (Hegger et al, 2008).

Environmental considerations in the selection of building envelope materials, and particularly the embodied energy of high performance insulation materials, are more critical than ever as we move towards the achievement of carbon neutral buildings.

Performance testing of the envelope is increasingly required, demanding that design, specification and construction are all very carefully undertaken.

Sustainable strategies for envelope design

- Respond to orientation to provide for heating and cooling and daylight strategies. The world about the building is not symmetrical. Modify the envelope to respond to the challenges and opportunities presented by different façade orientations.

- Design and detail the building envelope to minimize heat losses and achieve thermal comfort with respect to thermal mass and insulation, avoid thermal bridging and minimise air infiltration.

- Design for durability. Specify for long life and low maintenance to minimise the use of energy and materials over the life of the building.

- Specify materials with low embodied energy —more significant as we move towards carbon neutral buildings.

- Minimise heat loss through infiltration and provide controlled energy efficient ventilation with heat recovery.

- Integrate appropriate passive components to enhance the performance of the envelope.

- Integrate active technologies to provide energy from renewable sources.

- Keep it simple. Do as much as possible by architectural means before resorting to service installations to fine-tune the indoor environment.

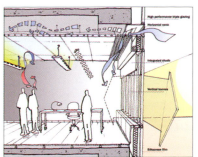

Envelope acts as mediator of climate, Tour Carpe Die, Paris. Architect: Robert A. M. Stern Architects. Source: Atelier Ten

Active façade at BRE Watford. Architects: Fielden Clegg Architects. Source: Dennis Gilbert

Considerations for façade design include:
- Thermal, solar and light transmission properties of the elements
- Control of openings, for heat losses and gains
- Potential for thermal collection and storage
- Glazing ratios.

The role the envelope is required to play in any particular building will depend on the heating, cooling, ventilation and lighting strategies adopted.

The following checklist may help to prioritise decisions in relation to envelope design and specification:
- Is it to be a slow or fast response building?
- Is the envelope to be used as a heat store?
- Is the primary objective to exploit daylight, to maximise heat gain, or to minimise heat loss?
- Are there particular problems of use, site or orientation to be overcome?

Choices about materials will be influenced by issues of embodied energy and of health.

Considerations for façade design

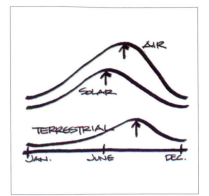

Annual solar and terrestrial air temperature.
Source: Bruce Haglund

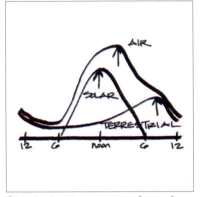

Diurnal solar air temperature. Source: Bruce
Haglund

Exposed slab in Offaly County Council building,
Architect: ABK Architects. Source: Christian
Richters

Sinusoidal slab in the BRE building, Watford,
Architect and source: Fielden Clegg Bradley
Studios

OPAQUE / SOLID ELEMENTS

The solid elements of the building envelope can perform both heating and cooling functions through use of thermal mass, insulation and protection of the internal environment from air infiltration.

Heating and cooling

Efficient thermal performance of the envelope in northern Europe means heat conservation. Buildings lose heat through their external fabric and by uncontrolled ventilation and infiltration.

In southern Europe walls may facilitate the undesirable transfer of heat to the inside. Traditionally, solid, brightly painted walls are used to reflect solar radiation, while the thermal inertia of masonry walls slows down unwanted gain and dissipates it at night keeping the interior cool.

For both heating and cooling functions, the thermal properties of an opaque wall can be controlled by:

- thermal conductivity and thermal storage capacity of material (thermal mass);
- thermal insulation;
- good detailing.

Thermal Mass

Studies analysing passive solar design of non-domestic buildings found that:

- high thermal mass is desirable to stabilise daytime temperatures and for night cooling, but may marginally increase heating cost in some buildings;
- thermal mass is best increased by maximising surface area, as increase in thickness is relatively ineffective;
- thermal mass delays the time at which peak temperatures occur;
- thermal mass should not be thermally isolated from circulating air (e.g. under a raised floor or above a suspended ceiling);
- adopting a night cooling strategy can enhance the performance of thermal mass.

Walls

Wall materials can be categorised in terms of low or high thermal mass. For example, masonry construction has good thermal inertia qualities, which slow down the building's response to changes in external conditions and limit internal temperature swings. Clay bricks, concrete blocks and rammed earth are examples of this kind of construction. A low thermal mass building is one with a timber- or steel-framed structure and lightweight cladding panels. This gives a fast thermal response to changes in external conditions and results in larger temperature swings.

In buildings occupied by day, thermal mass will absorb heat during the day and release it at night, reducing peak day-time air temperatures. Thermal comfort depends as much on mean radiant temperature as on air temperature, and the surface temperature of thermally massive elements will be lower than the air temperature at peak times, contributing further to comfort. In buildings not occupied all day, in cooler climates, a lightweight envelope with low thermal mass may be appropriate, as it can reduce response time and the heat required to provide comfort.

Floors

Suspended timber floors have less embodied energy than concrete floors (refer ISSUES, Environment), but a concrete slab (provided that it is not covered with a lightweight finish) can act as a thermal store, as the cross-section through the floor construction of the BRE building in England illustrates.

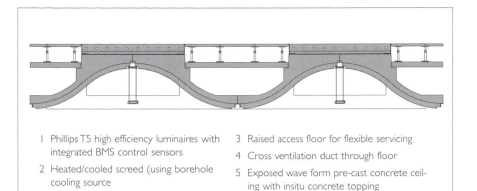

1 Phillips T5 high efficiency luminaires with integrated BMS control sensors

2 Heated/cooled screed (using borehole cooling source

3 Raised access floor for flexible servicing

4 Cross ventilation duct through floor

5 Exposed wave form pre-cast concrete ceiling with insitu concrete topping

Cross section through sinusoidal floor slab in BRE building, Watford. Architect: Fielden Clegg Bradley Studios. Source: Dennis Gilbert

Materials	Thermal Conductivity W/mK
Expanded polystyrene board	0.036–0.038
Expanded polystyrene cavity wall partial fill board	0.025
Glass fibre quilt	0.040
Glass fibre partial fill cavity slab	0.034
Mineral fibre quilt	0.037
Mineral fibre partial fill cavity slab	0.032–0.033
Polyurethane board	0.023–0.025
Polyisocyanurate	0.023–0.020

Thermal conductivity of some common insulating materials

Insulation

Walls, roofs and other opaque parts of a building must be provided with thermal insulation, both in cool climates to reduce heat loss and to maintain internal surfaces at a higher temperature than would otherwise be the case, and in hot climates to reduce external gains and to maintain internal surfaces at a lower temperature, thus improving comfort levels.

Reduction of heat loss by means of increased levels of insulation is still the most effective conservation measure, but it should be remembered that the law of diminishing returns applies in specifying insulation thickness.

Choosing the appropriate insulation material depends on the application, placement in element, life cycle analysis, and specific requirements such as compressive strength and environmental characteristics.

Building envelope insulation performance is best when a complete seamless layer of insulation is provided which eliminates thermal bridging, air infiltration and interstitial condensation. The air permeability or airtightness of the building envelope is evaluated by undertaking a blower door test, and the insulation integrity can be checked through thermographic imagery.

Airtightness should not be confused with what was commonly referred to as the 'breathing wall' but is now better known as 'diffusion open' construction. Envelopes constructed with natural materials are often detailed to be diffusion open, mainly to overcome moisture build-up that can occur within the construction; whether moisture arising during the construction process, or vapour associated with occupation resulting in interstitial condensation. Previously, breathing wall construction was intended to diffuse outwards whereas with modern intelligent membranes diffusion can happen in either direction (depending on the relative humidity of the air).

Walls

Insulation may be placed on the external or internal face of a wall or within the wall without, in theory, altering the overall insulation properties. The optimal position will be determined by the availability of thermal mass, occupancy patterns, and the responsiveness and control of the heating system.

Internal insulation

Internal insulation will separate the thermal mass of the walls from the space, and reduce both the response time and the energy required to bring the room up to comfort levels. There may be thermal mass available in other elements in the space which will dampen temperature fluctuations. Otherwise the application is appropriate for intermittently heated buildings.

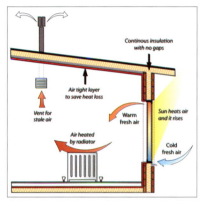

Achieving a jointless, sealed and airtight skin is particulary important to the achievement of energy efficient ventilation strategies. Source: Ballymun Regeneration Limited

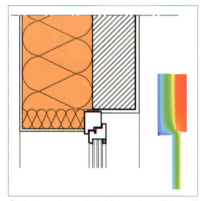

Reducing thermal bridging in solid wall insulation. Source: Isover

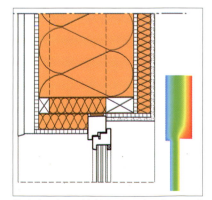

Reducing thermal bridging in timber frame wall insulation. Source: Isover

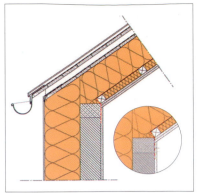

Reducing thermal bridging in insulation of masonry construction. Source: Isover

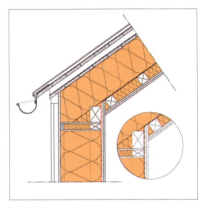

Reducing thermal bridging in insulation of timber frame construction. Source: Isover

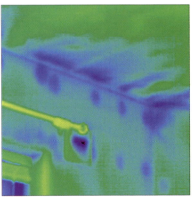

Infra red image of roof/wall junction. Source: Donal Lennon

Air permeability test. Source: Tõnu Mauring

The disadvantage of internal insulation is that it is prone to detailing problems such as thermal bridging and condensation.

External insulation

The higher internal thermal capacity available as a result of locating the insulation on the outside of the building means that fluctuations in air temperature are reduced, but the space will take longer to heat up and cool down. Thus the application is most suitable for continuously heated buildings, and low energy buildings with significant solar gains.

It's usually easier and safer to achieve high standards of insulation using external insulation; this is especially the case in retrofitting masonry walls without cavities. Effective vapour control and services distribution are two aspects which are facilitated. The disadvantage of locating the insulation externally is that the layers of finish on the outside of the insulation will be subject to larger temperature fluctuations, resulting in thermal stress and movement and requiring careful specification of finishes.

Cavity insulation

In some parts of Europe masonry cavity wall insulation is a standard form of construction. The cavity may be either partially or fully insulated depending on the details of construction, and the climate. Cavity insulation makes available some of the thermal inertia within the wall and substantially reduces the risk of air infiltration and condensation within the building. It also reduces problems from thermal bridges.

Roofs

Generally the position of insulation in the roof will offer similar advantages and disadvantages as mentioned for walls.

Pitched roofs are usually insulated just above ceiling level leaving the attic space unheated (if it is not occupied). The unheated space is well ventilated and risk of condensation is low. Insulation can easily be upgraded by adding another layer.

Flat roofs may be one of three types: the 'cold roof' is ventilated above the insulation, while in the 'warm roof' the insulation layer lies immediately below the roof covering and is unventilated. The warm roof has less risk of condensation, but as with external insulation, the layers of finish on top of the insulation will be subject to large temperature fluctuations, and to thermal stress and movement. The inverted roof uses a water-resistant insulant on top of (and protecting) the weatherproof membrane.

Floors

There is evidence that heat losses through solid ground floors are greater than standard calculations suggest. Heat loss from the slab is not constant over the whole area of the floor, the greatest being from the edge. Studies have shown that insulating the edges of the slab can have as good an effect as overall insulation, and the U-value calculation for the ground floor slab must take into account both the size and edge conditions of the slab.

Additional insulation of a suspended timber floor is usually provided in the form of either a continuous layer of semi-rigid or flexible material laid above the joists (and below the floor finish), or else semi-rigid material between the joists. The U-value is calculated as a combination of the floor finish, the air spaces and the overall insulation above the structural floor.

TRANSLUCENT ELEMENTS

Heating

Transparent insulation material (TIM) can admit daylight but without the heat loss associated with conventional glazing. In addition, its composition can still allow useful solar gain. The heating load in both new and retrofit applications can be reduced significantly with the application of TIM; however, care is necessary in its specification to avoid overheating problems.

Daylighting

Transparent insulation material sandwiched between sheets of glass in a conventional frame can replace traditional glazing where light but not vision is required. There are several categories of TIM and performance characteristics, such as light transmission, total solar energy transmittance (TSET) and thermal (Ug-values) can be varied by using other constructions and glass types. Ug-values of up to 0.4 W/m²K, light transmission from 60% to 21% and TSET of up to 12% are possible.

Okalux glass with transparent insulation. Source: Okalux Kapillarglas GmbH

Transparent insulation in Falls Leisure Centre, Belfast. Architect and source: Kennedy FitzGerald Architects LLP

Hostel at Windberg with transparent insulated façade. Architect: Herzog and Partner Architects

TRANSPARENT ELEMENTS

In a sustainable building the glazing elements are often the most interesting and complex. Glazing and window design are areas in which there have been considerable technical developments in recent years, with new materials emerging from research laboratories. It is now possible to specify the make-up of a glazing unit to meet the requirements for heat gain, heat conservation, light transmission and light direction, at different latitudes and for different orientations.

Good glazing and window design involves finding a balance between demands which are often conflicting such as passive heating and cooling functions, e.g. allow solar gain but keep out excessive solar heat, provide sufficient daylight without causing glare, allow controllable ventilation into the building but keep out excessive noise, allow visual contact with the surroundings but ensure sufficient privacy and ensure safety.

Heating

Direct heat gain through correctly oriented windows is the simplest and often the most effective manifestation of 'climatic' architecture. Glazing design and orientation should optimise useful solar gains and minimise heat losses during the heating season.

The design of glazed areas must balance heating, cooling and daylighting needs (refer EVALUATION; The LT Method).

Kalwall in Pearse Stree Primary Care Centre, Dublin. Architect: A+D Wejchert & Partners. Source: Peter Moloney

Kalwall in Metea Valley High School, Aurora, IL. Architect: DLR Group. Source: Kalwall Corporation

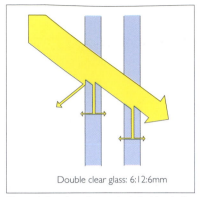

Transmission through standard double glazing system

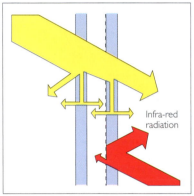

Infra-red radiation

Transmission through typical Low E glazing

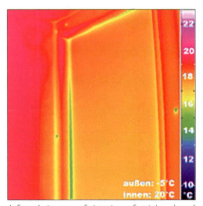

Infrared image of interior of triple glazed window. Source: Passivhaus Institute Darmstadt

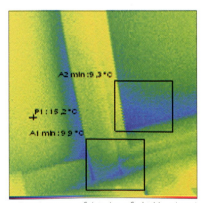

Infrared image of interior of double glazed window. Source: Passivhaus Institute Darmstadt

If south-facing glazed areas are to be larger than the size required for daylighting so as to increase solar gain, their U-value must be improved. But lower U-values in glazing are usually associated with some reduction in light transmittance. On the other hand, improving the U-value of the glazing will raise the mean radiant temperature in the space and so reduce the air temperature required for comfort.

An alternative approach is to use glazed areas no larger than those required for daylighting, but to install very high levels of insulation, taking particular care to eliminate thermal bridges and minimise infiltration losses. In such a building, the solar gains from conventionally sized windows should meet a significant proportion of the heating demand.

Thermal insulation

Glass is a poor thermal insulator. There are a number of ways to decrease heat lost through glazing:

- low-energy coating on the glass (Low E) decreases radiation heat loss;
- gases such as argon or krypton may be substituted for the air in the cavity to further decrease the convective heat loss of the pane;
- triple-glazing with low-e coating, with or without argon or krypton gas.

In addition to the thermal conductivity qualities of the glass itself, energy is lost through and around the fenestration by infiltration, and radiation and via the frame. Infiltration gains and losses can be significant but avoided by well-fitting frames and weather-stripping. Since the overall percentage of the area of framing in elevation can be 10–20% of the component area, the thermal insulation value of the frame is important.

Timber, used as a framing material, conducts less heat than other materials. Metal frames should be well insulated and have a thermal break, which will result in much lower heat losses. Weather gaskets are also important, and typically there will be two weather gaskets in high performance frames, the primary function of the outer one being for weathering with the inner one serving to improve air-tightness. Typically triple glazed windows are used in passive houses in central and northern Europe. The principal characteristics and advantages of using triple glazed windows are listed below:

- Three panes of glass separated by low conductivity spacers eliminates the risk of condensation at the bottom of the glass in cold weather;
- Low E coating on the inside of the two outer panes reduces thermal re-radiation;
- Insulating gases in both cavities reduces heat loss.

With triple glazing the solar transmittance is somewhat reduced in comparison with double glazing, due to the effect of the additional pane of glass. In designing a passive house it is important to ensure a minimum solar transmittance of 60% or higher to optimise the solar contribution towards heating the building, taking care to avoid over heating in the cooling season.

Cooling

Overheating in the cooling season is one of the most serious problems related to glazing and window design. The principal passive cooling techniques include the use of solar shading and ventilation.

Type of Pane	U-Value W/m²K	light transmission %	solar transmission %
Clear glass			
Single glass, 4 mm	6.0	88	83
Double glass with air (4-12-4)	3.0	80	76
Double glass with Low E coating & argon (4-12-4)	1.5	77	65
Triple glass with air (4-12-4-12-4)	2.0	72	67
Triple glass with Low E coating & argon	1.0	67	68
Triple glass with Low E coating & krypton	0.7	67	69
Vacuum pane with Low E coating (4-12-4)	0.5	77	65
Reflective glass			
Double medium reflective glass with Low E coating (6-12-6)	1.6	29	39
Double glass, bronze + low E coating with argon (6-12-6)	1.6	9	13

The optical and thermal characteristics of a range of glazing materials. (Data assembled from product literature of various manufacturers)

Solar shading

Heat gain through conventional windows can be significant. Depending on the orientation and geographic location, if sensible glazing ratios are adopted the need for shading may be reduced. However, where solar radiation is excessive for parts of the day in summer, the most effective way to reduce heat gain is to prevent or block solar radiation by using external shading. A wide and ever-growing competitive range of shading devices is available to the architect, including blinds, shutters, louvres and structural or add-on devices.

If external shading is not possible, the closer the shading is to the outside of the building the more satisfactory it will be. Use of plants for shading should also be considered (refer STRATEGIES; Landscape).

Shading devices can be classified as fixed or movable, internal or external. Overhangs, loggias and arcades are examples of fixed shading favoured in southern Europe for their provision of shade against hot summer midday sun, and are among the traditional built approaches. Louvres and overhangs can be fixed directly onto the façade. These systems, while durable and maintaining air movement, are limited in that they provide adequate shading for only part of the day in particular seasons, and limit the amount of daylight entering the space at other times of year when natural light would be welcome.

Moveable shading devices include shutters, which are widely used. Insulated shutters are an energy-efficient option. Manually or automatically controlled louvres can provide optimal light levels at all times of year, provided they are operated correctly. For large areas of glazing, semi-transparent, opaque or reflective external systems have proved effective. Some shading systems can incorporate photovoltaic panels to generate electricity (refer ELEMENTS; Shading, Light Directing Chromic Glazing and Photovoltaics for further information).

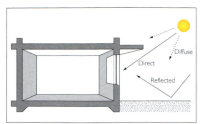

Direct, diffuse and reflected radiation

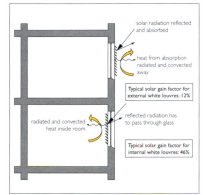

External versus internal louvres

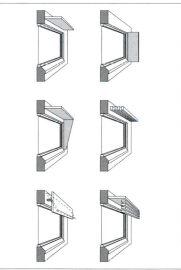

Typical fixed external shading devices

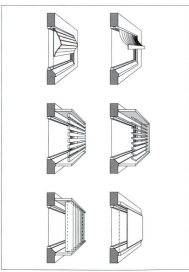

Typical adjustable external shading devices

Good daylight design

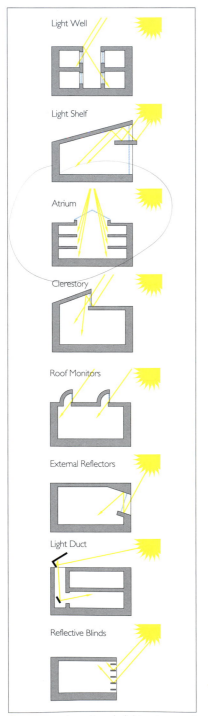

Transparent elements - daylight systems and devices

- Light Well
- Light Shelf
- Atrium
- Clerestory
- Roof Monitors
- External Reflectors
- Light Duct
- Reflective Blinds

Ventilation

Ventilation air may be supplied by natural or mechanical means, or a hybrid system containing elements of both. Natural ventilation is driven by wind or by buoyancy forces caused by temperature differences. To encourage cross-ventilation, there should be vents or openable windows on opposite sides of the building, without major obstructions to air flow in between. An open-plan layout is good in this regard.

Well-designed naturally ventilated buildings are generally shallow-plan, with the distance from façade to façade (or atrium) not greater than five times room height. For cellular rooms with single-sided ventilation, natural ventilation will be effective only to a depth of about twice room height. Room heights may need to be higher than those in a mechanically ventilated building. The space saved through not needing ducting in the ceiling or floor may offset any required increase in storey height.

Vents should be located so as to avoid cold draughts. A number of well-distributed trickle vents (which may be incorporated in windows) are better in this regard than a single open window. Proprietary self-regulating vents which provide the same air flow rate regardless of external wind speed are available. Vents which attenuate outside noise are also available, though their flow resistance is higher. Demand controlled ventilation, providing ventilation in automatic response to humidity sensors, combined with a passive ventilation system, can be very energy efficient.

In climates where night-time air temperatures in summer are significantly lower than day-time temperatures, night ventilation can be used in combination with thermal mass to provide cooling. There should be good thermal contact between the ventilation air flow and the thermal mass. Windows or vents used to provide night ventilation should not present a security risk. The duration of night cooling should be controlled in order to avoid over-cooling, which could result in the occupants feeling cold on the following morning, or even cause the heating to be turned on.

Daylighting

Artificial lighting accounts for about 50% of the energy used in offices, and a significant proportion of the energy used in other non-residential buildings. In recent years, use of daylighting combined with high performance lighting means that between 30–50% savings can be easily achieved while 60–70% savings are possible in some cases.

Thus, substituting daylight for artificial light will lead to substantial energy savings. Daylit spaces are often more attractive and more economical for working and living. In addition, a deficiency of daylight in our living and working environment can lead to health problems such as Seasonal Affective Disorder (SAD) and Vitamin D deficiency (refer ISSUES; Health, Comfort and the Environment).

Daylighting requirements will depend on the function of the building, the hours of use, type of user, requirements for view, need for privacy and ventilation requirements as well as the energy and environmental targets. The perception of adequate and comfortable daylight is influenced by the uniformity of daylight and the absence of glare.

Windows

As a rule of thumb, daylighting within a building will only be significant within about twice the space height of a glazed façade. Thus shallow-plan buildings provide more opportunities for daylighting (as well as natural ventilation and cooling) than deep-plan arrangements.

The level of daylighting at a point in a space depends to a large extent on the amount of sky visible through the window from that point. Thus the provision of a significant amount of glazing near the ceiling is beneficial from a daylighting point of view. For example, tall narrow openings will provide a better daylight distribution in a room than low wide ones. For spaces with dual aspect or on the top floor, openings in more than one façade or rooflights will also improve daylight distribution.

The shape and size of the window will depend on factors such as the depth of the space, and the orientation of the opening. High windows will ensure good daylight penetration into the back of the space, wide ones will give better view. Often, the glazing may be divided to cope with differing demands, a lower part may be provided for view and a higher part for daylight requirements. Each may be shaded differently.

Rooflighting is a highly effective source of daylight where practical.

Daylight systems and devices

Daylight devices can be used to distribute the light more evenly. Most are designed to reflect light onto the ceiling and to the back of the room while reducing excessive light levels near the windows, thus saving lighting energy and providing more comfortable conditions. Because of the eyes' adaptive response, the perceived need for artificial lighting is less in conditions of uniform lighting. There are several different light re-directing systems available which differ with respect to purpose, cost and maintenance. The selection of an appropriate system will be influenced by its passive or active nature and the appropriateness of user control.

Light re-directing systems include:

- Scattering the light: such as special glasses and holographic optical elements

- Re-directing the light: such as re-directing glasses, light shelves, laser cut panels , louvers and louvered blinds, heliostats, lightpipes

- Transporting the light: fibre-optic or other elements *(Hegger at al, 2010)*

Shading

If glazed openings have fixed overhangs to minimise solar gains in summer, these will also reduce daylight entry throughout the year. Movable shading or blinds will reduce daylight only while they are in place. While direct sunlight can be an attractive feature in a room (particularly in winter), if it falls directly on occupants or worktops it may be undesirable. Venetian blinds may be used to reflect sunlight towards the ceiling, thus avoiding discomfort due to direct sunlight and achieving greater penetration of daylight at the same time. Occupants may need instruction on how to use such blinds to best effect.

Ventilation

Where opening lights in glazing present problems, operable vents, whether located in opaque elements or integrated in a window assembly, are worth considering. With air flow control, insect and dust screens or acoustic baffles, they can provide a relatively inexpensive solution where noise or air pollution create difficult site conditions. Openable opaque panels can enhance ventilation rates in summer while avoiding excessive glazed areas.

Insulation

Insulating shutters which are closed after dark can be useful in reducing heat loss. Creating a well-sealed air-gap between shutters and glazing increases their effectiveness, but can be difficult to achieve. External shutters are preferable; internal shutters may lead to condensation on the glass during cold conditions, or, if left closed while the sun shines, set up thermal stresses which probably cause the glass to break. However, managing the operation of external shutters is not easy; in cold weather the occupants are unlikely to open windows to close the shutters. A louvred shutter operated from the inside can overcome this problem, but it may also interfere with light penetration during the day.

Good detail design requires detailed analysis

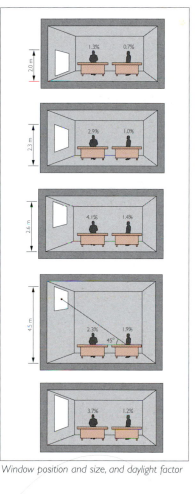

Window position and size, and daylight factor

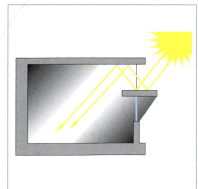

The light shelf shades the main part of the window but allows light to reach the back of the room by reflection between the shelf and the ceiling. Source: N. Baker, Optimising daylight design

Photovoltaic roof, Roaf House, Oxford. Architect: S. Roaf

Photovoltaic roof, Centre for Alternative Technologies, Wales. Source: London Permaculture

Integrated photovoltaic roof in Prisma, Nurnberg. Architect and source: Joachim Eble-Architektur

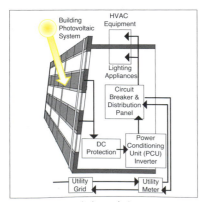

Building-integrated photovoltaic system

ENERGY PRODUCTION ELEMENTS

Photovoltaics

Photovoltaic technology represents a decentralized electricity generating system that can help a building provide its own energy requirements directly from sunlight.

An important focus of photovoltaic applications is their integration into the building envelope. Integrating PV panels into façade cladding systems is relatively straightforward and more cost effective than in the past. Photovoltaic modules in the form of building components can take on many additional functions as they are developed from glass modules to thin film cells, and applied to metal foils and plastic films to provide flexibility and semi-transparent modules.

Photovoltaic roofs in which the photovoltaic panels themselves serve as the roofing material, are increasingly seen in Europe. In the Sue Roaf House in Oxford, the PV panels are integrated into an aluminium glazing bar system, together with Velux roof lights and solar water-heating panels, while complete PV rainscreens were constructed in the Centre for Alternative Technologies, Wales.

Solar thermal panels

A typical solar panel consists of a flat collecting plate sandwiched between an insulating backing and a glazed front; evacuated tubes represent an important alternative. The optimum orientation in the northern hemisphere is south-facing on roof or walls, though any orientation within about 30° of south will perform almost as well as a south-facing collector. The optimum inclination depends on the application. For water heating an angle with the horizontal of less than the latitude of the site is usually best, to make good use of energy from the high-altitude summer sun. For space heating a higher inclination angle is best, since the sun is lower in the sky during the heating season. The path of the sun is not the only consideration in choosing collector inclination – diffuse solar radiation from the sky is also important (for further information refer ELEMENTS; Photovoltaics, Solar Thermal Panels).

SUNSPACES

Familiar to many in the form of the traditional domestic conservatory, the sunspace is a combination of both direct and indirect gain approaches to passive solar heating.

Heating and Cooling

The sunspace acts as a buffer zone for a house, significantly reducing heat loss. Even in the absence of direct solar gain it is a functional energy efficient device.

Sunlight entering the space via the glazing is stored in the solid elements as heat energy. The distribution of this heat can be achieved in a variety of ways. A masonry wall, forming a partition between the sunspace and the rest of the house, can provide sufficient thermal mass to store absorbed heat and release it later. A natural convection loop will be encouraged by inserting vents at floor and ceiling level. Likewise, a fan coupled with a thermostat will allow heat exchange between the sunspace and the rest of the house, when desired.

Where a sunspace has been added to the external wall of an existing building, it is less important to double-glaze, insulate or tightly seal the external envelope. At least two thirds of the fenestration should be openable to avoid summer overheating. If possible, provide movable insulation to cover the sunspace glazing at night or when the sky is overcast.

In new buildings sunspaces should be separated from adjacent heated spaces by insulated construction with tight-fitting doors or windows. When heat from the sunspace is available and needed, convected heat can quickly be admitted to the main spaces. At night-time or in cold weather, the sunspace can be cut off to serve as a thermal buffer.

A sunspace fitted with a heating system will be a source of energy loss instead of energy gain.

ATRIA

Heating and Cooling

Atria function as intermediate buffer spaces, and their ambient temperature levels depend on the specific losses from the glazed space to the outside, and the specific gains from the buildings to the glazed space.

Thermal gain from solar radiation has to be carefully evaluated because a large amount of thermal radiation can be re-transmitted to the outside, especially in the case of low absorbent opaque surfaces. An atrium may retain between 30–85% of transmitted radiation, depending on the adjacent building's thermal capacity, colours and geometry, and on the glazing transmission properties.

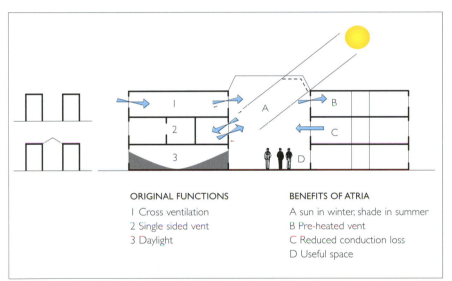

ORIGINAL FUNCTIONS
1 Cross ventilation
2 Single sided vent
3 Daylight

BENEFITS OF ATRIA
A sun in winter, shade in summer
B Pre-heated vent
C Reduced conduction loss
D Useful space

The environmental benefits of atria evolved from open space

Ventilation

Solar shading and ventilation is an effective combination to reduce atrium temperatures during summer, but natural cross-ventilation has to be carefully evaluated in order to ensure comfort on critical days.

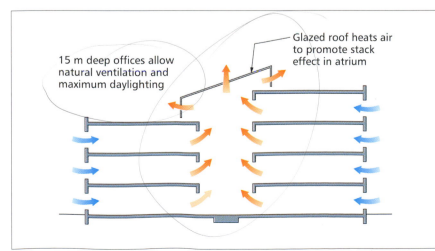

Glazed roof heats air to promote stack effect in atrium

15 m deep offices allow natural ventilation and maximum daylighting

Stack ventilation, Barclaycard Headquarters, Northampton. Source: Reproduced from CIBSE AM10: Natural ventilation in non-domestic buildings, by permission of the Chartered Institution of Building Services Engineers

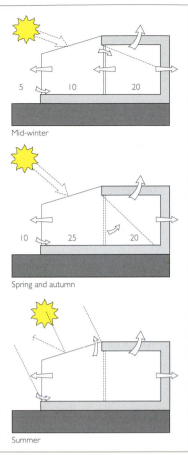

Mid-winter

5   10   20

Spring and autumn

10   25   20

Summer

Sunspace as energy efficient device

South Facing Conservatory in Hockerton Housing Project, Nottinghamshire. Source: Hockerton Housing Project Trading Limited

Public Atrium in Prisma, Nurnberg. Architect and source: Joachim Eble-Architektur

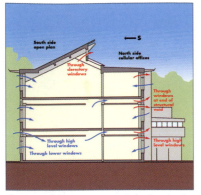

Cross ventilation on warm windy days in the BRE Environmental Building, Watford. Source: BRE

Stack ventilation on warm still days in the BRE Environmental Building, Watford. Source: BRE

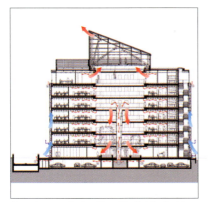

Day time ventilation, Riverside, Dublin. Architect and source: STW Architects

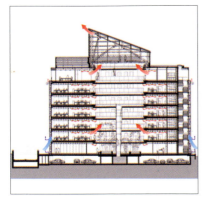

Night time ventilation, Riverside, Dublin. Architect and source: STW Architects

Appropriate ventilation systems can achieve a higher temperature in the atrium in winter without increasing the building's energy consumption. For example, exhaust air from the building may be used as an air supply for the atrium, and likewise exhaust air from the atrium can pre-heat the supply air to the building via a heat exchanger.

Daylighting

Atria can noticeably improve the quality of the adjoining internal spaces, which can enjoy all the advantages of daylight, without the accompanying climatic extremities. Improved technologies allow the architect greater freedom regarding the choice of construction, design and materials; even where longer payback periods are indicated there may be a strong case for employing such a system

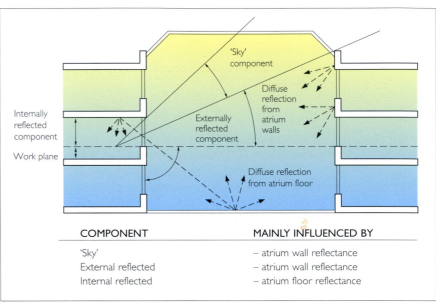

COMPONENT	MAINLY INFLUENCED BY
'Sky'	– atrium wall reflectance
External reflected	– atrium wall reflectance
Internal reflected	– atrium floor reflectance

The atrium as a source of daylight

FINISHES

In specifying the finishes for a building there are a number of issues to take into consideration. Many of these have already been raised in earlier sections and some will be treated in detail in later ones.

Low energy and environmentally friendly design strategies will inform the selection and specification of finishes. In general however, materials may be assessed under three main headings:

- The effect of the materials' production on the global environment;
- the environmental impact per kilogram of the processes of extraction, transportation, manufacturing, installation, demolition and disposal;
- The effect of the use of the material on building energy consumption, thermal and daylighting performance;
- The effect of the use of the material on the indoor environment: indoor air quality, visual and acoustic characteristics.

The first has already been covered in some detail elsewhere, as the information applies to strategies for the selection of all materials, and it is not intended to deal with it here (refer ISSUES; Comfort, Health, Environment and ELEMENTS; Materials).

BUILDING ENERGY PERFORMANCE

At the early stages of a building design, targets for the energy performance of the building will be determined and agreed. During construction and completion it is important that the finishes specification be consistent with these targets. The finishes selected will have a positive or negative effect on the energy and environmental performance of the building. It is important that the client and design team all should be aware that the theoretical performance of a low-energy design will in practice depend on the rigorous implementation of supportive strategies at later stages.

The role of finishes in the energy performance of buildings will relate in particular to thermal and daylight (light reflection and re-direction) performance.

Heating and Cooling
The passive solar design of the building may anticipate the use of elements such as walls or floor as a passive thermal store for either heating or cooling purposes. For these elements to function as designed they should be exposed to the source of heating or cooling and be in direct contact with air currents.

The finishes used may help or hinder the thermal function. Using a dark finish on floors will increase their capacity to absorb heat and act as a thermal store. Light coloured finishes will reflect light and also heat. Low density finishes such as timber or carpet act as insulating layers and inhibit heat absorption. Raised floors and suspended ceilings will counteract the use of thermal mass.

However some flexibility is possible. As has already been discussed (refer STRATEGIES; Envelope) an interior with high thermal mass would be slow to warm, and surface temperatures will remain depressed and ensure a cooler internal environment. This is ideal in summer in hot climates, but may be less attractive in the winter. Application of finishes such as timber will alter the thermal response time and the thermal capacity. In The Climatic Dwelling the example is used of tapestries in medieval buildings: 'in summer the wall hangings could be removed to reveal the heavy thermal mass of the masonry walls and their lower surface temperature' (O'Cofaigh et al, 1996).

Reflective finishes. Architect: A Campo Baeza

Material	Density kg/m³	Conductivity (k) W/m C	Resistivity (1/k)mC/W
Asbestos insulating board	750	0.12	8.3
Carpet			
• wool felt underlay	160	0.045	22.2
• cellular rubber underlay	400	0.10	10.0
Concrete	2400	1.83	0.55
Cork flooring	540	0.085	11.8
Fibre insulating board	260	0.050	20.0
Glasswool	25	0.04	25.0
Linoleum to BS 810	1150	0.22	4.6
Mineral wool			
• felted	50	0.039	25.6
	80	0.038	26.3
• semi-rigid felted mat	130	0.036	27.8
• loose, felted slab or mat	180	0.042	23.8
Plastics, cellular			
• phenolic foam board	30	0.038	26.3
	50	0.036	27.8
• polystyrene, expanded	15	0.037	27.0
	25	0.034	29.4
• polyurethane foam (aged)	30	0.026	38.5
PVC flooring and Rubber flooring		0.40	2.5
Wood			
• hardwood		0.15	6.7
• plywood		0.14	7.1
• softwood		0.13	7.7
Wood chipboard	800	0.15	6.7
Woodwool slab	500	0.085	11.8
	600	0.093	10.8

Thermal properties of some flooring materials. Source: Building Research Establishment ISBN No. 011 72155, Publ.No. 737645 C109/94

Some typical reflectances of matt paint finishes:	
White	.85
Pale yellow	.82
Bright yellow	.70
Pale orange	.54
Pale blue	.45
Bright orange	.28
Bright red	.17
Dark green	.09
Black	.05

Typical reflectances. Source: Esbensen

Arup Fitzrovia, London. Architect: Sheppard Robson. Source: Hufton and Crow Photography

Illuminance contours (Radiance) in an office with lightshelf. Source: Greg Ward

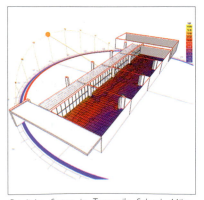

Daylight factor in Terragni's School, Milan. Source: Paul Kenny

DAYLIGHTING

Illuminance

Illuminance is a function of the amount of light entering a room and the colour and finish of the surfaces. When daylight enters a room it is reflected off the internal surfaces (walls, floor, ceiling, interior fittings). The colour and finish of the surfaces will affect both the quantity and quality of light in that space. In general, light colours have more reflectance while dark colours have more absorption. Use of light-coloured finishes on the ground and vertical surfaces will reflect light, thus contributing to higher levels of daylight while reducing the contrast between bright window areas and the surrounding surfaces. Conversely, darker surfaces cause a loss of light.

Reflectance

Values of reflectances to be achieved have to be agreed at an early stage. Basic lighting calculations will use assumed surface reflectances for walls, ceiling and floor. The final decision on finishes frequently takes place much nearer the completion of the project. Actual reflectances may differ markedly from those used in the lighting calculations, normally to the detriment of the illuminance. Reducing the reflectance factor of the walls of a space could reduce the horizontal illuminance on the working plane significantly and no longer satisfy the required specification. For working planes, or surfaces in the view of any workspace, shiny finishes should be avoided. As surfaces with very highly reflecting finishes may cause distracting reflections, semi-matt or matt finishes are better.

Improving the reflectance of a ceiling benefits light distribution and improves both horizontal and vertical plane illuminance.

Colours

The colours used will affect light absorbance and reflectance of surfaces as well as their thermal performance as discussed earlier. Colours should be assessed in regard to their relative absorbtance and reflectance and selected accordingly.

Internal fixtures and fittings

At the design stage, interior surfaces are often conceived as planar and monochromatic, but once occupied this is rarely the case. Walls may have pictures or shelving on them, while floors will be covered by furniture whose finishes will affect the daylight distribution. Office partitions, visual display units and artificial lighting systems will all introduce further shading/modelling effects.

INDOOR AIR QUALITY

Conservation of energy often means highly insulated and well-sealed internal environments. Choice of materials in energy efficient buildings affects indoor air quality to an even higher degree than in conventional buildings. Where materials with toxic ingredients are specified and there is out-gassing, the effects will be magnified by reduced air movement and ventilation, resulting in a wide range of impurities in the indoor environment. High concentrations of chemicals such as formaldehyde from fabric, furnishings, and particle-boards may be particularly hazardous for a sleeping or desk-bound person in a confined space (refer ISSUES; Comfort, Health, Environment and ELEMENTS; Materials).

Careful selection of building finishes is one way to improve indoor air, although it should be part of a broad strategy looking at ventilation systems, indoor plants, maintenance, and other factors.

The highest levels of pollutants are often found during construction and in the first weeks of occupation, as toxins diffuse out of the source materials. Other materials such as carpet and wall coverings may need to be protected during this phase to prevent them absorbing toxins and becoming sources of pollution themselves. The most toxic materials tend to be those that are unstable or that are applied in a wet state. Paints, sealants, preservatives, glues, cleaners and plastics such as PVC are among the worst offenders. Often, less damaging alternatives to standard products exist but may not be widely known or available. Materials present in small quantities may have a disproportionate impact on air quality. It may be a good idea to delay the installation of soft furnishings such as carpets until solvent-based products are dry. This prevents VOCs and other air pollutants being absorbed by the soft furnishings to be released later.

Finishes Specification

The science of materials and their specification is a complex area. Finishes are selected on the basis of many criteria such as cost, durability, appropriateness, function, aesthetics and so on. Impact on the indoor environment is only one of these issues. No publication of this type can hope to give a full discussion of the environmental advantages and disadvantages of the uses of common materials. There are many specialist publications and periodicals which do just that. There follows a brief resume of some generic types of commonly used finishes and the environmental effects of their use, with particular regard to indoor air.

Walls and Ceilings

Plaster

Most walls and ceilings are finished with plaster unless the structural materials used are self-finishing. Plaster is available in a number of forms, 'wet' trowel applied, 'dry-walling' board, tiles. The raw material for plaster may either be gypsum (whose processing is highly energy intensive), or lime mortar. Flue gas gypsum is a by-product of electricity production and its use avoids disposal of the material as waste. Natural gypsum is extracted with some environmental effects but the material is non-toxic and benign. Lime mortar is a natural compound with a low energy manufacturing process.

Paints and stains

Paint contains a wide range of toxic ingredients and solvents. The function of paint is both decorative and functional. An environmental objective might be to reduce the need for painted finishes of any kind, especially in little used, residual or service spaces. Internal surfaces can be protected by the use of plant oils, waxes and plant derived shellacs.

Where paint is used internally it should be water-borne, plant based and contain the minimum of toxic or polluting ingredients. It may be necessary, in some building types, to use a solvent-borne, plant based paint. Typical plant based solvents are gum turpentine and oils such as linseed (*Woolley et al, 1997*) (refer ELEMENTS; Materials for more detailed information on paints and wood finishes).

Paper

Paper is widely used, especially in domestic applications. Un-coated paper is preferable to vinyl coated, but harder to maintain. Vinyl wallpaper is increasingly popular because it is washable but the coating is PVC, with the attendant indoor air implications.

Ceramic tiles

Tiles are a durable wall finish and frequently used in areas such as bathrooms and kitchens. They are made from clay with additives for colour and hardness. Highly glazed tiles can be relatively high in embodied energy content due to the firing process. The indoor air impact depends on the selection of adhesives. The environmental choice for tile adhesives is one with little or no organic solvent content: mortar for floors and water-based for walls.

Wood

The use of wood as a wall or ceiling finish material is less common outside domestic applications, but the comments about wood in floors largely apply here also. European

Health:
Reduced toxins benefit everyone, including those with allergies and chemical sensitivities.

Environment:
Reduces landfill, groundwater and ozone depleting contaminants.

Effective:
Low-VOC products perform well in terms of coverage, scrubability and hideability.

Water-Based:
Easy cleanup wtih soap and warm water.

Little or No Hazardous Fumes:
Low odor during application; no odor once cured. No off-gassing.

Occupancy:
Painted areas can be occupied sooner, with no odor complaints.

Not deemed Hazardous Waste:
Cleanup and disposal greatly simplified.

Benefits of non toxic paints.
Source: eartheasy.com

Materials/Products	Range of Formaldehyde emission rates $\mu g / m^2 / day$
Medium - density fibreboard	17,600 – 55,000
Hardwood plywood panelling	1,500 – 34,000
Particleboard	2,000 – 25,000
Urea - formaldehyde foam insulation	1,200 – 19,200
Softwood plywood	240 – 720
Paper products	260 – 680
Fibreglass products	400 – 470
Clothing	35 – 570
Resilient flooring	<240
Carpeting	NP – 65
Upholstery fabric	NP – 7

Formaldehyde emissions from a variety of construction materials, furnishings and consumer products. Source: Balaras

Softwood timber panelling, the Irish Energy Centre, Dublin. Architects: UCD Energy Research Group, University College Dublin

softwood is environmentally benign but softwood ceilings may need an applied finish, such as oil or wax, and the impact on indoor air will depend on its composition. Good quality timber, well detailed, can be left unfinished and allowed to breathe.

Floors

Floor finishes are available in a wide range of natural and synthetic materials such as stone, wood, tile, vinyl and linoleum sheet, wool or nylon carpet. Concerns relate to the source of the material (renewable or not), the embodied energy content and the effect on indoor air quality as a result of the composition of the material and the use of adhesives.

Stone

The advantage of stone (such as slate, marble or terracotta) is its great durability and attractive appearance. The environmental impact of stone-based products is less than that of most other materials although granite does emit a higher level of radon than most other construction materials (Martinez et al, 1996). The small amount of granite used inside buildings is unlikely to be a cause for concern.

Granolithic floors

Aggregates bedded in concrete (a poured terrazzo floor for example) are extremely hard-wearing, and require no adhesive or sealant finish after laying. Any environmental concern about these relates to the use of concrete (refer ELEMENTS; Materials).

Wood

Wood, if recycled or from a certified sustainable source, is a non-polluting material, but it is often protected or coated to increase its durability, and may be fixed using adhesive. Wood finishes may be carcinogenic (Martinez et al, 1996). The degree of toxicity will depend on the amount of ventilation and the extent of harmful synthetic coating. Finishes should be specified which are based on wax, oils or eco-friendly varnishes.

Wood dust from working with timber may be toxic, immuno-damaging or carcinogenic (Green Building Digest, 1995); safety at work legislation in many countries limits exposure to hardwood dust.

Wood-based products such as plywood, blockboard, chipboard, and fibreboard may contain phenol and urea formaldehyde resins, which will increase the levels of toxicity in the indoor air. Stricter controls on manufacturing and processing techniques and site installation practices reduce the hazard. The use of fibreboard instead of plywood for sheathing, because it contains no formaldehyde or toxic glues, is now standard practice; but it should be carefully detailed, as it does not have the same qualities as other boards in bending or water resistance.

Wood finishes

Synthetic varnishes are more durable than natural ones, but are sources of VOCs. Non-toxic wood finishes, such as linseed oil, beeswax and shellac, and paints are widely available. The term non- toxic is used in the broadest terms and includes natural paints, Zero VOC and Low VOC.

Carpet

Synthetic carpets are a recognised source of VOCs from the pile, adhesives and backing, and most fabric dyes are derived from petrochemicals. Combined with other sources of VOCs around the home, new carpet emissions could result in concentrations above threshold limit values, particularly in poorly ventilated buildings.

Nylon is often blended with wool to improve wear. It is safe during use but produces toxic fumes when incinerated. Other synthetics used in carpet manufacture and associated with toxic emissions are polyester, polypropylene, polyurethane and acrylic. The most environmentally benign carpets are those made with animal (wool or goat) or vegetable (sisal, seagrass, coir, cotton and hessian) fibres, and on natural backings such as jute or latex, which are undyed or unbleached and which have not been treated with insecticides.

PVC/Vinyl

The main environmental impact of vinyl flooring production is the generation of large quantities of toxic waste; the raw ingredients are known carcinogens and powerful irritants (Green Building Digest, 1995). PVC is discussed in detail in ELEMENTS; Materials.

Cork

Cork is a relatively benign material in terms of its harvesting and production. Cork granules are moulded using binding agents. Cork flooring will require a protective coating to prevent discolouration from dirt. The specifier should beware that natural binders may be replaced by those containing formaldehyde, with effects on indoor air quality. Some composite products incorporate vinyl backing or surface coatings. In conclusion, cork is only a good organic material if oil or wax coating is used.

Linoleum

Lino is made with cork, linseed oil, wood flour, pigments and hessian. It performs as well as vinyl for comparable cost. It is a completely natural and environmentally benign material, which even contains a naturally occurring bactericide.

Adhesives

One critical environmental dimension of the specification of wall and floor finishes is the use of adhesives. Many adhesives in common use are synthetic, with out-gassing both during application and immediately following installation, usually from inorganic solvents. In addition, some adhesives can cause skin irritation during application. Rubber, cellulose, animal or vegetable derivative adhesives may be substituted and there are many naturally derived products available to suit most applications of materials

---

Floor coverings which are least likely to add to the quantity of pollutants in the indoor air are:

- Smooth coverings: linoleum, cork in tile or sheet form, latex (rubber) matting.

- Stone, and ceramic tile e.g. quarry tile.

- Timber from a renewable resource or particularly recycled.

- Natural carpet, on a hessian backing, with felt underlay. (Carpet should be tacked in place rather than using solvent-based adhesives.)

Natural floor coverings

Treatment of Timber

First choice:
no preservative

Second choice:
Water based boron or zinc, copper, and /or fluoride compounds

Try to avoid:
Chrome or arsenic compounds, permethrin

Avoid:
Lindane, pentachlorophenol, tributyl tin oxide and creosote

Treatment of timber. Source: Woolley et al, Green Building Handbook, Vol 1.

Treatment Application methods

Smoking

Spraying

Dipping

Pressure impregnation

Brushing

Spreading/mastic-gunning pastes

Drilling and injecting jellies

Drilling and inserting rods

Application methods in order of decreasing risk. Source: Woolley et al, Green Building Handbook, Vol 1

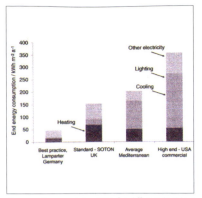

Range of energy intensities for different building types. Source: Eiker 2010

Typical breakdown of energy use in Great Britain for a naturally ventilated office building, an air conditioned office building and a large hotel

CO$_2$ emissions per unit of energy for different fuels

Fuel	kg CO$_2$/kWh
Natural gas	0.20
Oil	0.27
Coal	0.30 – 0.35

CO$_2$ fuel emissions

SERVICES, EQUIPMENT AND CONTROLS

A building's performance depends to a considerable extent on the interactions between the microclimate, envelope, fabric, occupants and its services. Energy-efficient building requires an integrated design approach involving the architect and the design team, ideally from the very start of the design process. This is particularly true in the case of buildings designed for passive solar heating, daylighting, natural ventilation and natural cooling. Good integration of mechanical and electrical services with passive systems is required to obtain maximum benefit from ambient energy.

Services, equipment and controls can play an important role in modern buildings, particularly in commercial and institutional buildings. Although the predominant ethos of this publication is towards minimisation of mechanical and electrical services, many building designs are such that even after load minimisation, mechanical and electrical services have to be considered, often predicated by climate, building end-use or client expectations. For a typical commercial building, the range of services that need to be assessed is potentially quite extensive and may include services from some or all of the following categories: heating, cooling, ventilation, lighting. The various service options are listed in the table below.

Heating	Cooling	Ventilation	Lighting
Furnaces/Boilers-Gas/Oil/Biomass	Natural	Natural	Natural
Electric Resistance	Night Cooling	Mechanical	Incandesent
Electric Heat Pumps	Mechanical Cooling –Vapour Compression Water Chillers	Hybrid Systems	Fluorescent (FL)
CHP-Cogeneration CCHP-Trigeneration	Mechanical Cooling - Thermal Absorption/Adsorption	Heat recovery	Compact Fluorescent (CFL)
District Heating	Evaporative Cooling		Light Emitting Diodes (LED)

Building Mechanical and Electrical Services

The concept of energy intensity is used when assessing the role of building services. Energy intensity (or energy consumption) is often expressed in kWh/m^2/yr and includes all building end-energy consumption. As energy intensity is normalised only with respect to floor plate area, it will vary with climate region, building type and end-sector. The potential of low energy building design is illustrates in the range of energy intensities from different building types *(Eicker, 2010)*.

HEATING

Eicker notes that many existing office and administrative buildings have approximately the same energy consumption associated with the provision of heat as residential buildings. For public buildings in southern Germany, heating typically accounts for approximately 220 kWh/m^2/yr, which will be climate dependant *(Eicker, 2010)*. Zimmermann and Andersson report, that for naturally ventilated offices in the UK, energy intensity values were found to in the range from 200 to 220 kWh/m^2/yr *(Zimmermann and Andersson, 1998)*. Moreover, Eicker notes that heat consumption associated with commercial buildings can be reduced without difficulty to 100 kWh/m^2/yr by adoption of increased insulation standards and even to as low as 15 kWh/m^2/yr, if PassivHaus standards are implemented.

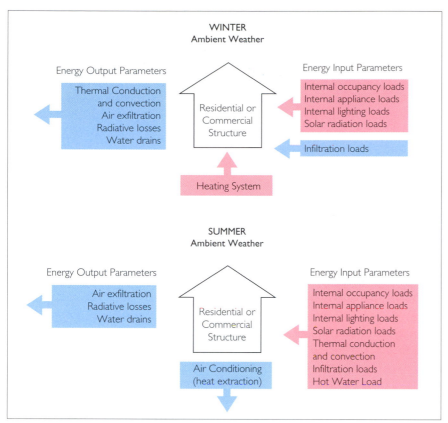

Typical energy gains and losses in winter and summer

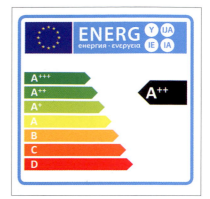

Rating scheme used by SEDBUK, the rating testing agency for the UK. Source: SEDBUK 2010

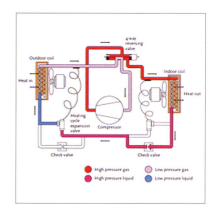

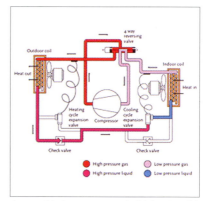

A reversible heat pump cycle (a) heating, (b) cooling. Source: Welch, 2009, CIBSE

Boilers

Boilers can be fuelled typically by oil, gas or biomass. Modern gas and oil boilers that incorporate condensing flues are capable of efficiencies in excess of 90% and should be considered as a default design option for any heating installation. Manufacturers typically cite two efficiencies, a steady state efficiency and a seasonal efficiency. The steady state efficiency describes the performance when the boiler is operating under continuous load, and is usually determined under laboratory conditions. In practice, a boiler will cycle on and off, with the proportion of off-time increasing as the heating load decreases. On-off cycling leads to additional energy losses, therefore giving rise to a lower average efficiency. More recently the advent of modulating boilers capable of altering their heat output by varying the rate of fuel supply, allow more efficient operation. Given the large market, boilers can be sourced from a wide range of manufacturers in serveral countries and are often classified according to different standards.

Electrical Resistance

The efficiency of electric resistance heating at the point of end-use is 100%. However, given that in most countries electricity is still generated primarily from fossil fuels at overall efficiency levels that vary from 30 to 55%, the amount of primary energy used per unit of electrical resistance heating is approximately three times the energy delivered to the building (Harvey, 2006). Use of resistance storage heaters may offer certain economic advantages, if low cost off-peak electricity is used, however it should be noted that this will not result in improved efficiencies or reduced carbon footprint until electricty from carbon-free sources is more generally available.

Heat Pumps

Heat pumps use electrical or mechanical work input to upgrade low-grade heat to more useful high-grade heat. Most heat pumps utilise the principle of vapour compression within a thermodynamic cycle to achieve this objective. Heat driven systems are also available based on a different thermodynamic cycle (the absorption cycle) and can use gas, waste heat, or solar thermal as the driving mechanism. In recent

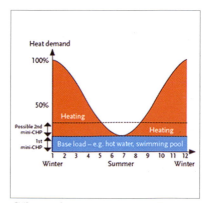

CHP sizing for thermal load. Source: Evans and Dwyer, 2010, CIBSE

Inland Revenue Headquarters, Nottingham. Architect Michael Hopkins. Source: Dennis Gilbert

Glazed solar stairs tower, Inland Revenue Headquarters, Nottingham. Architect Michael Hopkins. Source: Dennis Gilbert

Double skin façade, Riverside, Dublin. Architect and source: STW Architects

Double skin façade providing ventilation in Riverside, Dublin. Architect and source: STW Architects

years, reverse cycle split air-conditioning systems are increasingly being deployed in buildings which are capable of both heating or cooling. Heat pump performance is assessed using the concept of coefficient of performance (COP), which is the ratio of useful heating (or cooling) duty to power input to the compressor. For heating, well designed air-source heat pumps should have a seasonal COP_h of between 3 and 4 for air source heat pumps. This means that, for every 1 kW of electricity consumed by the heat pump, between 3 and 4 kW of heating is produced. Heat pump COP is strongly influenced by the temperature difference between the heat source (ambient air, water, ground) and the heat sink (building air or water circuit), such that the greater the temperature difference, the poorer the COP. Therefore, to achieve maximum efficiency, the sink and source temperatures should be minimised. High temperature sources, such as waste heat, if combined with low temperature heating systems, (e.g. underfloor heating, low temperature radiators) give the best COP_h. When heat pumps are used with existing radiators, the radiator size will have to be increased so as give the same heat output with the lower water temperature *(Welch, 2009)*.

CHP or Cogeneration or CCHP or Trigeneration

Combined Heat and Power (CHP or Cogeneration) or Combined Cooling Heating and Power (CCHP or Trigeneration) is an efficient way of producing cooling, heat and electricity simultaneously within commercial buildings. CHP can deliver overall system efficiencies well in excess of 85%. CHP units are likely to utilise as prime movers gas turbines, gas reciprocating engines or Stirling engines *(DEFRA, 2010)*. CHP can result in savings of up to 50 per cent of CO_2 emissions compared with conventional sources of heat and power *(ICHPA, 2010)*. Moreover, CHP can offer energy cost savings by reducing the amount of electricity imported from the grid and by displacing fuel used by other heating and hot water-generating appliances in the building. For every unit of electricity generated by the CHP plant, around two units of potentially usable heat are produced. This heat can be used to help satisfy space-heating needs or to support the production of domestic hot water. CHP units are normally selected to match the base heating load of the building so as to maximise the running hours. The success of all forms of CHP depends on effective integration with the building's existing load demands *(Evans and Dwyer, 2010)*.

COOLING

Cooling can be achieved by either natural or mechanical means.

Natural Cooling

Natural cooling systems (natural and night ventilation) have the potential to maintain comfortable conditions in summer for a wide range of buildings and climates. If natural cooling alone is not adequate, then ventilation rates may be increased mechanically. If this is not sufficient, artificial cooling will be required. However, before ruling out natural cooling as an option, all means of reducing internal and solar gains and enhancing natural ventilation during peak temperature conditions should be assessed. Naturally cooled buildings have lower capital and operating costs and provided they can meet thermal comfort requirements, many occupants prefer them. Effective management is critical for air conditioning systems. Without it, efficiency falls and discomfort increases. Natural cooling systems do not normally require such a commitment in terms of operation and maintenance. If mechanical ventilation or artificial cooling is required, consideration should be given to combining it with natural ventilation in a 'mixed-mode' or 'hybrid' system. This may involve the provision of natural cooling in some parts of the building and mechanical ventilation/cooling in others (zonal mixed-mode). Alternatively, both natural and mechanical systems may be installed in the same zone, with the mechanical system being used only when the natural cooling system is unable to meet requirements (daily mixed mode or seasonal mixed-mode).

Natural Ventilation

Natural ventilation is achieved by supplying and removing air to an indoor space by natural forces. Two types of natural ventilation are used in buildings: stack ventilation and wind driven ventilation. The differential pressures generated by buoyancy in a building give rise to the stack effect and are relatively small (0.25–2.5 Pa), whereas differential pressures due to wind are greater (2–30 Pa). The impact of wind on the building structure creates a positive pressure on the windward side of a building and negative pressure on the leeward side. In many applications, wind pressure will vary considerably therefore creating complex air flows and associated turbulence which may give rise to localised discomfort within the building. Vernacular and traditional buildings in different climatic regions usually rely on natural ventilation for maintaining human comfort conditions in the building space. Use of natural ventilation to cool buildings at night is also effective as a pre-cooling mechanism particularly in buildings where significant thermal mass exists (e.g. exposed concrete).

Ceiling fan providing air movement. Source: Passiefhuis Platform VZW (PHP)

Mechanical Ventilation and Cooling

Mechanical fans may be used to enhance natural ventilation, e.g. in a stack ventilated atrium, roof-mounted extract fans may be utilized as required. Ducted mechanical ventilation systems may also be used for cooling. However, because of the relatively high flow rates which may be required for cooling, system pressure drops will be high resulting in additional fan electrical power requirements. Mechanical ventilation can also be used with night ventilation systems to increase building cooling.

Ceiling Fans

The air movement generated by a ceiling fan may produce the same cooling effect as a temperature reduction of 2–3°C, and at only a fraction of the energy consumption of a typical air conditioning system. Air movement below such fans must remain within acceptable limits.

Heat recovery ventilation control unit. Source: Passiefhuis Platform VZW (PHP)

HVAC (Heating Ventilating and Air Conditioning)

HVAC is the use of electro-mechanical systems which combine heating and cooling, humidification or dehumidification along with mechanical ventilation as a means of maintaining space thermal comfort. Design of HVAC systems is a sub-discipline of mechanical engineering, based on the principles of thermodynamics, fluid mechanics, heat transfer and psychrometrics. HVAC systems are often used in medium to large commercial buildings, particularly in climates where external conditions are such that air conditioning is necessary HVAC systems are energy-intensive. If air-conditioning must be used, it should be specified only for those parts of the building where it is essential. If artificial cooling is unavoidable, factors which can minimise the required capacity and operating hours include: shallow building plan, well-insulated building shell, air-tight construction, solar gain minimisation by solar shading, internal load reduction by the use of low energy lighting and energy efficient equipment. Excessive amounts of glazing on façades exposed to the summer sun should be avoided.

The efficiency of an artificial cooling system may be expressed in terms of the ratio of the heat removed from occupied spaces to the electricity consumed by the complete system, similar as defined for a heat pump. Seasonal average values depending on the HVAC technology, and vary from 6.0 or better for well designed mechanical centrifugal chillers to 1.5 for thermal absorption systems. Applications with significant potential are the use of absorption chillers for space cooling driven either by waste heat from combined heat and power plant or by active solar thermal systems. The economics of such projects will be favoured by a demand for heat throughout the year; e.g. space heating in winter, space cooling in summer and hot water during all seasons. Finally, a layout which minimises the lengths of required ductwork and pipework, thereby minimising resistance to flow, increases system efficiency. Locating plant rooms close to the areas of greatest cooling load may be useful in this regard.

Building type Room/activity	Operative temperature (°C)
Residential	
Living room	21
Bedroom	18
Staircases	16
Offices	
General	20
Private	20
Stores	15
Factories	
Sedentary work	19
Light work	16
Heavy work	13
Schools and Colleges	
Classrooms	18
Lecture rooms	18
Coffee shops and bars	18
Canteens and dining rooms	20

Recommended indoor temperatures during heating season (northern Europe)

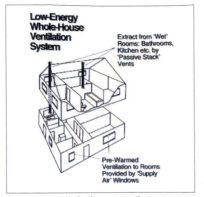

Low energy whole house ventilation system.
Source: EU RDPClevs

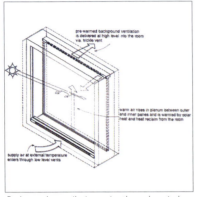

Preheated ventilation air through window.
Source: EU RDPClevs

BedZed, London. Architect: Bill Dunster. Source:
Tom Chance

Passive ventilators with heat recovery, Bedzed,
London. Source: Andrea Rota

Internal Design Temperatures

Air-conditioning systems are usually designed for summer peak conditions and operate on part-load for the majority of their working life. Under part-load conditions their efficiency is less than full load conditions. Where comfort temperatures are expressed as a range, for example 24–26ºC, the system should be sized for the upper end of this range rather than the midpoint. Allowing temperatures to rise above conventional comfort levels more often can reduce plant size and energy consumption. Design internal temperatures for summer and winter are based on data provided in ISO 7730, which is derived from laboratory-based assessments of comfort perceptions. However, as outlined in Section 2: ISSUES, field research has shown that there is often a discrepancy between the comfort conditions predicted by these methods and those observed in practice. In many cases people are satisfied with higher temperatures in hot weather and lower temperatures in cold weather, than those suggested by ISO 7730. Particularly if opportunities for adaptive comfort are provided, the selection of design temperatures need not be as stringent as ISO 7730 would suggest. Opportunities for adaptation tend to be more numerous in naturally cooled air conditioned buildings, as occupants seem more tolerant of fluctuations where they have a degree of control. Examples of design features allowing occupant control of the internal environment include adjustable thermostats, trickle vents and blinds, openable windows and a flexible layout which allows occupants to modify the position of desks and seating to suit themselves.

VENTILATION

As levels of thermal insulation improve and as occupant expectations regarding air quality rise, the proportion of total building heat loss accounted for by ventilation has become more important. Required ventilation rates depend on various factors including occupant activity and accommodation type. For example, in offices, a ventilation rate of 5–8 litres per second (l/s) per person is often recommended. Ventilation rates above those required give rise to an energy penalty. Since both the driving forces for infiltration (wind pressure and stack effect) and the internal ventilation requirements vary, a relatively airtight building envelope and controllable ventilation rates are required to meet occupant needs without wastage. A basic level of ventilation is required to provide occupants with oxygen, and to dilute and remove carbon dioxide and odours. However, ventilation must also remove other pollutants (water vapour, formaldehyde, etc), thus higher ventilation rates will be required if these are present in significant quantities. An important element in an energy-efficient ventilation strategy is to minimise the required ventilation rate by avoiding the emission of pollutants in the building (refer ISSUES; Health). Where the emission of pollutants within the building is unavoidable, it is more energy-efficient to remove these at source than to increase whole-building ventilation rates. Sources of such pollutants in office buildings include some photocopying machines and printers which emit ozone and tea-rooms and canteens which emit water vapour. Pollutants may be removed at source either through local extract or by locating the source close to a window through which air would normally leave the building (e.g. on the downwind side). If natural ventilation is unable to fully meet ventilation needs in particular circumstances (e.g. calm weather), extract fans may be used to increase ventilation rates. These fans should be controlled to ensure that they are not switched on when not needed.

Mechanical ventilation systems may be categorised as supply, extract or balanced. In mechanical supply-only systems, air leaves the building through exfiltration and therefore heat recovery is not feasible. Mechanical extract and balanced systems provide opportunities for heat recovery. In extract systems, heat may be recovered from the stale air by means of a heat pump and used for water heating. In balanced systems, heat recovered may be used to heat replacement fresh air via a crossflow heat exchanger or a thermal wheel. The economics of heat recovery in balanced systems improve with the severity of the heating season. Heat exchangers can have seasonal efficiencies from 70% to 90%. If a building with a balanced mechanical ventilation system is leaky, much air will leave by building fabric exfiltration. Furthermore, infiltration will increase ventilation air supply rates above required levels. Thus, particularly in balanced ventilation systems, an air-tight construction is required for effective operation. The ventilation system should be designed to facilitate easy cleaning and maintenance. Once in operation, the system should be properly maintained, with filters changed and heat exchange surfaces cleaned regularly, otherwise efficiency will fall and air quality will deteriorate, possibly giving rise to health concerns due to the growth of micro-organisms.

LIGHTING

Electric lighting contributes to internal heat gains in buildings, which reduces the building winter heating load, but increases the summer cooling load. Globally, lighting consumes about 19% of the total generated electricity (IEA, 2010). Within offices and commercial buildings, it can account for up to 25% of the total energy consumption. Historically, annual electricity consumption associated with office lighting varies from 20 to 40 kWh/m^2, however recent lighting developments means that this demand is decreasing to levels closer to 10 kWh/m^2.

Region	Average lighting power density (W/m^2)	Annual lighting energy consumption per unit area (kWh/m^2)	Average operating period (h/a)	Lighting system efficacy (lm/W)	Commercial building floor area (billon m^2)	Total electricity consumption (TWh/a)
Japan/Korea	12.6	33.0	2583	62.7	1.7	54.6
Austria/NZ	16.5	31.7	1924	43.5	0.4	12.7
North America	17.4	59.4	3928	50.1	7.3	435.1
OECD Europe	15.5	27.7	1781	46.1	6.7	185.8
OECD	15.6	43.1	2867	49.6	16.1	688.2

Average Lighting Consumption Data. Source: IEA, 2010

Type of lamps	Belgium	Germany	Spain	Belgium	Germany	Spain
	Existing office lighting			New office lighting		
Fluorescent lamps	80%	99%	70%	95%	100%	85%
CFL	10%	5%	15%	16%	10%	20%
T8 LFL	80%	90%	75%	52%	45%	50%
TS LFL	10%	5%	10%	32%	45%	30%
Other	20%	1%	30%	5%	0%	15%

Luminare Fittings in Existing and New Office Buildings. Source: IEA, 2010

Lighting energy consumption can be reduced by a number of strategies including: minimization of power density, use of light sources with high luminous efficacy, use of lighting control systems and utilisation of daylight. The quality of light must be maintained when installed power for lighting is reduced. The luminous efficacy of a light source is defined as the light output per unit of power input. Its units are lumens per watt (lm/W). Typical luminous efficacies for different lamp types are shown below.

Lamp Type	Characteristics							
	Luminous efficacy	Lamp life h	Dimming Control	Re-strike time	Colour Rendering Index	Cost of installation	Cost of operation	Applications
GLS	5-15	1000	excellent	prompt	very good	low	very high	general lighting
Tungsten halogen	12-35	2000-4000	excellent	prompt	very good	low	high	general lighting
Mercury vapour	40-60	12000	not possible	2-5 min	poor - good	moderate	moderate	outdoor lighting
CFL	40-65	6000-12000	with special lamps	prompt	good	low	low	general lighting
Fluorescent lamp	50-100	10000-16000	good	prompt	good	low	low	general lighting
Induction lamp	60-80	60000-100000	not possible	prompt	good	high	low	places where access for maintenance is difficult
Metal halide	50-100	6000-12000	possible but not practical	5-10 min	good	high	low	shopping malls, commercial buildings
High pressure sodium (standard)	80-100	12000-16000	possible but not practical	2-5 min	fair	high	low	outdoor street lighting, warehouse
High pressure sodium (colour improved)	40-60	6000-10000	possible but not practical	2-6 min	good	high	low	outdoor, commercial interior lighting
LEDs	20-120	20000-100000	excellent	prompt	good	high	low	all in near future

Lamp types – performance and characteristics. Source: IEA, 2010

The chart below gives potential future scenarios concerning likely efficacy developments. Particular attention should be paid to developments in CFL and LED technologies, as well as relevant legislative changes.

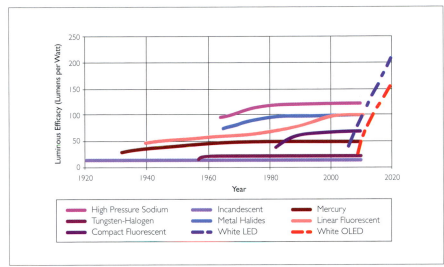

Development of luminous efficacies of different light sources. Source: IEA, 2010

Another measure of the efficiency of a lighting fixture or luminaire is the total emitted luminous flux as a proportion of the luminous flux emitted by the lamp it contains. The directional distribution of the emitted light, and the luminance of the luminaire, are also important design considerations. Light-coloured room surfaces will reflect more light than dark ones (refer STRATEGIES; Finishes). If surfaces of high reflectance can be assumed at the design stage, required electric lighting capacity, and thus capital costs, will be reduced. The provision of localised lighting (task lighting) on work surfaces, with a lower level of general (ambient) lighting in other parts of the room, is more energy-efficient than general lighting only, since not all of the space needs to be lit to the high level required at workplaces.

Controls and Building Energy Management Systems

In many buildings there is considerable potential for energy savings through switching off lamps when they are not needed. Since occupants cannot in many cases be relied upon to switch off or dim lamps as required, automatic controls have an important role to play in energy efficient lighting. Time control can be used to switch lights off automatically when the building is normally unoccupied. Occupancy control involves the use of motion detection sensors. Daylight linking controls may be used to dim or switch off lamps in response to daylight levels. Such controls are in many cases necessary if significant daylight savings are to be achieved. Localised switching involves the provision of opportunities to control lighting in small areas independently by means of switches which are close at hand. Lamps controlled by a single switch should be rationally related to daylight penetration and occupancy, e.g. lamps providing general lighting in an open-plan office should be controlled in rows parallel to the window wall, while lamps over each workplace could be controlled individually. The control strategy most suitable to a particular building or room will depend on the circumstances, in particular the occupancy patterns. In many cases, the better strategy is for the controls to switch lights off only, leaving occupants to switch them on as required. There has been poor experience with some over-complex controls and controls which can irritate or frustrate the user. The integration of various controls as part of a Building Energy Management System (BEMS) can yield the following additional benefits:

• More sophisticated control procedures can be programmed.

• Monitoring of energy consumption, and targeting of opportunities for energy saving, are facilitated.

• Routine maintenance requirements may be flagged, helping the operator to maintain energy efficient operation and to avoid disruptive equipment failures.

RENOVATION

Increasing consciousness of the economic and environmental advantages of building renovation is spreading as European targets to save 20% of energy consumption by 2020 impact in each EU Member State. The Recast EPBD includes a provision for ensuring all new buildings will be very low energy before 2021. However, a major acceleration in the refurbishment of existing building stock is needed if Europe is to achieve its objectives.

Given that measures to upgrade buildings provide the most cost effective way to reduce carbon emissions, while creating employment and contributing to economic savings, there is a strong need for accelerated action for the refurbishment of existing building stock, given that 50% of that stock will still be standing in 2050 (EUROACE, 2010).

The benefits to owners and occupants of a thorough re-evaluation of a building's energy performance are potentially far-reaching: improved comfort, health, productivity, enjoyment, aesthetic quality, prestige and capital value, together with reduced running costs and security from energy price fluctuations. Some of these benefits are difficult to quantify, but they are nonetheless apparent to clients. Public programmes to require performance labelling of buildings are designed to influence market behavior and support retrofitting of energy improvements. The potential for architectural improvement is considerable and may extend to the re-organisation of the functional and spatial arrangement of the building or the combination of adjacent buildings and spaces.

A significant proportion of European residential dwellings are blocks of apartments consisting of prefabricated concrete blocks or panels. Many of these buildings are in poor condition and need major renovations.

The economics for the individual owner of energy-saving measures for single-family dwellings are fairly well understood, but upgrading other building types involves assessing a range of options in increasing order of cost and complexity. As with new build, an integrated approach will produce better results than a piecemeal one. In the context of national and international commitments to mitigate greenhouse gas emissions, the cost-effectiveness of reducing energy demand in the building sector is compelling; ambitious programmes are emerging in most countries to overcome the various obstacles to radical improvement in the energy performance of the building stock.

TO RETROFIT OR NOT?

Sometimes there will be a choice to be made between retrofitting and commissioning or buying a better building; sometimes retrofitting will be unavoidable. In either case there are similar questions to be answered: can the required internal environment be achieved? How much energy will be saved? What will be the reductions in CO_2, CFCs and other pollutants? Can the proposed measures be applied at no extra risk? Will they be durable? Will additional maintenance be required? Are there other, non-energy benefits? Will the measures be cost-effective?

The cost-effectiveness of any intervention is increased if it is implemented in phase with the normal renewal of the building and its fittings; running maintenance, routine redecoration and replacement of out-worn equipment, interior fit-out or total building refurbishment.

As a first step, the energy performance of the existing building in a 'free-running' state should be evaluated for representative periods of the day and year, together with an investigation of any building defects (such as cold bridging or condensation) to understand how the building performs and to provide a reference, base case from

Façades prior to refurbishment Renewable Energy House, Brussels. Source: EREC

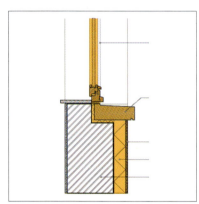

Retrofit strategy for Renewable Energy House, Brussels. Source: EREC

Refurbished Renewable Energy House, Brussels. Source: EREC

which to design. The thermal performance of the existing building envelope should be analysed in terms of unwanted heat loss or gain through walls, windows, doors and especially the ground floor and the roof. Particular attention should be paid to the effectiveness of existing cold bridges, especially at balconies and floor to external wall joints where insulation may be deficient, and to energy losses due to unwanted infiltration of cold external air (or warm air during summer).

Then consider the adverse or beneficial microclimatic conditions occurring around the building. Just as with a new building, patterns of solar radiation, temperature, precipitation, wind flow and strength, topography, vegetation, surrounding buildings and the nature of local activities should be studied and interpreted in terms of environmental conditions and opportunities. The spaces between buildings may be exploited to good effect, for example, through landscaping to optimise micro-climatic conditions for energy saving and comfort, or by structures which link buildings and provide additional enclosed areas. Examples of interventions include changes to ground contours (earth berming, etc.), planting of trees and other vegetation for shelter or shading and changes in the reflective characteristics of external surfaces to improve daylight levels indoors.

BUILDING ENVELOPE

Alternative forms of construction for the building envelope are covered in (refer STRATEGIES; Envelope). This section looks at the options which are likely to be relevant in renovating existing buildings.

Walls

Insulation may originally have been placed within the wall construction and, if well fitted, may still be effective, although certain insulation types can deteriorate with age. However, it may be desirable to apply additional insulation to improve comfort and reduce energy use. In multi-storey buildings this will usually involve a choice of internal or external insulation systems.

Internal insulation should generally be used only if the façade must not be altered, occupancy is intermittent, or, in the case of multi-unit buildings, where not all the owners want to upgrade. It is usually cheaper than external insulation, but it reduces room size and involves the replacement of skirtings, architraves, pipework, wiring and any other fixed items, and, in addition, precludes the use of the building's thermal mass as a heat store. Water vapour control is practically difficult, and it is almost impossible to solve the problem of cold bridges.

Cavity fill insulation has no effect on internal or outside appearance or on room size, and can be applied without disturbing the occupants. It permits the inner leaf to function as a thermal mass and, depending on construction, can eliminate cold bridging. The insulation is well protected, and a range of proprietary systems are available. However, it must be carried out by skilled operatives and without a thermographic survey it is difficult to ensure that the wall is evenly insulated. Some zones may be impossible to insulate such as wall-to-roof or column-to-beam junctions, head and cill positions, for example. Bridging the cavity may exacerbate damp penetration.

External insulation combined with cladding or rendering systems, although sometimes initially more expensive than internal insulation, has the following advantages:

- It completely wraps the building with insulation, thus eliminating cold bridge problems.
- It allows the thermal mass of the building to be used to moderate indoor temperature variations by acting as a heat store.
- The building can remain occupied during installation.
- It can improve the appearance and weather resistance of the building envelope.

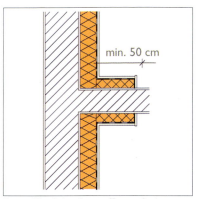
Internal insulation. Source: Zsuzsa Szalay

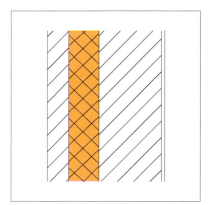
Cavity wall insulation. Source: Zsuzsa Szalay

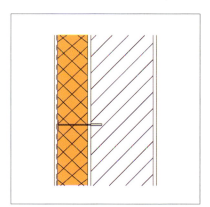
External insulation. Source: Zsuzsa Szalay

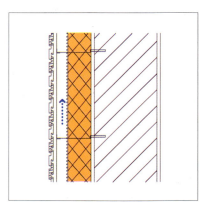
Ventilated façade insulation. Source: Zsuzsa Szalay

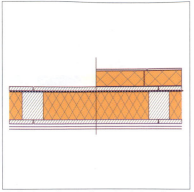

Pitched roof attic floor insulation. Source: Zsuzsa Szalay

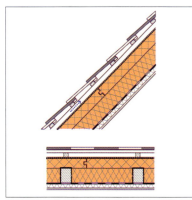

Pitched roof external rafter insulation. Source: Zsuzsa Szalay

Pitched roof internal rafter insulation. Source: Zsuzsa Szalay

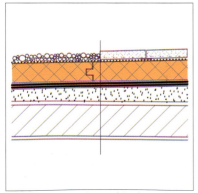

Flat roof warm or inverted insulation. Source: Zsuzsa Szalay

- It can result in lower maintenance costs.
- Where renovation of the façade is necessary, the extra cost of the insulation system can often be recovered in a few years.

External wall insulation systems fall into three main categories:

Thin-layer insulation or 'coat method':

Normally the cheapest option, thin-layer insulation, usually in the form of rigid panels, is fixed to the façade and a reinforced render or plaster coat of special composition is applied to give a weather-proof external layer with a range of possible finishes. Care is needed in detailing and installing the render coat, especially around joints, corners and window and door openings. Many proprietary systems exist.

Ventilated façade insulation

The insulation is fixed to the existing façade and finishing panels are then installed using a spacer grid. The panels have openings which allow the outside air to ventilate the space between the panels and insulation. In summer the airflows through the void cool the surface of the insulation, thereby reducing heat gains through the wall. However, these airflows can also increase heat loss in winter if unrestricted.

Pre-finished modules

Similar in thermal operation to ventilated façade insulation, pre-finished modules arrive on site ready for installation using special fixing systems which simplify the mounting operation and help to ensure a good quality of workmanship. The result is an external surface which does not require any further work.

Roofs

Heat losses from roofs are high because of their relatively large surface area and because of night-time radiation to the sky. Adding insulation is often quite easy and pay-back periods are short. Water vapour and condensation must be controlled by appropriate use of vapour barriers and ventilation.

Pitched roof attic floor insulation is an easy, low-cost action where insulation material, usually fibreglass quilt, mineral wool or rigid foam plastic panels, is placed horizontally. Where the attic space is insulated the new insulation can be applied between the rafters -remembering to allow for ventilation of the structure.

In general, proprietary pitched roof systems (such as the metal deck systems used in industrial premises, which may already have some insulation) can be upgraded by the application of additional internal insulation. The relatively durable decking systems are often in good condition and continue to provide an effective rain screen.

In flat roofs, cold deck construction should be avoided. Warm or inverted deck constructions allow the roof slab to act as a thermal store and the risk of interstitial condensation is reduced. An inverted deck has the advantage of protecting a sound weatherproof layer against thermal stress, but, if the existing roof finish has reached the end of its useful life, a warm deck solution may have an attractive payback period.

Floors

The cost of placing insulation under existing concrete floors is not likely to be justifiable unless they need to be replaced for other reasons - damp, deterioration, or inadequate load-bearing capacity, for example. Heat loss can sometimes be reduced by ensuring effective land drainage around the building perimeter and adding vertical external insulation below ground level. Another alternative is to place insulation over an existing floor and cover it with a screed or proprietary flooring system.

Suspended floors are usually easier to insulate and proprietary systems for various forms of floor construction are available.

Windows and Doors

In colder climates, transmission losses through glazing, cold bridging through frames, and ventilation losses through joints are all issues to be addressed. Improvements in these areas will not only reduce building heat loss but, by eliminating draughts and the 'chill factor' of cold glazing, will also reduce the room temperature needed for comfortable conditions.

The more layers of air trapped between glass panes, the lower the heat transfer through the window. It is often possible to fit secondary glazing within existing frames with only minor adaptations. This secondary unit could incorporate one of the advanced types of glazing described in ELEMENTS. If there are existing double-glazed frames in good condition, replacing the existing glazing with units which incorporate a 'Low E' coating and a gas-filled cavity may be appropriate. Transparent insulation materials (TIM) may be an option for openings where heat losses outweigh heat gains but daylight is essential. Insulated blinds or shutters are an inexpensive method of reducing heat losses after dark.

In general, but particularly in windy areas, poor airtightness in existing window and external door frames results in heat gain or heat loss. Draught stripping can help, but where frames are seriously damaged or aged, they should be changed for new well-sealed ones.

Infrared image of heat loss reduction. Source: Energy Heritage; a Guide to Improving Energy Efficiency in Traditional and Heritage Homes © City of Edinburgh

Secondary glazing. Source: Zsuzsa Szalay

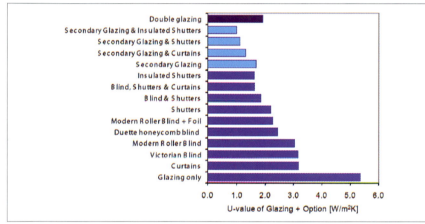

Measured values of a historic Scottish window, Glasgow Caledonian University. Source: Paul Baker

Materials

As with a new building, careful, informed selection of materials and components used in buildings can improve environmental conditions indoors, and can have a significant, cumulative effect on the health of the environment.

Services

In any sustainable retrofitting programme there are two fundamental tasks in relation to services. First, reduce demand. Then make sure that where additional resources are needed they are supplied and used efficiently. Where mechanical heating or ventilation must be provided, the energy required should be supplied from renewable sources where feasible. The use of mechanical air conditioning should be avoided if at all possible.

Control systems

Better controls can have a substantial impact on energy consumption and are sometimes justified as stand-alone options. Thermostatic radiator valves can save 10% over manual controls. A metering and recording system will give owners or occupiers the information and motivation to manage and reduce their energy consumption. Generally, the more efficient a control and metering system, the higher its investment cost. The introduction of smart meters provides the opportunity for significant energy savings through motivation of the consumers towards more careful use of energy.

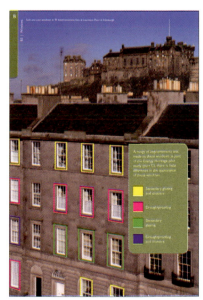

Retrofit study Lauriston Place, Edinburgh. Source: Energy Heritage; a Guide to Improving Energy Efficiency in Traditional and Heritage Homes © Changeworks

HAZARDS

In assessing renovation strategies, care must be taken to avoid or minimise the hazards which may arise. Renovated buildings are often occupied while work proceeds and the occupants are exposed to pollution and other hazards resulting from demolition and stripping out processes, as well as from the newly installed materials.

Problems can be identified and controlled through analysis of the potential causes of indoor air pollution. The technique will be common to all projects while the sources of pollution will, of course, be unique to the specific project in hand.

A typical sequence of management of the refurbishment project should include at least the following:

- analysis of the existing building to identify possible sources of pollutants;
- organisation and management of the refurbishment process to minimise pollution levels during demolition and disposal;
- procedures to measure and assure indoor air quality at all stages of the work.

CONSTRUCTION AND COMPLETION

During renovation, close supervision and briefing of the construction team is essential. On completion building managers and occupants should be provided with concise, easily understood explanations of how thermal and lighting systems can be operated most effectively, information about what is required of them in using the building and the likely results of failure to operate or maintain the building and its energy systems appropriately. Sustained good management is essential.

Renovation Checklist

Space heating and ventilation

Reducing demand	• insulate fabric
	• reduce infiltration
	• utilise solar gain
Improving efficiency	• consider efficiency of heating appliances
	• improve controls

Space cooling and ventilation

Reducing overheating	• reduce solar gain
	• improve efficiency of lighting and other heat producing equipment
	• use natural ventilation
Improving efficiency	• ensure the efficiency of pumps and fans
	• improve controls
	• specify efficient cooling plant (if cooling plant is unavoidable)

Lighting

Reducing demand	• improve daylighting
	• rationalise space usage
Improving efficiency	• redesign artificial lighting layout
	• specify efficient lamps, luminaires and ballasts
	• improve controls

Water

Reducing demand	• use treated water for human consumption only
	• harvest rainwater for suitable uses
	• improve water storage and pipe layout
	• install water meters
Improving efficiency	• specify water conserving fittings

Building management

Reducing demand	• educate building users
	• ensure good 'housekeeping'
Improving efficiency	• set targets and monitor performance
	• ensure effective maintenance and operation
	• consider a range of energy management and monitoring systems

---

SECTION 4: ELEMENTS

COMPONENTS

INTRODUCTION

Any list of types of components used in sustainable building could be very long. Hundreds of different solutions have emerged during the history of green architecture, but few are well tested over many years in different situations.

This manual is aimed at building designers who are approaching these concepts for the first time. We have therefore selected technologies which are well known, at least by those familiar with green design, and widely available on the market. The non-specialist can easily apply these tried and tested solutions.

COMPONENTS
Introduction
Building Envelope
Controls
Renewable Energy
Heating and Cooling Systems

MATERIALS
Introduction
Life Cycle Design
Wood
Straw and Plant Fibres
Earth
Stone
Cement
Concrete
Brick, Tile and Ceramics
Glass
Metals
Paints, Adhesives and Preservatives
Sealants
Synthetic Materials

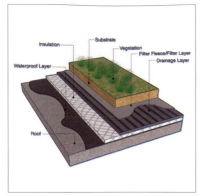

Grass roof layers

Grass roof on the Skellig Intepretive Centre, Ireland. Architects: Peter and Mary Doyle

BUILDING ENVELOPE

Green Roofs

Placing soil and green plants on a flat or pitched roof to create a 'green roof' is an ancient vernacular tradition that has become popular again in recent years. However, a modern green roof is not simply a conventional roof with soil on top; it is a complex structure with multiple layers providing different functions.

There are several types of green roof which each create different habitats, affect storm-water runoff to varying degrees, and have different levels of impact on the building's thermal performance. Green or living roofs can be planted with a single simple plant such as Sedum, or cultivated with a mixture of grasses and plants creating a bio-diverse roof.

The roof structure may need to be strengthened to support the extra weight of the soil, which has a density of roughly 2 t/m³. The roof deck may be flat, or pitched to an angle below about 30°. Protrusions such as nail heads must be avoided. A waterproof membrane, generally made of ethylene-propylene-diene monomer (EPDM) or another synthetic rubberised material, is laid loosely over the deck. A geotextile mat lies on top of the membrane, which prevents soil slippage and provides a barrier to roots. The soil, typically about 200mm deep, is seeded and/or planted with whatever mix of plants is desired. The deeper the soil, the wider the variety of plants that can be used. A biodegradable matting is often placed on top of the soil to prevent it from blowing or washing away before the plants are established. At the edge of the roof is a drainage zone typically consisting of a gravel-filled channel to prevent moisture build-up *(Talbott, 1993)*.

There are a number of benefits with the use of green roofs in an urban environment. One such is the use of green roofs as part of a sustainable urban drainage systems (SUDS) strategy. Green roofs have the capacity to store rainwater within the plants and substrate and release it back into the atmosphere through evapo-transpiration and evaporation following a rainfall event. Green roofs provide attenuation of stormwater within the roof and reduce the volume of stormwater which is discharged to drain, thereby reducing the risk of surcharging within existing stormwater drains. This is especially relevant within existing urban areas where it may be easier to retrofit compared with other SUDS methodologies such as underground attenuation.

In addition to reducing the impact of stormwater problems, green roofs can provide a haven for wildlife in a city, can deliver aesthetic benefits, and may moderate local microclimates if present over sufficient area. The insulation value of soil is dependent upon its moisture content and density; conductances range from 0.7–2.1 W/mK, giving a U-value of 0.15–0.4 W/m²K for a 200mm layer. The lifespan of the roofing membrane may be longer than other types of roofing materials, but this is probably outweighed by the higher initial cost. Green roofs also reduce exterior noise, although if this is a problem then other measures such as sealed double glazing are likely to take priority. The soil of a green roof provides a substantial amount of thermal mass, but since this lies outside the insulated building envelope it will be only weakly coupled to the rest of the building.

Architectural integration
Providing access for maintenance is a possible issue. Structural design may be affected, as mentioned above.

Economics
A green roof involves considerable extra expense, which is unlikely to be recouped through energy savings alone; however, where SUDS strategies are required and the available area within the site is limited for surface or underground stormwater attenuation, green roofs may provide an economical solution.

BUILDING ENVELOPE

Trombe Walls

The Trombe wall is an example of solar heating by indirect gain. It consists of a 150–500mm masonry wall on the south side of a building. A single or double layer of glass or plastic glazing is mounted approximately 100–150mm in front of the wall's surface. The exterior surface of the wall is painted a dark colour to absorb solar heat, and the glazing prevents this heat from being lost to the outside. Thus, the Trombe wall gradually heats up during the day, with the heat penetrating slowly from the exterior to the interior surface of the wall. As the interior surface of the wall heats up it radiates heat to the adjacent interior space. If the wall is the right thickness, this time lag means that the heat from the afternoon sun will start to warm the space in the evening, just as temperatures begin to drop.

If more rapid heating is needed, vents at the top and bottom of the wall may be opened, allowing heat to circulate by convection into the interior from the glazed space in front of the wall. These vents must be closed at night to prevent the cycle reversing and heat being lost from the interior. Heat loss at night can also be reduced by drawing a curtain across the outside of the Trombe wall, inside the glazing.

Architectural integration

A full height Trombe wall has the disadvantage of blocking sunlight from the south and presenting a blank, dark-coloured face to the outdoors. It is worth considering a half-height Trombe wall from this point of view, since it would permit sunlight to enter the space. The loss of usable floor space caused by a thick Trombe wall is also worth considering from an architectural viewpoint.

Economics

The economics and suitability of a Trombe wall system are dependent upon many factors including climate, construction type, cost of materials and energy prices.

Transpired Solar Collector

A transpired solar collector (TSC) provides pre-conditioned air for a building's active or passive heating and ventilation system, thereby reducing its heating and cooling loads. A TSC system consists of a south facing dark coloured perforated sheet metal façade. The sheeting is mounted on the building's structural wall, creating a 100-150mm gap between the TSC sheeting and the building. Outside air is drawn through the collector's perforations by ventilation fans within the building. As the air is drawn through the TSC, its temperature is increased through heat transfer from the metal sheeting. The heated air flows to the top of the wall, where it is distributed to the building's interior through the ventilation system. During the cooling season, collector bypass vents can be opened allowing the wall to dump heat, thus reducing cooling loads.

Architectural Integration

Transpired solar collectors can be incorporated into the south-facing façade of large buildings.

Economics

A transpired solar collector system can provide a simple, economical and low maintenance method for the preheating of air for a building resulting in reduced heating and cooling loads.

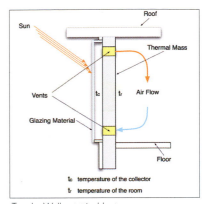

Trombe Wall – typical loop

SolarWall system by Conserval Engineering at Sainsbury Distribution Centre, Pineham. Source: SolarWall

Double façade with integrated shading. GSW Headquarters, Berlin. Architect: Sauerbruch Hutton. Source: Annette Kisling

Double façade, GSW Headquarters, Berlin. Architect: Sauerbruch Hutton. Source: Lorna Browne

BUILDING ENVELOPE

Double Skin Façades

The double skin façade is an architectural technology designed to combine the aesthetic features of a high glazing ratio (over 90%) with the energy efficiency and comfort of a solid envelope.

Many buildings of the past 50 years, particularly office buildings, are noted for using large areas of external glass in a non-loadbearing 'curtain wall'. This is mainly an aesthetic device, made possible by cheap energy; steel or aluminium frames supporting a non-structural envelope, and comfort-control technologies, particularly air conditioning.

The double skin façade typically consists of two separate glass skins enclosing an air space. One or even both skins may be double-glazed. Shading and light directing devices may be situated between the two skins, which may be controlled by a building management system or by the occupant as in the GSW Headquarters in Berlin, and ventilation air circulates in this space. If well designed, the outer façade should protect the interior from wind, rain and noise, allowing the inner windows to be opened to provide natural ventilation. Daylighting is another benefit, although excessive light, particularly when it comes from one side of a deep space, can create glare problems. The aim is that the thermal performance of a well-designed double façade should approach that of a solid envelope. Double façade systems are becoming increasingly common as part of the retrofitting and upgrading of existing multistory buildings. The use of a double façade can reduce the heating and cooling loads on a building, enable natural ventilation, and provide an acoustic barrier to exterior noise pollution.

Concerns in relation to the use of double skin façades include fire protection (due to the circulation of air between floors in the air space between the façades), and the reflection of noise between rooms.

The implementation of a double skin façade as an energy efficient strategy for either existing or new buildings requires extensive detailed design and building simulation in order for the strategy to be successful. The detailed design of a double skin façade is critical, and in the most successful examples, extensive simulation has been carried out using computer analysis, scale models and full-scale prototypes.

Recommendations
Adequate analysis of the design using computer and scale models and full-scale prototypes is likely to be essential if a design that performs well is to be achieved.

Economics
The incorporation of a correctly designed double skin façade can be an attractive option for the upgrading of existing highly glazed buildings, or where a high glazing ratio is required in a new building. However, the energy required for heating and cooling in buildings which are not highly glazed and have a serious level of thermal insulation is likely to be lower than in a highly glazed building with a double skin façade.

If the starting point is an extensively glazed building, then adding a properly designed second skin can result in energy savings (heating and cooling), and provide improved thermal and visual comfort, improved sound attenuation, and exterior solar shading, which is protected by the building's second skin *(Blomsterberg, 2007)*.

BUILDING ENVELOPE

Light Re-directing and Chromic Glazing

Redirecting light

Prismatic glazing and holographic film are products that redirect light. In prismatic glazing the direction of incoming daylight is changed as it passes through an array of triangular wedges, some of which may have specular or silvered surfaces, and whose geometry can be designed for particular conditions. It can keep out unwanted direct sunlight, while redirecting diffuse daylight onto the ceiling and farther back into the room. Light coming from different angles can be handled selectively, with assemblies custom-made for site latitude and façade orientation.

Holographic film can also be designed to handle sunlight coming from well-defined angles. High-angle sun on south façades, or low-angle sun on east and west façades, for example, can be either blocked or redirected. Up to four images containing different 'instructions' can be combined in one layer. A view out is retained, but from some viewing angles there is a rainbow effect.

Chromic glass

Chromic glass when activated can turn from a clear transparent state to a semi-transparent or opaque state, and vice versa. It is used to control solar radiation entering the building, preventing overheating and glare. As a result, bulky solar control measures, such as louvres and mechanical roller blinds may be eliminated and maintenance costs reduced.

Chromic glass changes its light absorption and transmission characteristics in response to changes in light (photochromic) or temperature (thermochromic), or to an electrical charge (electrochromic). Control of electrochromic glazing can be incorporated in a building energy management system. Photochromic and electrochromic glass have reached technical maturity, but costs are high.

Architectural integration

Light-redirecting and chromic glazing products can be creatively used by building designers, combining performance with appearance.

Recommendations

Chromic glass which changes state without the user's intervention isn't normally appropriate for eye-level window panes, but it may be used for roof glazing or placed above and below the normal viewing level.

Economics

Prismatic sheets themselves are inexpensive to manufacture, but the overall construction cost of the window is higher than for conventional glazing. The cost of chromic glazing systems is reducing as active research and commercial interest in the technology increases.

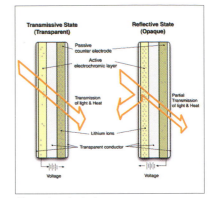

Electrochromic glazing

Light directing glazing at the Design Centre, Linz. Architect: Herzog and Partner Architects

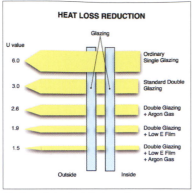

U-value of standard glazing units

High performance triple glazed window

High Performance Windows

The key performance characteristics of windows are insulation value (U-value, in W/m²K) and transmission of light. A conventional, single-glazed window with clear float glass will transmit approximately 83% of the light that falls upon it, and will have a U-value of roughly 6.0 W/m²K. Double glazing typically provides a U-value of around 3.0 W/m²K with a transmissivity of about 80%.

High-performance triple glazed windows with a U-value (including the frame) of between 0.85 and 0.70 W/m²K are now available. These high performance windows deal with the three modes of heat loss (conduction, radiation, and convection) and infiltration or exfiltration of air by using triple pane insulating glazing with low-emissivity coatings, sealed noble gas filled inter-pane voids and insulated glass spacers in conjunction with thermally broken window frames, together with effective weather stripping.

Gas-filled multiple glazing

Standard double and triple glazing units are filled with air. Sealed glazing units containing noble gases (such as argon and krypton) provide significantly better insulation values by reducing heat transfer through the unit. An argon-filled window will typically have an insulation value about 20% better than an identical air-filled unit, without affecting transmission of light *(Esbensen, 1998)*.

Low-emissivity coatings

In a cold climate, heat from the interior space is absorbed by the glass in a normal window, which heats up and re-radiates the heat. After being absorbed and re-radiated several times the heat reaches the outside and is lost. The re-radiation process can be reduced by coating one or more panes with a low-emissivity (Low E) coating.

Low E glazing has a thin and almost transparent coating of metal oxide, which substantially reduces the ability of the glass to radiate at certain wavelengths, thus reducing heat transfer through the glass. The solar heat gain coefficient (SHGC) of the glazing indicates the degree of control of radiation transmission:

- Low E glasses with a low SHGC reflect solar radiation, and so are suitable for climates dominated by cooling.
- Low E glass with a high SHGC allows solar radiation to pass through the glazing into the building, as is appropriate for climates dominated by heating.

Frames

The quality of the seal around a window's edge varies depending on the frame material, the gasket or sealant, and the age of the window. Windows may be compared by rate of air infiltration. The conductivity of the frame is also an issue (particularly in smaller windows), metal frames conducting more than wood or plastic.

Recommendations

The U-values of windows should be specified as being for the whole assembly including the frame, rather than 'centre-of-glass' values, which applies only to the glass.

Economics

As part of an integrated design, high-performance windows can provide improvements in comfort and significant energy cost savings.

BUILDING ENVELOPE

Shading Devices

Shading devices can be used to reduce glare and heat gain during the day, and heat loss at night, provided they are appropriate to location and orientation.

Interior/Exterior Shading Devices

Exterior shading is more effective in reducing heat gains (by up to 80%) because it intercepts and reflects solar radiation before it strikes the glass. Exterior shading devices are more expensive to install and to maintain and play a major role in the aesthetic character of an elevation.

Interior shading devices such as blinds are less expensive and more easily adjustable. They protect a room's occupants against the immediate effects of sunlight and glare, but are not particularly effective at reducing solar heat gain as the solar radiation has entered the building before it is effected by the shading device.

Integral shading installed within a double or triple glazing unit, with ventilation of the void to the outside, combines the advantages of both types. Heat gains are dissipated to the outside, and the shading is protected from the severity of the outdoor climate.

Fixed/Adjustable Shading Devices

Fixed horizontal overhangs exclude high-angle sunlight, but reduce daylight penetration and are not appropriate for east and west orientations. Thus, they are most appropriate where light levels are high and overheating is a problem, such as in southern Europe. Continuous overhangs provide much more shade than those which extend across the width of the window only.

Light shelves can be used to redirect sunlight into the back of the room, and also to protect the front of the room from direct radiation.

Low-angle direct sunlight is more difficult to screen. Fixed vertical fins, if they are to be really effective, exclude a great deal of daylight and obstruct the view. Steel mesh sunscreens are almost 'transparent' but they too reduce the amount of daylight penetrating the windows.

Adjustable shades avoid some of these problems. Retractable awnings, adjustable exterior blades, curtains, roller blinds or venetian blinds can be left open for much of the time and closed only when the sun-angle demands it. On east or west-facing façades, horizontal louvers need to be almost completely closed to block sunlight, but vertical louvers can be left partially open to admit reflected or diffused light from the north, while still blocking sunlight. Fully automated systems, which respond to changes in sun angle, temperature and/or light levels, may be necessary, particularly for exterior systems.

Recommendations

Solar shading should be designed using daylight modelling of year-round site-specific data such as sun paths and taking into account the overshadowing effects of adjoining buildings. Both fixed and adjustable shading devices can have significant impact on the aesthetic character of a building and should be considered during the early stages of the design process.

Economics

As part of a good design, shading devices can be an economical investment.

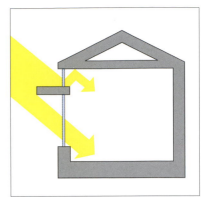

Light shelves can redirect light and provide solar shading

Clakamas High School, Portland. Architect and source: Boora Architects

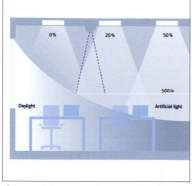

Constant lighting control can regulate the strip lighting to compensate for the lack of daylight assuring the target light intensity. Source: Siemens

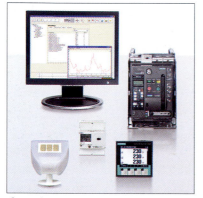

Comprehensive energy management at the application, power distribution and automation level can reduce energy consumption. Source: Siemens

CONTROLS

Lighting Controls

In a complex or sophisticated daylight design, particularly one with exterior adjustable daylighting devices, integrated automatic lighting control systems are probably essential. In a conventionally lit commercial building, controls alone can make a 30–40% saving in lighting use. Care in the specification of control systems is necessary. Technical difficulties with the positioning and sensitivity of sensors, rapid changes in daylight levels due to fast-moving clouds, and the response of the occupants must all be anticipated.

Occupancy sensors

Occupancy sensors can help to optimise the use of background lighting. These sensors will operate the lights only when people are in the area. There are two types of occupancy sensors: infrared and ultra-sonic. Ultra-sonic sensors are best in rooms with partitions or dividers. Infrared sensors are better for open areas. Some sensors use both methods. Integrated units that include a sensor and a relay in a single housing in a standard electrical box are quite reasonably priced for residential applications.

Balancing artificial light

In rooms receiving natural light, there can be an intermittent need for artificial light depending on how bright it is outside. A fluorescent light with a 'daylighting ballast' (which includes a light-sensitive photocell) will vary light output according to the levels in the room, maintaining sufficient light at all times while eliminating the wasteful use of artificial light when daylight levels are already high.

Outdoor lighting

Photocells can also be used in outdoor lighting, for example, to activate lights at dusk and switch them off at dawn. For added efficiency, the photocell can be combined with an infrared or ultra-sonic motion detector. In this way, the lights are switched on only when daylight levels are low and there is motion in the vicinity.

Timing devices and dimmer controls

Timers turn lights on and off at predetermined times and are useful where regular cycles of light and dark are appropriate. Dimmers will only save energy when used consistently, and can often be combined with other forms of lighting control.

Recommendations

- Limit the number of light fittings controlled by any one switch.

- Provide clear and understandable layouts for light switch panels.

- Zone light fittings and controls in relation to distance from windows.

- Make light switches accessible. Hand-held remote control switches are useful where changes in partition layout are frequent. Simple local switching of this kind can produce 20% energy savings.

- Use automated controls (timers, time delay switches, movement sensors or sound detectors, daylight sensors, voltage/current controls).

Economics

Lighting controls can provide significant savings as part of a well-designed lighting scheme.

RENEWABLE ENERGY

Renewable energy comes from sustainable sources such as wind, hydro, solar, biomass, wave and tidal energy.

Wind

Wind turbine technology has developed rapidly over the last 30 years and onshore wind is now one of the most cost-effective renewable energy sources. Wind turbines convert the kinetic energy of the wind into electrical energy with the use of an electrical generator connected to the rotary blades of the turbine. Wind turbines are mostly installed in groups which make up wind farms, which supply electricity to the grid like conventional power stations. Many turbines being installed at present are in the size range 500 kilowatts (kW) to 2.5 megawatts (MW).

Wind turbine

Annual power output is dependent on the wind speed at the site. Thus, the economic returns from wind turbines are much better on exposed coastal or upland sites than in sheltered areas. Wind turbines produce electricity variably when wind conditions are suitable, and there are periods when no electricity is being produced. Planning permission and a connection to the grid are also required before a wind farm can start operating.

Small scale hydro plant. Source: Dulas Ltd

Wind energy is one of the most efficient energy sources in terms of land use. Only 1–2% of the land on which a wind farm stands is occupied by turbine foundations and access roads; the land between the turbines can be used for agricultural or other purposes. Offshore wind farms are also being developed.

Small scale or micro-turbines can be used on a domestic scale for the production of electricity. Micro-turbines can produce between 300W and 100kW of electricity, but are unlikely to be appropriate within an urban environment due to wind turbulence caused by surrounding buildings.

Small scale wind turbines can be designed to feed into off-grid or grid connected systems. In an off-grid system the electrical power from the wind turbine as direct current (DC) output is transferred to batteries for storage and later use. If power is required as alternating current (AC), then an inverter is used downstream of the batteries. In a grid connected system the DC power is converted to AC and surplus electricity is sold to the grid.

Economics

The economic viability of a wind energy system is dependent upon the capital cost of the system, the local cost of electricity and availability of incentives such as feed-in tariffs, local wind velocities, and the developer's energy demands.

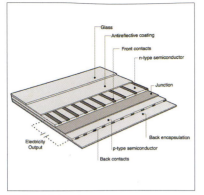

Photovoltaic panel

Integrated photovoltaic façade in Tobias Grau
GmbH Head office, Rellingen. Architect: BRT
Architects. Source: Schueco International KG

RENEWABLE ENERGY

Photovoltaics

Photovoltaic (PV) devices convert sunlight directly into electricity. They are clean, quiet, low-maintenance and efficient in their use of solar energy. The main obstacle to the wider use of PVs at present is its cost per watt produced. However, this cost has been falling steadily, and PVs are likely to become much more widely used in the next ten years as costs fall still further and the technology is improved. The potential of PVs is enormous. Studies in Germany and Britain have found that between a quarter and half of these States' respective electricity needs could be supplied by PVs mounted on buildings alone.

Photovoltaic systems generate a direct current (DC) output, which can be used directly as DC or converted to alternating current (AC). DC output can be used directly or stored in battery systems.

Photovoltaics are used in two types of installations, 'off-grid' and 'grid-connected.' Off-grid or stand-alone installations are those where the photovoltaic cells and the devices which they power are not connected to the electricity grid. The electricity may either be used as it is generated (for example, in a solar-powered pump) or it may be stored for later use in batteries. Off-grid PVs are used in isolated rural locations for already cost-effective applications such as refrigeration, emergency phones and water pumps, but are also familiar in urban applications such as street warning signs and parking meters.

A grid-connected installation usually dispenses with the cost of storing electricity. Surplus power is supplied to the grid as it is generated and bought back when it is needed. The economics of grid-connected PV installations are governed by the market conditions in the country in question, and whether there are incentives such as feed-in tarriffs.

The most common photovoltaic cells are currently based on silicon. Photovoltaic panels are available as mono-crystalline silicon, polycrystalline silicon and thin film amorphous silicon. Crystalline panels in both mono-crystalline and polycrystalline form are typically more efficient than amorphous silicon PVs, however they are more expensive to manufacture than amorphous panels. The recent development of technologies such as dye-sensitised solar cells may radically reduce the cost of PV cell technology.

Architectural integration

Traditionally PV cells were installed on pitched roofs in the same way as solar thermal panels, with the generation of electricity as their sole function. New developments mean that it is now possible to integrate cells into the building fabric, as part of the roof, walls, shading devices and even windows. The term building-integrated photovoltaics (BIPV) describes this combination of PV modules with building elements. Established examples of such integration are the incorporation of PV modules into roof tiles or as part of a solar shading strategy.

Recommendations

When designing a PV system the following should be considered:

• Local climatic condition including shading by adjoining buildings.

• The efficiency of PV panels decreases with an increase in temperature. Ensure that the panels are sufficiently vented to facilitate cooling.

• Safe access should be provided for regular cleaning of the panels.

Economics

The cost and reliability of photovoltaic systems continues to improve significantly as active research and commercial investment in the technology increases.

RENEWABLE ENERGY

Bioenergy/Waste

Heat, transport fuel and/or electricity may be produced from various types of waste, including agricultural wastes, forestry wastes, municipal refuse and sewage. There are many examples of commercial projects using these fuel sources throughout Europe.

Energy may also be derived through direct or indirect combustion of fuel generated from cultivated biomass. Biomass can be defined as any plant-derived organic material that renews itself over a short growth cycle. The most common type of biomass used for direct combustion is wood, in either treated or untreated forms. Typical examples of cultivated woody biomass include short rotation forestry, short rotation coppice and the perennial grass miscanthus.

Short rotation forestry (SRF) involves fast growing trees such as ash, beech, willow, poplar and alder with an eight to 20 year harvesting cycle. The felled timber is often chipped and used for energy production by direct combustion. Once the timber is harvested the trees can be replanted, or in the case of willow allowed to regenerate as coppice.

Short rotation coppice (SRP) involves the growth of multiple shoots from saplings or the stumps of felled trees which are usually the by-product of SRF. The tree stumps produce multiple shoots of high yielding trees such as willow and poplar in relatively short cycles (often three to five years). The coppice is harvested and allowed dry to reduce its moisture content before being used for energy production by direct combustion.

Miscanthus giganteus, commonly known as elephant grass, is another short rotation crop which is being grown as a commercial energy crop within Europe. Miscanthus giganteus is a tufted perennial grass which grows up to four meters high and can be utilised for energy production by direct combustion on its own or with other fuel sources. Miscanthus can also be used for the production of biofuels such as ethanol.

Processed woodpellets

Miccanthus Giganteus grass

BIOMASS FUEL	Energy Density by Mass	Energy Density by Mass	Bulk Density	Energy Density by volume
	GJ/tonne	kWh/kg	kg/m³	MJ/m³
Wood chips (dependent on moisture content)	7-15	2-4	175-350	2000-3600
Log wood (20% moisture content)	15	4.2	300-550	4500-8300
Wood (solid oven dry)	18-21	5-5.8	450-800	8100-16800
Wood Pellets	18	5	600-700	10800-12600
Miscanthus (bail)	17	4.7	120-160	2000-2700

(Pennycook, 2008)

Biomass Boilers

Biomass boilers range in size from small domestic wood burning stoves to large industrial automated boilers suitable for large buildings or group/district heating schemes. Biomass boilers can require longer startup times than traditional fossil fuel boliers and are slower to shut down.

Biomass fuels have a lower energy density in comparison to fossil fuels such as oil or gas; storage requirements for biomass fuels on site are significantly greater. Biomass is usually locally sourced and alternative sources of supply should be available to ensure security of supply into the future. Biomass boilers produce small volumes of waste ash which requires access to a suitable disposal route.

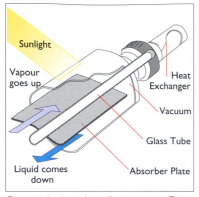

Evacuated tube solar collector: more efficient than flat plate collectors

Labels in diagram: Sunlight, Vapour goes up, Heat Exchanger, Vacuum, Glass Tube, Absorber Plate, Liquid comes down

Evacuated tube solar collector array

RENEWABLE ENERGY

Solar Thermal Systems

Solar thermal systems are devices which collect the energy of the sun and deliver it as useful heat, mostly for domestic hot water. They are in widespread use in many parts of the world, and in Europe particularly in Greece, Germany, Austria, Scandinavia and the Netherlands.

A solar thermal system contains components which collect the sun's heat, distribute and store it. There are three main types of solar collector:

- Unglazed collectors consist of black plastic or metal pipes through which the fluid is circulated. They are very simple and cheap to make but can only reach temperatures of about 20°C above ambient air temperature. They find application in swimming pools.

- Flat plate collectors consist of a glazed insulated box containing a absorber through which the fluid circulates. They can produce temperatures up to 70°C above ambient.

- Evacuated tube collectors comprise an array of glass tubes each containing a partial vacuum and an absorber which collects solar energy and transfers it to the heat transfer fluid. These collectors can produce temperatures of 100°C or more above ambient.

Solar collectors need to be mounted so as to catch the sun, generally facing south and tilted for water heating at an angle to the horizontal that is roughly equal to the latitude of the site. In Europe, this means a tilt of 35–65°. A south-facing pitched roof is ideal, in the northern hemisphere.

The distribution and storage parts of a solar thermal system are very similar to those of a conventional heating system. The distribution medium is usually based on either air or water. The heat storage unit will often be larger than in a non-solar system because of the need to store heat during cloudy periods. A backup heat source such as a wood, oil or gas boiler is usually necessary.

Solar thermal systems are an economical and clean source of energy. In most parts of the EU, a solar thermal system can supply at least 50% of a household's energy for hot water at virtually no running cost. A typical DHW system for a household will have 2–5m^2 of collector area, although less is needed in southern than northern Europe, and a 200–300 litre water storage vessel.

Architectural integration
The impact of a roof-mounted solar thermal collector on the building's architectural appearance is no greater than that of, for instance, an attic window. Some systems, particularly in southern Europe, make use of the thermosyphon effect to circulate the water, which means that the tank has to be placed above the collector, on the outside of the roof. While the use of an electric circulating pump is avoided, this can lead to much greater architectural impact.

Recommendations
Check that shadows from surrounding buildings and trees do not obstruct sunlight falling on the collectors, especially in winter when the sun is low in the sky. Solar systems can in stagnant conditions reach high temperatures and pressures. Systems should be designed with pressure venting safety systems, and industry standards and installation codes should be followed.

Economics
Solar thermal systems can provide significant savings as part of a well-designed domestic hot water system.

HEATING AND COOLING SYSTEMS

Ground Coupled Air Systems

Ground coupled air systems are used to partially heat or cool a space by drawing outside air into a building through underground ducts or pipes. The process is based on the fact that the earth below a certain depth maintains a near constant temperature. Air is drawn through underground pipes where it either captures or dissipates heat to or from the ground, depending on the temperature differential between air and ground temperatures. During summer months, for instance, dissipation of heat to the surrounding ground occurs as the air is drawn through the underground pipe before entering the building. A typical ground coupled air system consists of one or more tubes of appropriate diameter and length buried horizontally in the ground.

The performance of a ground coupled air system is dependent on site specific factors including:

- Ground temperature
- Soil moisture content
- Thermal conductivity of the pipes
- Thermal diffusivity of the soil
- Length and diameter of pipe
- External air temperature
- Air velocity and turbulence within the pipe

The system of air circulation may be either open or closed loop. In a closed circuit, both intake and outlet are located inside the building and the indoor air is circulated through the tubes. In an open loop system the air is drawn in from outside. Either open or closed loop circulation systems can be used to reduce the cooling or heating load on a building.

Recommendations

- The length of the pipes should be at least 10m.
- The pipe diameter should be between 200–300mm.
- The pipes should be between 1.5–3m deep, or where average ground temperatures are about 5–6°C different from air temperatures.
- The air velocity should be between 4–8m/s.
- Tubes can be made from various materials (PVC, stainless steel, concrete, etc.) but must be impermeable to groundwater, and should not release dust or toxins into the air.
- When transferring heat to the ground, condensation may occur inside the tube. Adequate drainage must therefore be installed, and the velocity of air inside needs to be calculated with particular attention to reducing the risk of condensation. The presence of stagnant water within the pipe can lead to a risk of mould and fungal growth.

Economics

Ground coupled air systems are simple, low-maintenance systems; however the economics of ground coupled air systems are dependent upon the local climatic conditions, geology, the nature of the site and the building in question. 'Parasitic' electrical energy required by any fans must not be overlooked.

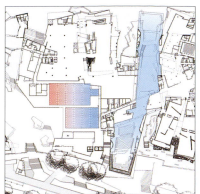

Ground coupled system at Federation Square, Melbourne. Architect: Lab and Bates Smart Architects. Source: Atelier Ten

Construction of ground coupled system at Federation Square, Melbourne. Architect: Lab and Bates Smart Architects. Source: Atelier Ten

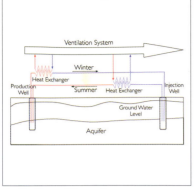

Aquifier Thermal Energy Storage

Drilling a Borehole. Source: Passivhaus Institute Darmstadt

HEATING AND COOLING SYSTEMS

Aquifer Thermal Energy Storage

Aquifer thermal energy storage (ATES) utilises the relatively stable groundwater temperatures found in underground aquifers to reduce space cooling requirements within a building or as a source of heat for pre-conditioning ventilation air.

An aquifer thermal energy storage system utilises two separate wells, which tap into an underground aquifer. During the cooling season water is extracted from one 'production' well at ground temperature and pumped through a heat exchanger, which is used to deliver cooled water to the building's HVAC system. The groundwater having passed through the heat exchanger is pumped into the second 'injection' well.

The ATES system can be reversed during the winter months, and some of the energy removed from the building and stored within the aquifer during summer can be re-introduced into the building to reduce the heating load.

Aquifer Thermal Energy Systems can be combined with other technologies such as ground source heat pumps.

Recommendations

* The borehole wells should be between 30–150m deep.
* The boreholes wells should be 100–150m apart.
* Extraction of water from aquifers may require licensing.

Economics

The economics of an ATES system are dependent upon site specific geology, climate, regional utility costs and the size of the building loads.

HEATING AND COOLING SYSTEMS

Gasification Wood Boilers

Notwithstanding their use of a renewable energy source, traditional wood boilers tend to have a low combustion efficiency and produce a large amount of air pollutants, such as particulates (soot), carbon monoxide, oxides of nitrogen and sulphur and volatile organic compounds.

Gasification wood boilers mitigate these and some other disadvantages connected with traditional technologies for the use of wood in heating, and help to ensure adherence to emissions standards.

The most efficient and cleanest combustion of wood is obtained when the flame does not come into contact with fuel, other than that being consumed. This type of consumption is generally obtained when the flame is directed downwards at the top of the fuel. An appropriate furnace design, assisted with a small fan, provides a good air flow, while inverting the flame so that it burns towards the top of the fuel. The fuel heats up, sublimes (becomes gaseous) and rises into the flame, at which point its actual combustion takes place. The result is a controlled burn that starts at the top of the furnace and progresses downwards, providing clean, efficient combustion (an efficiency of 90% and emission levels similar to those of natural gas.)

Advanced boilers can be programmed to work on standby until full heat is required, and can be loaded with wood to last up to 24 hours, depending on capacity. Gasification wood boilers typically have a peak capacity of between 30kW and 100kW, making them suitable for domestic and commercial applications. They can also be combined with fossil fuel-based heating systems.

Condensing Gas Boilers

In a condensing gas boiler, heat from the combustion of fuel passes through the primary heat exchanger where approximately 80% of the energy is transferred to the return water. The flue gas is then recirculated through a secondary heat exchanger by utilising a fan. The flue gas contains water vapour (steam), which is a by-product of the combustion of the hydrogen content of fuel. The secondary heat exchanger through which the return water passes before entering the primary heat exchanger, absorbs heat within the flue gas reducing its temperature to approximately 55°C. This causes the flue gases to condense, releasing latent energy to the secondary heat exchanger.

The temperature of the return water is increased within the secondary heat exchanger and therefore the burner has to impart less energy to raise the temperature at the primary heat exchange to the desired level. This results in improved efficiency and a reduction in fuel consumption.

Condensing boilers are most efficient when the temperature of the return water is low as it increases the rate of condensation within the flue gas. In a condensing boiler most of the energy transfer to water occurs during the fuel combustion process, with 5% efficiency added during the secondary heat exchange as the flue gas cools. An additional 5% efficiency due to latent energy transfer can also be achieved at this stage resulting in an overall efficiency of about 90%.

The condensate from a condensing boiler is slightly acidic (pH 3–5), so additional care should be taken when specifying the drainage systems used to accept the condensate.

Economics

Both gasification wood boilers and condensing gas boilers are high efficiency heating systems and therefore require less fuel and cost less to operate than traditional boilers.

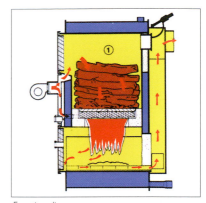
Function diagram

Gasification wood boiler

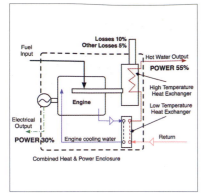

The principle of a CHP unit

CHP unit, Source: Platignum Environmental Limited

HEATING AND COOLING SYSTEMS

Combined Heat and Power

Combined heat and power (CHP), or cogeneration, is the simultaneous production of usable heat and electricity in the same power plant.

In most power plants and generators, approximately 40% of the energy from the combusted fuel is converted to electricity; the remainder is given off as heat to the environment. A further 8% of the electricity (about 3% of primary energy) is typically lost during transmission and distribution to the end user. The waste heat from the generation process can be used to provide space heating or domestic hot water. The waste heat when used with an absorption chiller can also provide space cooling.

A CHP plant is an electrical generator situated close to a location with a large demand for heat, such as an industrial site, hospital or hotel. Both the electricity and the 'waste' heat from the generator are usually supplied to the same end-user. The overall efficiency of a CHP process is about 87%, that is, 87% of the primary energy is delivered as heat or electricity.

CHP can be used in almost any type of building: commercial, industrial, institutional or residential. In the industrial sector, sites with large process heating requirements, such as the chemical, brewing and paper industries, tend to be the largest and most effective applications for CHP. In offices or homes, CHP can be used in the form of 'district' or 'community' heating.

Small CHP systems, consisting of an internal combustion engine burning gas or oil with an output ranging from 15kW to 1MW electrical output, are the most common. Systems like these are marketed as a complete package by specialist firms and can be located in the existing boiler room of a building. Micro-CHP gas-fired systems for individual dwellings are also emerging.

CHP plants can also be designed for tri-generation, which greatly increases the usefulness of the heat generated by a CHP unit. Within this process, waste heat from the CHP unit can be used to generate chilled water via an absorption chiller. The use of tri-generation results in waste heat from the CHP process being available all year round for the generation of both space heating and domestic hot water during the winter months and space cooling along with domestic hot water during the summer months.

Architectural integration

CHP requires space for not only the installation of the equipment but also adequate space for regular scheduled maintenance of the equipment. When specifying the location of the CHP plant within a building or complex, the designer should be aware of the effects of noise and vibration as well as the requirement for the provision of exhaust stacks and air intake systems.

Economics

The economics of CHP are site and machine specific. They are governed by the site's energy demand profile, the plant's capital and maintenance costs, operating hours and energy prices. Applications are growing considerably.

CHP is considered particularly suitable for swimming pools which have a continuous heating demand for pool and domestic water as well as a high pumping demand; and for hospitals which operate 24/7, require high ambient temperatures and also have a high demand for domestic hot water and electricity.

HEATING AND COOLING SYSTEMS

Phase Change Cooling

Phase change materials (PCMs) have the ability to absorb, store and release large amounts of energy in the form of latent heat rather than sensible heat. Thus, PCMs absorb large amounts of heat without an increase in their own temperature as they change phase from solid to liquid. The phase change occurs at a particular temperature which is dependent upon the composition of the material.

PCMs can store greater amounts of thermal energy per unit mass than conventional building materials and can be used to add thermal stability to lightweight construction without adding physical mass. Phase change cooling unlike other systems does not remove unwanted heat from a space, but rather stores the heat within the building by absorbing it in PCMs, thus reducing the temperature rise within a building.

PCMs can be used for cooling a building in three ways:

- Passive cooling: Cooling through the direct heat exchange of indoor air with PCMs incorporated into building materials such as plasterboards, floorboards and furniture.

- Assisted passive cooling: Passive cooling with an active component (for example, a fan) that accelerates heat exchange by increasing air movement across the surface of the PCM.

- Active cooling: Using electricity or absorption cooling to reduce the temperature and/or change the phase of the PCM.

(Kendrick, Walliman, 2006)

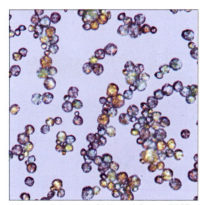

Microscopic images of Micronal. Source: BASF – The Chemical Company

The first two methods are passive systems, where heat is absorbed or released when indoor or outdoor temperatures rise or fall beyond the PCMs melting point. The third method comprises active systems, where the absorbed heat energy is stored in containment, thermally separated from the building by insulation. This creates a situation where energy can be used on a demand basis.

Architectural Integration

PCMs can be impregnated or encapsulated into building materials such as wall and ceiling plasterboard, concrete blocks and floor tiles, which significantly increases the thermal capacity of these materials.

Within lightweight steel and timber buildings these materials can be used to improve the thermal energy storage capacity. This can increase human comfort by decreasing the frequency and extent of internal air temperature swings, such that the desired internal temperature is maintained for longer periods of time.

Recommendations

With the development of new low cost, high efficiency linear crystalline alkyl hydrocarbons a number of different commercial phase change materials suitable for building applications have become available. However, the use of PCMs is still not common within the construction industry and experience of longer-term performance is limited.

Economics

The cost of using materials with embedded phase change materials can offset savings provided by utilising lightweight construction techniques. These materials can also be effective in certain situations for retrofitting existing buildings.

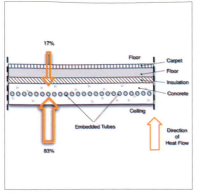

Concrete core system

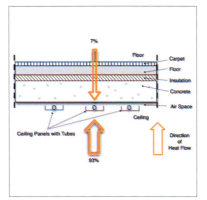

Suspended ceiling panel system

HEATING AND COOLING SYSTEMS

Radiant Heating/Cooling Systems

Radiant heating/cooling systems supply heating and cooling, in an energy-efficient manner, by changing the temperature of the walls, ceiling and/or floor of a space instead of heating and cooling the air. This works because the temperature experienced by the human body is approximately equal to the average of the radiant temperature and the air temperature. The radiant temperature is the weighted average temperature of all the objects which surround the body. High temperature radiant heating is also common is certain large-volume spaces.

A radiant heating/cooling system generally consists of an array of pipes or tubes installed in or behind the surface of the walls, ceiling or floor of an interior space.

The three main types of radiant heating/cooling systems are:

- core systems, where water is circulated through plastic tubes embedded in, for example, the slab of a concrete ceiling, wall or floor. This employs the thermal mass of the slab in smoothing out heating and cooling loads.

- panel systems, consisting of usually aluminium panels, with metal tubes connected to their rear. The system has minimal thermal mass but a very swift response time and is most often used with suspended ceilings.

- capillary systems, consisting of a fine grid of small-bore plastic tubes installed under wall or ceiling plaster or embedded in gypsum board. They provide an even surface temperature and have an intermediate heat storage capacity between the other two types of system. They are suitable for retrofit applications.

Compared with conventional heating systems, a radiant heating/cooling system will usually occupy a large part of the surface area of the space, such as the whole ceiling or wall. The surface temperature change necessary to produce comfort for the occupants is relatively small. The heating and cooling load is generally supplied by a low-temperature boiler, an efficient refrigeration system, a passive cooling system or a heat pump with a high coefficient of performance.

Architectural integration

Architectural implications are limited to providing each room with the necessary unobstructed wall or ceiling surface. The choice of internal wall, ceiling and floor finishes should be considered when using radiant heating and cooling systems.

Economics

Radiant heating and cooling systems can in some instances significantly reduce the ductwork and associated controls associated with traditional HVAC systems, resulting in significant savings.

MATERIALS

INTRODUCTION

There is a large variety of materials which can be used in the construction of buildings, and careful selection of environmentally sustainable building materials is an important means of incorporating sustainable design principles into buildings.

To perform a complete analysis of the environmental impact of all the components and materials in a building would be prohibitively time-consuming and expensive. However, a responsible architect should weigh up environmental considerations alongside other criteria. To do this the architect requires an understanding of the environmental impact of materials, and that is what this chapter aims to provide.

SUSTAINABILITY CONSIDERATIONS IN MATERIAL SELECTION

There are several issues that should be considered by any architect who is concerned about the environmental impact of the materials that will go into his or her building. A brief checklist might run as follows.

For materials used in quantities of 250kg or less, consider the following issues:

- Impact of the material's production: habitat destruction, toxins released;

- Lifespan of material;

- Eventual destination of the material after building's life. Re-use is better than recycling, which is better than incineration or landfill;

- Reduction/separation of construction waste and avoidance/careful disposal of toxic waste.

For bulk materials, consider all the above issues, but also:

- The nature of the resources involved: renewable or non-renewable, scarce or abundant;

- Emissions of CO_2 (in kg/kg) during production or, if information is not available, embodied energy (in kWh/kg);

- How far and by what mode(s) the material will be transported, and associated emissions/energy use.

The design of the building as a whole cannot be separated from the choice of materials and components which will go into it, as their selection profoundly influences both design and performance. Building materials have environmental impacts associated with the manufacture, processing, transportation, construction, maintenance, demolition and recycling or disposal of the materials themselves. In life cycle analysis we attempt to identify understand and quantify at every stage of the material's life cycle the impacts due to the material or component. Further, whole building environmental impact analysis is by now well established to integrate such analyses with other holistic considerations, and in Section 5 several sustainable building rating systems are described which evaluate the environmental performance of building design, materials and components, construction methods and building operation.

LIFE CYCLE DESIGN

As part of the life cycle review of a material, each of the phases of the process is examined, from collecting or extracting raw materials, manufacturing, transportation and installation, to end of life reuse or disposal of the material or component. The cradle to cradle life cycle can be organised in three distinct phases: manufacturing, use and disposal/reuse.

Manufacturing

This phase includes the extraction, refining, manufacturing and transportation of materials; it has the potential to cause the greatest environmental impacts and an understanding of these impacts is critical in the selection of environmentally sustainable materials.

The collection and extraction of many of the elements which make up building materials involves mining or harvesting natural resources, and can have a significant effect on the environment. The extraction of materials such as metals and stone requires the mining of finite resources from the earth, which then need further refinement resulting in large volumes of often toxic waste and small volumes of refined material.

The harvesting of organic materials such as timber has a less damaging effect on the environment. However, timber can only be classified as a renewable resource if the growth of new timber is in balance with or in excess of the rate of harvesting. The extraction of materials in their raw form from both finite and renewable sources can result in severe environmental damage such as the loss of habitat, soil erosion, water pollution and air pollution.

The manufacturing of building materials which involves the conversion and combining of raw materials into specific building products can also be responsible for environmental damage due to water and air pollution arising from manufacturing processes, as well as consuming large amounts of energy in the manufacturing process. The total amount of energy consumed in the collection and processing of a material is its embodied energy. The greater a material's embodied energy, the greater is the amount of energy required in its production; which often results in a higher cost to the environment.

Because of the sheer quantity of materials used in the construction industry, the environmental impact of transporting them is a cause for concern. The energy needed to transport bulk materials is generally a function of distance travelled, mode of transport, and mass of material hauled. Materials with very low density (such as insulation), however, tend to use disproportionate amounts of energy for transport, due to their bulk. The table below gives estimates of the environmental impact of different modes of transport. The use of locally sourced materials can reduce the impact of transportation; although it may not always be possible to use the local, designers should keep in mind the environmental costs of transporting materials such as decorative stone over long distances.

TOTAL EMISSIONS AND PRIMARY ENERGY USE BY DIFFERENT MODES OF FREIGHT TRANSPORT				
Emissions: g per t per km	Water	Rail	Road	Air
CO_2	30	41	207	1206
CH_4	0.04	0.06	0.3	2.0
NO_x	0.4	0.2	3.6	5.5
CO	0.12	0.05	2.4	1.4
VOCs	0.1	0.08	1.1	3.0
Energy: kJ per t per km	423	677	2890	15839

Note that several important environmental impacts, such as noise, particulates, and oil spills, are not included. For environmental impact equivalent to hauling 100 tonne-kilometres by road, it is possible to move roughly 400 t.km by rail, 700 t.km by water, or 17 t.km by air.

(Whitelegg, 1993)

Use

This phase in a material's life cycle starts with the assembly of the building and extends throughout its useful lifespan. During the construction phase large volumes of waste material can be generated on site. The design and utilisation of different materials and construction methods can have a significant effect on the volume of waste created.

The building may be carefully designed to use as far as practicable, standard units and sizes of material; this reduces labour (cutting and trimming) as well as minimising waste. Careful site practices can also help to avoid damaged materials. There are those who would outlaw site skips to encourage each trade to minimise their waste. The key to successful and profitable recycling of unavoidable site waste material is separation of waste types at an early stage. Separate bins for different recycling categories should be maintained on site, as close as possible to the building work. Toxic waste (such as left-over paint, adhesives and chemicals) should, of course, be handled with care and disposed of according to the manufacturer's instructions.

Disposal/Reuse

This phase in the material's life cycle includes its removal following the expiry of its usefulness within the building. The material may be removed and reused in its existing form, be recycled and incorporated into new products, or disposed of offsite.

Until relatively recently, many materials from demolished buildings were simply reused on the same site. However, with modern materials such as reinforced and prestressed concrete, composite assemblies of different materials, and strong adhesives, this is much more difficult to achieve. Apart from the wider consideration of planning some degree of redundancy in order to facilitate adaptation to extend the useful life of the building as a whole, modern buildings should be designed to facilitate recycling and minimise wastage of their materials following demolition. This means arranging to assemble materials so that they may be easily disassembled rather than destructively demolished (an example might be using lime mortar so that bricks can be readily cleaned and re-used); using materials that are valuable for recycling (such as metals) rather than those that are difficult to recycle (such as many plastics); and ensuring that proper drawings and records are kept so that those entrusted with demolition will know how to undertake the job.

The majority of demolition waste (often 95% by weight) consists of inert bulk materials such as brick, concrete and stone. These may be recycled into aggregate, although bricks and stone can also be re-used in new building provided they can be separated and cleaned adequately. It is important to avoid cross contamination of waste streams during the demolition process if possible, as this can add significantly to the cost of recycling materials.

The most valuable elements of a building being demolished are those that can be removed whole. These can range from structural elements such as trusses and girders to interior installations such as furnishings and appliances. The capacity of a material to be reused in a new product is classified as its recyclability value. Metal has a high recyclability value as it can be segregated relatively easily, and can be reformed at a fraction of the cost and energy input of the original manufacturing of the material.

Life Cycle Assessment Framework, ISO 14040/14044

Many diverse methodologies have been developed for carrying out life cycle analysis (LCA) of materials and products, which has resulted in difficulties in evaluating and comparing the environmental performance of materials and products. In response to these problems the International Organization for Standardization (ISO) has developed a framework for conducting and reporting life cycle analysis.

ISO 14040:2006 Environmental management – LCA Principles and framework
ISO 14044:2006 Environmental management – LCA Requirements and guidelines.

Forest Stewardship Council (FSC) logo. Source:
© 1996 FSC A.C.

Student Hostel at Windberg. Architect and source:
Herzog and Partner Architects

Access to high quality information is vital to enabling professionals to investigate the wider effects of their building practices. Labelling systems and sources of environmental information are becoming available within the international market following the introduction of the ISO 14000 suite of standards.

ISO 14000 ENVIRONMENTAL MANAGEMENT STANDARDS	
ISO 14000	Includes general guidelines for principles, systems and tools for environmental management
ISO 14001	Provides specific guidelines for implementation of environmental management systems
ISO 14010	Provides general principles and guidelines for environmental auditing
ISO 14020	Eco-Labelling
ISO 14031	Environmental performance evaluation/environmental auditing
ISO 14040	Life Cycle Assessment

International Standards Organisation

WOOD

Wood is a highly popular building material: light, strong, durable, easy to work, beautiful and with a timeless tradition and a mature skill base. It is also a renewable resource, given proper forestry practices. However, according to the World Wildlife Foundation (WWF), the international timber trade is now the primary threat to the world's forests. Forests vary enormously in type and quality; measurements of forested area can be highly misleading, equating rich natural forests with monocultural plantations.

Usually, the oldest forests are the richest in wildlife, with numerous rare and indigenous species. They also contain the highest proportion of mature trees and are therefore most attractive to timber companies. Most natural forests around the world are under serious threat. The disappearance of tropical forests is well known, but temperate and boreal forests, including the few remaining old-growth forests in Europe, are also disappearing fast, mainly because of logging operations. Illegal logging is widespread in many countries, as is displacement of indigenous people to make way for forestry operations.

It is not always easy to select wood and wood products that come from suitably managed forests. Many different labelling systems and claims of 'sustainability' exist, but most are not rigorously tested and are thus meaningless.

The Forest Stewardship Council (FSC) is an international body that exists to verify certification systems for properly managed forestry. To carry the FSC logo, certification systems must verify that management in their forests follows the following ten principles:

Principle 1   Compliance with all applicable laws and international treaties

Principle 2   Demonstrated and uncontested, clearly defined, long–term land tenure and use rights

Principle 3   Recognition and respect of indigenous peoples' rights

Principle 4   Maintenance or enhancement of long-term social and economic well-being of forest workers and local communities and respect of worker's rights in compliance with International Labour Organisation (ILO) conventions

Principle 5   Equitable use and sharing of benefits derived from the forest

Principle 6   Reduction of environmental impact of logging activities and maintenance of the ecological functions and integrity of the forest

Principle 7   Appropriate and continuously updated management plan

Principle 8   Appropriate monitoring and assessment activities to assess the condition of the forest, management activities and their social and environmental impacts

Principle 9   Maintenance of High Conservation Value Forests (HCVFs) defined as environmental and social values that are considered to be of outstanding significance or critical importance

Principle 10 In addition to compliance with all of the above, plantations must contribute to reduce the pressures on and promote the restoration and conservation of natural forests.

Wood products

Only products which carry the FSC logo should be treated as being from properly managed forests. Non-FSC-approved claims of 'sustainable' or 'environmentally friendly' production should be treated with great caution.

Wood from properly managed forests still carries a considerable environmental impact because of energy used during its extraction, transport and processing. Air-dried timber will use less energy than kiln-dried timber.

An alternative to using FSC-certified wood (which is becoming easier to source within Europe) is to use either locally produced wood or wood reclaimed from a known source (such as a building that is being demolished). Both have the advantage of involving less transportation energy and allowing architects to inform themselves about the provenance of the material.

Straw bale construction at the Centre for Alternative Technologies (CAT), Wales. Source: CAT

Wood products

Wood is a major constituent of a wide range of products used in building. In most cases similar comments can be made for the wood-derived portion of these products as for wood itself, with the proviso that it is even less easy to be certain of the wood's provenance. Many products, such as chipboard, fibre-board and even synthetic structural beams, make use of waste off-cuts and chips of timber. While this is no guarantee that the timber itself comes from a sustainable source, it does at least ensure that the timber is being used efficiently. Plywood, however, makes use of large-dimension timber which is unlikely to be sustainably produced.

The other components of wood products vary widely. Panel products such as blockboard, plywood and chipboard are bound together with organic resins. These do not usually have significant emissions to the indoor environment because they are effectively inert if properly manufactured.

Paper is another product that includes a significant amount of wood in its manufacture. Compared to the paper used by a building's occupants, however, the paper used in the building itself is not likely to have a serious effect on the environment. There is still considerable debate about the environmental costs and benefits of recycled paper. Paper based not on wood pulp but on other fibres such as hemp and kenaf is probably most sustainable.

STRAW AND PLANT FIBRES

Straw consists of the stems of grain crops such as wheat, oats, barley, rye and rice left over after the grain has been harvested. Straw may seem an unlikely candidate for a building material, but it is steadily growing in popularity because of its ready availability, low environmental impact, and excellent insulating properties: standard sized straw bales have an insulation value of approximately 0.012 W/mK.

Rammed earth construction, Mexico

Basalt cladding, Museum Modern Art (MUMOK), Vienna. Architect: Ortner and Ortner

Straw can be used in building in several ways. It is used in varying proportions as a binder in earth bricks and structures. Since the invention of the baler in the late nineteenth century, straw bales have been used as building blocks for highly insulating walls. This practice began in Nebraska, US, where some early strawbale buildings are still standing; more recently it has become popular in other countries.

Experience indicates that concerns about moisture and pests can be satisfactorily addressed by correct design; fire is not a problem because tightly packed, baled straw does not burn. In some buildings the bales themselves bear the weight of the roof, in others the bales are simply used as in-fill in a post-and-beam structure. The walls are usually staked together with steel or bamboo rods driven through the bales, and plastered inside and out.

Straw and other plant fibres are also used as the raw material for panel products, which can be used in a wide range of applications. The fibres are compressed together at high temperatures (about 200°C) and bond strongly without adhesives. Reeds, straw and other plant stems are also a traditional roofing material. Thatched roofs are attractive and low-impact, but highly labour-intensive and require skilled workers.

The environmental impact of straw and other plant fibres is generally very low. They are mostly agricultural waste products, although some may be grown especially for building. Huge amounts of waste straw are either burnt (producing air pollution) or, more beneficially, tilled into the fields to improve soil structure. The main environmental impact will be due to consuming fuel for transportation. The fuel needed per kilogram-kilometre will be higher than average because of the low density of the fibres. But if plant fibres are taken from a local source, their environmental impact will typically be low.

EARTH

Earth consists of various grades of pulverised stone (ranging from small cobbles to silt) and clay, which is the active ingredient or 'glue' that sticks the soil together. Organic material, such as is present in topsoil, is undesirable in earth for building. Water is the other main ingredient. Clay content varies widely; most soil is likely to have too much clay (which can cause cracking as the earth dries) rather than too little (which can cause crumbling). Extra sand or straw can be added to balance excess clay. To increase the structural strength of earth it may be 'stabilised' with asphalt, lime or cement.

Earth was one of the first building materials and is still one of the most widely used. Even today, one third of the human population resides in earthen houses; in developing countries this figure is more than half *(Minke, 2006)*. Earth is used in building in several different ways. Perhaps the simplest is where it is 'puddled' with water and other ingredients and the building's walls are built up by hand without forms. This is known as 'cob' in Anglophone countries. In sunny climates, earth is moulded into bricks, sometimes mechanically compressed, and sun-baked. This method, known as 'adobe' in Hispanic countries, may have originated in the Middle East as long ago as 10,000 BC, and is still used very widely. The earth can also be packed into forms in situ and compressed by machine or hand to give it great strength, a method called 'rammed earth' or 'pisé'. The forms are usually wood or metal, but even automobile tyres have been used. Rammed earth walls can resemble concrete in their hardness, strength and durability, depending on the degree of compression. Another method with a long tradition is 'geltaftan,' where a specially designed earth building is packed with fuel and used as a kiln for firing pottery, being baked to great hardness in the process. Earth walls can be a metre or more thick, or they can be no thicker than a comparable structure in brick or concrete.

Even if the walls are not made of earth, earth may be piled around the building (as a 'berm') or over it (as a 'green roof'), or the structure may be sunk into the ground. In each case the earth provides insulation and thermal storage. The ultimate in 'earth-sheltered' building may be dwellings that are actually artificial caves dug into the ground; there are examples in many European countries.

Earth is not a particularly good insulator and its conductance varies with moisture and density. CIBSE Guide A: Environmental Design is a good source of information (CIBSE, 2006). It is, however, a very good thermal store. The possible extra structural strength needed to support a 'green roof' is likely to negate any cost savings from the use of earth as an inexpensive insulator.

Earth is a flexible and forgiving building material; clay content in particular can vary between about 10–25%. However, as with all building materials, the techniques of building with earth are particular to the material and expert advice should be sought.

Concrete, Habitat '67, Montreal

STONE

Stone forms the basis of traditional architecture in many places and is still widely used. It is particularly useful for its high thermal mass, strength and durability (depending on hardness) and beauty. Stone is non-renewable but abundant, although some types are scarce. The quarrying process is disruptive to natural environments, and using reclaimed stone will reduce this impact. However, the greatest environmental impact of stone is likely to be due to haulage. The natural and traditional solution to this problem is to use locally quarried stone; or from quarries accessible by water. The former also allows the architect to remain informed of any concerns about the impact of quarrying operations. Manufactured and synthetic stone are sometimes used as a less expensive alternative to natural stone, particularly as a facing to concrete blocks. The manufacturing process for these materials is quite energy-intensive, and their overall environmental impact is probably similar to that of concrete.

Extruded terracotta blocks

CEMENT

Cement is a general term for binding agents whose ingredients include lime (calcium oxide). By far the most widely used form of cement in Europe is Portland cement. To make Portland cement, calcium carbonate (usually in the form of limestone), silicates (from sand, clay or fly ash, a by-product of coal-fired power plants) and trace ingredients such as ores of aluminium or iron, are mixed together and burnt at temperatures of up to 1500°C. The result is a mixture of chemical compounds of calcium, silicon and oxygen with some iron and aluminium; the exact mix determines the properties of the cement. About 5% gypsum (calcium sulphate) is then added. Because of the high temperatures required, the process is highly energy-intensive. In addition, the chemical reaction producing lime from calcium carbonate (calcining) releases carbon dioxide.

Other environmental impacts of cement production are mainly due to the highly alkaline nature of cement dust. When released into the air or water (e.g. from equipment washing), it can present an environmental hazard, since alkaline water is toxic to fish and other aquatic life. Cement dust and wet concrete may also present dangers to workers' health due to its alkaline nature.

The total amount of embodied energy and embodied carbon within cement varies depending on the composition of the cement, efficiency of the kiln and the type of fuel used in the manufacturing process. One estimate from the Inventory of Carbon and Energy (Hammond and Jones, 2008) states that Portland cement contains 4.6 MJ/kg of embodied energy and 0.83 kgCO$_2$/kg of Embodied Carbon.

Ground Granulated Blastfurnace Slag (GGBS) is a latent hydraulic binder that can be used in conjunction with Portland cement to produce blastfurance cement. GGBS is a by-product of the steel industry created when slag from a blastfurance is rapidly quenched in water. This quenching process optimises the cementitious properties of the

Glazed façade

Glazed façade. Source: Quinn Dombrowski

GGBS and produces small granules, which are then ground to a fine powder called GGBS cement. GGBS cement can be used as a direct replacement for Portland cement on a one to one basis by weight. GGBS cement when used as a cementitious replacement for Portland cement reduces the embodied energy within the mix to 3.01 MJ/kg and the emodied carbon to 0.45 $kgCO_2$/kg based upon a replacement level of 50%.

A key strategy of the environmentally aware architect should be to minimise the amount of cement used. Careful design helps, for example in the use of pier foundations or pre-cast concrete; so does effective management of construction to avoid mixing excess concrete which will be thrown away. Lime and fly ash (see below) can be substituted for concrete in some applications.

CONCRETE

Concrete, the biggest end-user of cement, consists of roughly 12–14% cement and varying amounts of water (6–7%), sand (25–35%) and gravel, crushed stone or other aggregate (48–53%). Fly ash which is a by-product of burning coal for the production of electricity can be substituted for 15–35% of the cement when mixing concrete.

Sand and gravel are non-renewable resources which are quarried or dredged, involving a significant impact on the local environment. Although considerable resources remain untapped, many of these will not be developed because of environmental considerations. Crushed stone requires an additional input of energy in the crushing process. Reclaimed and recycled aggregate and industrial waste products (including crushed concrete) can be used as part of the mix to reduce quarrying and transportation. Transportation will probably be the major environmental impact of the aggregates. However, carbon dioxide emissions from the production of the cement typically form the bulk (at least 85%) of overall CO_2 emissions due to concrete. One estimate from the Inventory of Carbon and Energy states that standard concrete contains 0.95 MJ/kg of embodied energy and 0.13 $kgCO_2$/kg of carbon. In comparision, a concrete block with a compressive strength of 8 Mpa contains 0.60 MJ/kg of embodied energy and 0.061 $kgCO_2$/kg of carbon (*Hammond and Jones, 2008*).

The other major environmental consideration in the use of concrete is disposal. Concrete forms about half of all waste from construction and demolition. It can often be crushed for reuse as aggregate, but re-use has been too rare. Concrete blocks are basically identical to other forms of concrete in their environmental impact per kilogram, except that they need to be cured before use. High-pressure steam is often employed for this purpose, using more energy.

Specialised forms of concrete include aerated concrete, which uses aluminium sulphate powder in the mix. This reacts with the lime to produce hydrogen gas, which forms bubbles in the concrete. While the aluminium sulphate adds an environmental impact to the process (due to the large amounts of energy used in its production) the resulting concrete has a higher strength-to-weight ratio and the overall environmental impact for a given structure is likely to be lower than for ordinary concrete. Composite insulating blocks are formed of insulating foam in between layers of concrete. The main concern here is to avoid the use of ozone-depleting CFCs and HCFCs as foaming agents in the insulation. Another possible concern is the difficulty of recycling or re-using composite blocks at the end of the structure's life, because the concrete cannot be separated from the insulating foam.

BRICK, TILE AND CERAMICS

Ceramics such as brick, tile and sanitary ware are made by baking clay at high temperature. Clay is a highly abundant, although non-renewable material. Clay quarrying can have a detrimental impact on local environments, but the main environmental impact of ceramics is due to the fuel burnt during the firing process. The energy used in this process will vary, however the energy contained within a typical brick has been calculated as 3.00 MJ/kg and up to 9.00 MJ/kg for glazed ceramics *(Hammond and Jones, 2008)*.

The embodied energy in MJ/kg within a brick is up to three times that of concrete. Therefore, it is one of the most energy-intensive of bulk building materials. Reclaimed bricks are an alternative, in which there is a thriving market in many places.

GLASS

Glass refers to materials, usually blends of metallic oxides (predominantly silica) which do not crystallise when cooled from the liquid to the solid state. It is the non-crystalline or amorphorus structure of glass that gives rise to its transparency *(Lyons, 2007)*. Glass is made from silver sand, sodium carbonate and sulphates, all of which are non-renewable resources but none of which are scarce. The manufacturing process is highly energy-intensive, with typically 0.85 kg of CO_2 per kg of glass produced *(Hammond and Jones, 2008)*.

However, the actual mass of glass in most buildings is relatively small. It has been estimated that a three-bed roomed, detached house contains about 100kg of glass, compared with over 25 tons of concrete (the main structural material) *(Howard, 1991)*. The environmental impact of the glass is outweighed by its importance in influencing day-lighting and thermal performance. Glass is generally recyclable, and the small proportion traditionally recycled is increasing.

METALS

Metals are obtained by mining, which is often detrimental to the local environment through large-scale physical alteration and toxic emissions. Most mine sites require expensive rehabilitation after closure before the land can be reused.

The process of extracting metal from ore is highly energy-intensive and the amount of embodied energy within metals varies greatly due to large variations in ore grade. Figures for embodied energy and embodied carbon sourced from the Inventory of Carbon & Energy (ICE; v.1.6a) complied by the Sustainable Energy Research Team (SERT) at the University of Bath are detailed below.

Anodised aluminium cladding, Royal Ontario Museum, Toronto. Architect: Daniel Libeskind

Pre-patinised copper cladding, Science Centre NEMO, Amsterdam. Architect: Renzo Piano

METAL	Embodied Energy MJ/kg			Embodied Carbon kgCO$_2$/kg		
	Typical	Primary	Secondary	Typical	Primary	Secondary
Aliminium	155	218	28.8	8.24	11.46	1.69
Copper	40-55	70	18-50	2.19-3.83	3.83	1.96-2.75
Iron	25	-	-	1.91	-	-
Steel	24.4	35.3	9.5	1.77	2.75	0.43
Zinc	62	72	9	3.31	3.86	0.48

(Hammond and Jones, 2008)

Although metals are a non-renewable resource, they are generally recyclable, and construction and demolition waste should be separated in order to facilitate this. Non-separated waste can be recycled but the cost is much higher. Recycling saves a significant proportion of the energy used in the extraction process. The recycled content of metal is not always easy to estimate but it is a reasonably good measure of the metal's global environmental impact.

Corten steel cladding, Quebec

Zinc cladding, Model Arts and Niland Gallery, Sligo. Architect: McCullough Mulvin Architects

Aluminium

Aluminium is extracted by electrolysis of the ore, bauxite, a highly energy-intensive process as the material must be heated to approximately 1650°C. A large volume of waste material results, with high levels of heavy metals. However, aluminium is highly recyclable and recycling requires only a fraction of the energy needed for electrolysis from ore. It is highly durable and resistant to corrosion, although specifiers should be careful to avoid contact with acids, alkalis, or other metals; for instance, rainwater which has been in contact with copper must not be allowed to reach aluminium components. During the construction process care should be taken to avoid contact with wet concrete and mortar, which due to its alkalinity causes the rapid corrosion of aluminium.

Copper

Copper has been widely used over the centuries for roofing, cladding, ornament, piping and cables. Copper is derived from copper ores such as chalcocite and chalcopyrite which typically have concentrations less than 1%. Copper has natural biocidal properties, which make it suitable for exterior use, but leads to toxic runoff. Copper pipes are still used in water supply, although banned in some places (such as Sweden); they are generally being supplanted by plastic. Copper can cause severe corrosion to zinc, aluminium and galvanised steel. Copper is highly durable, corrosion-resistant and very recyclable.

Lead

Lead has been widely used for centuries for roofing, cladding, flashing and pipework. Lead is a highly toxic material and a cumulative poison whose use in buildings is increasingly discouraged. It is also a material in very short supply, although easy to re-use. A high proportion of lead is recycled.

Steel

Steel is the most widely used metal in construction. It is produced from iron ore in conjunction with heat distilled coal (coke), limestone, magnesium and other trace elements. Steel can be produced in either a basic oxygen furnace or an electric arc process. Both production processes are highly energy-intensive.

The recycling of scrap steel is widespread, although not as easy as with other metals. Steel is not corrosion-resistant, and in many situations in order to prevent rust it needs to be treated with paint or another coating, whose impact should be considered separately.

Zinc

Zinc may be used in sheet form, and is a less toxic alternative to copper for many applications. Zinc tarnishes in the presence of air with firstly the creation of a thin oxide film, which is then converted into a zinc carbonate in the presence of water and carbon dioxide. Zinc sheeting can be pre-patinised under factory conditions if the light grey surface finish is required immediately on site. In urban environments the presence of sulphur dioxide can prevent the formation of a zinc carbonate film on the surface of the zinc, which will lead to corrosion of the metal. In addition zinc should not be used in contact with copper or where discharges of rainwater from copper roofs occur. Zinc sheeting is available as a pure metal as well as an alloy with the addition or small quantities of titanium and copper. The titanium alloy improves the lifespan of the material.

Zinc is often also used as a coating for other metals. By its nature this zinc coating has to be strongly bonded with the other metal, so neither is likely to be readily recyclable. The processes of zinc coating (galvanisation) frequently involves the use of chromate solution, which is highly toxic. The coating processes are also energy intensive. However, galvanisation is a very effective way to lengthen the life of steel and other metallic components.

PAINTS, ADHESIVES AND PRESERVATIVES

Paints, adhesives, preservatives, sealants and cleaning agents encompass a very diverse range of substances. They are typically present in relatively small quantities in buildings, but can have a disproportionate effect on the environment. Although their manufacture often involves the use of oil and gas both as fuel for the manufacturing process and as feedstocks, CO_2 and other fossil fuel related emissions are not a major environmental concern here because of the small quantities involved compared to other materials *(Howard, 1991)*.

Toxic emissions during manufacture, use, and disposal are a greater concern. These products should be treated as toxic waste and disposed of accordingly. Furthermore, the quality of the building's interior environment can be seriously affected by the careless use of these products. Indoor air quality (IAQ) should be a major concern of designers, particularly because buildings are becoming more airtight, and the use of organic solvents, office appliances and mechanical ventilation are on the increase.

Eco Labels

An 'eco-label' identifies a product that meets specified environmental performance criteria or standards. The EU Ecolabel award scheme is the eco-label of the European Union and was introduced on a voluntary basis in 1992 to promote products which have a reduced environmental impact (compared with other products in the same product group) and to provide consumers with accurate and scientifically-based information and guidance on products.

The EU Ecolabel scheme sets the criteria for each product on the basis of a 'cradle to grave' assessment of the environmental impact of the product group. This means that the complete life-cycle of a product is analysed, starting with the extraction of the raw materials, progressing through the production, distribution and use phases and ending with disposal after use. The EU Ecolabel is awarded only to those products which have been certified as having the lowest environmental impact in a product range.

Paint

Paint consists of a solvent (the 'base'), bonding agents, fillers, and additives such as pigments, drying agents, polishers and anti-foaming agents.

Each of these ingredients, and particularly those containing heavy metals, can potentially be hazardous to health and the environment .

Water-based paints, although not readily available for some applications, are environmentally preferable to those using organic hydrocarbons, which are hazardous to painters and occupants. Most hydrocarbon-based paints used alkyd resin as a binder. 'High solids' alkyd paint is preferable to traditional alkyd paint because it contains less organic solvent. 'Natural paint' generally consists of ingredients of biological origin, which are naturally degradable; these paints still use organic solvents such as turpentine, however, and tend to be more expensive and less effective than conventional paints. Acrylic paints are primarily water-based, containing 10% or less organic solvents, but tend to contain harmful preservatives. In all cases, high gloss paints require more solvents than those with a less glossy finish.

Adhesives

Concerns with the environmental impact of adhesives mainly focus on the release of VOCs from organic solvent based adhesives and curing agents, for example those used in epoxy resin systems. Adhesives which use organic solvents should be applied with care and proper ventilation, or avoided altogether in favour of water based adhesives or mechanical fixing systems. The widespread use of adhesives can make disassembly of the building for reuse and recycling more difficult.

EU Eco label

Blue Angel Eco Label

Nordic Swan Eco Label

Minergie Eco Label

Wood preservatives

Wood preservatives are added to wood to prevent the growth of fungi and to repel insects from attacking the wood. Wood preservatives are available in a wide range of different forms: paints, sticks, pastes and even smokes. Their active ingredients range from the relatively mild to the highly toxic; they include compounds based on copper, chromium, arsenic, zinc, boron and fluorine; also creosote, pentachlorophenol, dieldrin, lindane, tributyl tin oxide and permethrin.

Decay is normally a symptom of a building defect or moisture build-up, rather than an inevitable product of time. Each source of moisture should be balanced by a means of removing it. Preservatives can often be avoided altogether, if proper detailing is observed, a durable wood is chosen and where necessary a protective finish is applied and maintained. Localised preservation with solid implants in vulnerable places such as the corner joints of window and door frames, is preferable to overall treatment.

Preservatives ranked from least to most environmentally damaging	
Least Damaging	Borates
	Quaternary ammonium compounds, zinc soaps, azoles
	Chromium copper boron (CCB), zinc copper fluoride (ZCF)
Most Damaging	Chromium copper arsenic (CCA), improsol (bifluoride), creosote oil

(Anink et al, 1996)

Borates are the most environmentally benign form of preservative, although they suffer from leaching in the wet; where they will be in contact with water, they may need to be combined with a water-repelling treatment. Preservation treatment should always be carried by suitably qualified operatives.

SEALANTS

Because of their flexibility and ease of application, sealing compounds are used very widely for sealing joints, cracks and other gaps; some might say over-used. A wide range of products is available. Sealants may be in the form of tape or other solid, or as a fluid. Fluid solvents may be plastic or elastomeric. As with all building products, the environmental impact of the sealant should be weighed against its durability, since the more often it is replaced the more impact it will have.

In general, sealants are used in small amounts and do not have very great environmental impact. The main things to avoid are: sealants that use ozone-damaging chemicals (CFCs and HCFCs) in foaming; polyurethane (PUR) and polyvinyl chloride (PVC) sealants, both of which have significant environmental impacts; and use of sealants which contain organic solvents, such as non-water-based acrylic sealant.

Cleaning agents

An often forgotten part of the construction process is the cleaning of the building after completion but before occupancy. This is usually the responsibility of the contractor but it is often contracted-out to specialist cleaning firms who may not be fully aware of previous efforts to ensure a non-toxic, healthy building. Cleaning agents that are non-toxic and biodegradable should be specified.

SYNTHETIC MATERIALS

Synthetics are manufactured by a range of chemical processes, mainly from petroleum. It is also possible, although rare, to make them from plant-derived renewable resources; they are then known as bioplastics or biosynthetics. The cracking and polymerisation processes by which synthetics are manufactured can involve the release of organic materials into the environment. Other additives such as chlorine and cyanide are also used, and these may involve toxic emissions. Only a small proportion of the world's petroleum is used to make synthetics. The amount of energy used in the process is relatively large; estimates vary widely, between 50–100 MJ/kg. However, the quantities used in the building process are generally quite small and this means that embodied energy is not a major concern. An example of the embodied energy and carbon contained within a range of synthetic materials is detailed below.

Material	Embodied Energy MJ/kg	Embodied Carbon kgCO$_2$/kg
	Typical	Typical
Bitumen	47.00	0.48
Expaned Polystyrene	88.60	2.50
Acrylonitrile butadiene styene (ABS)	95.30	3.10
General Purpose Polystyrene	86.40	2.70
Thermoformed Expanded Polystyrene	109.20	3.40
PVC Injection Modeling	95.10	2.20

(Hammond and Jones, 2008)

Most synthetics are not readily biodegradable and this presents a long-term disposal problem. On the other hand, when they do degrade, or when they are otherwise destroyed or damaged by fire, UV radiation, etc, the resulting products in some (but not all) cases are a toxic hazard. Recycling is possible in some cases but generally only where waste is separated.

Synthetics are extremely useful in many applications; they are mostly waterproof, flexible and inexpensive. In most cases, their environmental impact is not serious enough to outweigh their usefulness, but disposal should be considered carefully because their non-degradable nature can lead to problems.

Bitumen
Bitumen is widely used in roofing and weatherproofing. It is produced from low-grade petroleum fractions. It is theoretically recyclable as long as it is not polluted with other materials, but this is usually the case. Normally bitumen is mixed with rock dust or applied to cloth, glass fibre or polyester sheeting to form mastic, sheeting or shingles. It does not generate environmental problems during use. Care must be taken with hot bitumen/asphalt application with respect to the health and safety of workers.

EPDM (Ethylene-Propylene-Diene Monomer)
EPDM sheet is used in flat roofs, for lining reservoirs, and in gaskets and flashings. It is produced by polymerising and then vulcanising the ethylene, propylene and diene monomers. Various organic solvents, which could cause environmental hazards if released, are used in the process. It cannot be recycled although 'down-cycling' to form low-grade filler is possible.

EPS (Expanded Polystyrene) and Extruded Polystyrene
Polystyrene is used in insulation and sheet glazing. The production of polystyrene involves some emissions of styrene and benzebe, moderately harmful organic compounds. The blowing process by which EPS is expanded uses pentane (a moderately toxic organic solvent).

SECTION 5: EVALUATION

INTRODUCTION

Owners, designers, regulators and occupants all variously assess proposed and completed buildings with regard to comfort, functionality, cost and aesthetics. In addition to these fundamental parameters, buildings are evaluated based on their environmental performance in areas such as energy consumption, air quality, daylighting and recycled materials. The evaluation of the environmental and energy performance of buildings is a necessary component of the overall design process; in the European Union the requirement to label buildings according to their energy performance has given particular impetus to building energy evaluation in recent years.

At the design stage, alternative strategies must be considered and the most appropriate solution chosen. The architect evaluates environmental behaviour, energy performance, daylight, indoor comfort, acoustics and materials. Simulation-based analysis is often useful and, in large and complex buildings, may be indispensable. Monitoring the performance of the completed building can involve assessing comfort and environmental quality, energy and water inputs and waste outputs. This section provides advice on design and evaluation tools and systems for rating the sustainability of buildings.

INTRODUCTION

DESIGN EVALUATION TOOLS

BUILDING PERFORMANCE SIMULATION TOOLS

ENVIRONMENTAL RATING SYSTEMS
BREEAM
LEED
CASBEE
Green Star
DGNB

LIFE CYCLE COST

DESIGN EVALUATION TOOLS

Design tools include a diversity of aids, from those used to inform the design process by indicating trends in energy use associated with strategic design decisions, to tools to predict the energetic performance of detailed architectural and engineering proposals. They may be manual or computationally-based. Design tools can greatly assist where specialist or expert knowledge of a topic is not available or where the required study of an issue would be prohibitively complex or time consuming. Most are based on either mathematical or empirical relationships. However, the user does not necessarily have to understand these formulae in order to use the tool. With the help of guidance documentation and/or training, he or she may carry out studies of a particular proposal and the energy consequences for a building or component design.

However, tools also have their limitations. They are too often mistakenly used with the assumption that they can predict reality. This can be a most misleading assumption and is often the basis for serious misuse of design tools. While some sophisticated tools can achieve quite accurate predictions, all are based on assumptions and approximations which can introduce errors. Similarly, users will bring to a tool their own assumptions and simplifications of the design issue. For the potential user of a design tool, awareness of the assumptions and simplifications made within the tool's theoretical analysis method is important.

DESIGN TOOLS AND ENVIRONMENTAL EVALUATION					
E - Early		I - Intermediate		D - Detailed	
Issue	Drawing	Manual Calculation	Computer Calculation	Scale Model	Computer Simulation
Insulation		E	I		D
Overshadowing	E			E	I/D
Thermal Performance		E	I		D
Daylighting	E	E	I	E	D
Ventilation		E	I		D
Infiltration		E	I		D
Comfort			E		D
Building Fabric		E	I		D
Services Systems		E	I/D		D
Energy Consumption		I			D
Total Performance					D

Energy and environmental issues are interrelated, in that they can directly or indirectly affect both one another as well as overall performance. The aim is to achieve an optimal balance. No one tool can do this automatically, as most answer specific questions. Evaluation forms an integral part of an iterative process also involving analytical and design expertise. Diverse appropriate tools are useful at many stages of the process. For example, to predict how alternative forms of wall construction will perform, the architect must select materials, dimensions and obtain thermophysical characteristics for each alternative. Each construction should be input and results calculated. Only then can constructions be compared thoroughly, and the better one selected. If the design tool (e.g. building simulation software) has a database of materials and constructions matching those to be compared, the input required is reduced.

In trying to identify the most appropriate design tool to meet a user's requirements it is useful to first ask what functionality is required from the design tool. Functionality issues include the way in which data is input, the method of calculation, what energy related functions are important and in what output format results are required. By first addressing these issues the search for an appropriate design tool will be made simpler. When addressing functionality issues it is important to remember that it is not always a case of 'the more functions the better.'

Data output varies considerably depending on the type of evaluation method used. Simpler tools often provide only an outline of results to act as design pointers, but which may be very valuable strategically. Indeed, it is useful to distinguish between design tools and evaluation tools: the most critical decisions, on matters such as form, orientation and planning which will impact profoundly on energy performance, must be made at a stage when detailed information is by definition not available.

INPUTS

Climatic Data

Energy performance is affected by altitude, latitude and longitude, ground topography and surrounding structures, local microclimate, etc. External temperature is a basic requirement for most tools analysing energy related matters, but can be required as hourly, daily or monthly values. Other data may include wind speed and direction, solar radiation and humidity. Standard weather data sets (such as Test Reference Years) have been developed and are widely used within building performance simulation software.

Building Geometry

Building geometry specifies the shape and sizes of the volumes which make up the building. Simpler tools only accept vertical wall and window elements, horizontal floors and flat, sloping or pitched roofs. However, as detail increases, the complexity of geometric models accepted by tools increases.

In detailed models perhaps the most important element of geometrical data input is the building material description. Many building performance simulation tools provide built-in databases of the properties of common materials as individual components, or as typical constructional elements such as walls, windows, etc. This significantly reduces the requirement for the designer to input data.

Standard Calculations

There are many different theoretical calculation methods to model energy use/consumption, lighting, daylighting, ventilation, infiltration, running costs, etc. It is essential to use a method consistent with national or European standards. The differences between comparative methods are often negligible, but some regulatory bodies require particular standards to be used, particularly when demonstrating compliance with Building Regulations or sustainable building rating systems.

Services Systems

Many intermediate and high-level tools offer a wide range of systems describing services within a building. However, for detailed studies of complex services systems, specific tools and expert consultants are probably more appropriate.

Computer Aided Design

The use of sophisticated three-dimensional (3D) modelling tools is widespread amongst architects and engineers, driven by a rapid increase in computing power and the development of building information management (BIM) software. These modelling tools create accurate 3D geometric models of buildings, which can then be imported into performance simulation software for analysis.

MANUAL EVALUATION TOOLS

Architectural Model

Architectural scale models of card or other materials, when built to include the site and surroundings, can be used to study insolation and overshadowing. When used with a simple hair dryer and a fine-grained powder such as light sand, site models can be helpful in identifying exposed and sheltered external areas in the prevailing wind. When reasonably carefully constructed, internal models can give good representation of daylight distribution and of relative daylighting levels. Powerful insights into daylighting performance can be acquired with the assistance of heliodons and an artificial sky.

Stereographic Sun Chart

To assess solar availability on a site, shading from adjacent buildings and vegetation must be determined. This chart projects a view of the sky onto a horizontal plane. For each latitude there is a specific stereographic diagram, used to indicate which sections of the sky are free of obstructions and, consequently, the relative importance of the periods when solar light will be blocked.

The LT Method

The LT Method uses energy performance curves drawn from a mathematical model where most parameters are given assumed values. Only a few key design variable relating to building form and façade design, glazing ratio, surface to volume ratio, etc, are left for the user to manipulate. The resulting energy breakdowns of heating, cooling and lighting give an indication of the relative importance of various energy components. A key strength of this tool is that in a transparent fashion it enables the architect to appreciate how these design variables may be manipulated to improve the energy performance.

BUILDING PERFORMANCE SIMULATION TOOLS

With the introduction of performance certification within Europe there is an increasing interest in performance-based building design methodologies. These methodologies place emphasis on clear statements of requirements and on quantifying performance in use, rather than the more traditional compliance with prescriptive regulations. In principle this leaves the decision on how best to achieve the required performance to those who should know; to the industry rather than to the regulator. Increasingly stringent and performance-based regulations are leading to a greater reliance on building simulation and analysis as a fundamental part of the design process.

With simple tools, it is likely that once the use of the tool is understood, re-use at a later date may only require a brief review of the user documentation. However, the more complex the tool the more likely it is that the user will need to remain fully familiar with all aspects of the application or re-training will be required. This may result in simulation models being used too late in the design process by staff not directly involved in the project design; with an emphasis on evaluation rather than design.

A number of computational tools now exist which have been developed for designers rather than environmental engineers, and improved user interfaces allow for a closer integration of these tools into the design process in a more interactive and dynamic way. Performance modeling is best seen as a continuous process, which gets more detailed and refined as the project advances through the design stages. Some examples are set out below.

The following table outlines the type and level of analysis which building simulation tools can provide during the various project stages:

Design Stage	Building Model Detail	Level of Analysis
Concept Design	Building site location, massing orientation, prevailing wind direction, default assumptions	Assessment of impacts of design alternatives, orientation and solar exposure, overshadowing, etc.
Preliminary Design	Building geometry, construction, initial layout, and M&E equipment, intermediate assumptions	Evaluation of proposed design schemes, intermediate analysis, regulation compliance
Developed Design	Building geometry, detailed envelop design, construction method, detailed internal layout, M&E equipment, detailed assumptions	Evaluation of design energy performance, detailed analysis, preliminary regulation compliance
Detailed Design	Detailed Building Model	Estimated energy performance and regulatory compliance
Construction	Detailed Building Model	Analysis of the effect of change and construction detailing
Operation	Detailed Building Model	Comparison with actual building energy performance

CONCEPT DESIGN

A building's energy performance is affected by altitude, latitude and longitude, topography, surrounding structures and local microclimate. The use of a simplified design tool can provide valuable insights during the early stages of design. A simple energy model with single zoning per occupancy type (e.g. lecture hall, laboratory) can be used to understand the effects of site location, building mass and orientation; by using this methodology, numerous design concepts can be compared against each other and less efficient options eliminated based on site-specific conditions. But it is a mistake to consider simplified tools as unsophisticated. Energy is but one of the very many dimensions shaping the emerging design concept, and considerable subtlety is required of useful early stage design tools.

PRELIMINARY DESIGN

During the preliminary design phase of a project the use of energy modeling can provide valuable information to the design team. By analysing the major drivers of energy use within the proposed building, appropriate energy strategies can be determined and energy priorities decided. For example, where cooling loads are identified as an issue the architect can concentrate on optimising the design to minimize solar gain; the reduction of internal gains is likely to be a matter for a later stage in the design development. By examining different building orientations and form, solar gain through windows can be reduced, thereby reducing the building's cooling load. The designers could also examine the possibility of changing the solar heat gain coefficient of the glass, or introducing solar shading. Very many solutions are possible, and the performance modeling and analysis can facilitate identification and resolution of the key energy design determinants.

DEVELOPED DESIGN

At this stage in the design process an energy model allows the design team to analyse individual components. This parametric analysis can provide quantitative information on the impact of design modifications such as altering window specifications, deciding the appropriate U-value for composite wall constructions, finalising the detailed design of external solar shading, optimising HVAC control strategies, etc.

CONSTRUCTION

Energy modeling can be useful during construction to evaluate the effects of the practically inevitable site changes on the predicted energy performance of the building, and to evaluate if the building will still be in compliance with building regulations or the specification. Following the completion of the construction stage, 'as built' simulations may be run to provide documented evidence of compliance with sustainable building certification schemes such as LEED (Leadership in Energy and Environmental Design).

OPERATION

Following the completion of the construction stage, commissioning, and preferably after two or three years' operation, 'as built' simulations should be compared with monitored building data; this can provide valuable information to the design team on the usefulness of the energy model.

ACCURACY AND VALIDATION

As noted before, results from design tools are never accurate: the model upon which the tool is based incorporates assumptions and approximations, and is to some degree a simplified representation of the building. Even the most detailed calculations will demonstrate varying degrees of error compared to the real building. Designers may misuse a tool as a result of inadequate understanding.

For example, the heat loss performance of building fabric can be up to three times higher than the predicted U-values due to poor workmanship. The occupants will use the building in different ways than expected, perhaps using it for more hours and with more energy-intensive equipment.

The true value in the simulation model is more often the capability to compare alternative schemes and to identify relative differences in energy performance, which will tend to be more accurate than absolute values.

SELECTION AND USE

There is a wide variety of commercial building simulation software available, which have been developed to provide users with key building performance indicators such as energy demand, daylighting analysis, temperature, air speed and humidity. Each simulation program provides a particular set of tools which can be utilised for building performance analysis. A small sample of some of the tools available are listed below.

Simulation Tool	Developer
EnergyPlus	US Department of Energy
ECOTECT	Autodesk
Energy10	Sustainable Buildings Industry Council (in co-operation with NREL, LBNL, Berkeley Solar Group)
EcoDesigner	Archicad
Green Building Studio	Autodesk
IES Virtual Environment	Integrated Environmental Solutions

ENVIRONMENTAL RATING SYSTEMS

The demand for a holistic, whole-building environmental impact analysis has resulted in the development and implementation of sustainable building rating systems designed to foster and recognise the design of more sustainable buildings, the development of more sustainable construction methods and materials, and to promote more sustainable building operation.

Sustainable building rating systems are defined as methodologies which examine the performance or expected performance of a 'whole building' and translate that examination into an overall assessment that allows for comparison against other buildings *(Fowler and Rauch, 2006)*.

A number of sustainability rating systems have been developed to provide frameworks for the assessment of overall building designs by identifying specific performance criteria. These systems are mostly voluntary, and apply point-scoring ratings under various different criteria to the design of the site, building envelope, systems and components, and the building's operation. They provide designers, property interests, building owners and occupants with a wide-ranging analysis of the measurable impacts a building will have on the environment, and help promote best practice through the awarding of various certification levels.

There are several different sustainable building rating systems which have been implemented around the world. Each of these rating systems differs in structure, terminologies and performance assessment methods. There is a lack of a unified methodology and therefore, it is not possible to compare the environmental performance of two buildings evaluated under two different rating systems due to differences of emphasis and method.

The following list is a selection of the more established sustainability rating systems.

Assessment Method	Organisation	Commencement Date
BREEAM	Building Research Establishment Environmental Assessment Method (UK)	1990
LEED	Leadership in Energy & Environmental Design (USA)	1998
CASBEE	Comprehensive Assessment System for Built Environment Efficiency (Japan)	2001
GREEN STAR	Green Building Council Australia	2003
DGNB	German Sustainable Building Council	2007

BREEAM (BUILDING RESEARCH ESTABLISHMENT ENVIRONMENTAL ASSESSMENT METHOD)

BREEAM was developed in the United Kingdom in 1990 and is one of the longest established building environmental assessment methods. Versions are available for several other countries. The assessment method is designed to assist designers and construction professionals in identifying and mitigating the negative environmental impacts of buildings they design and build. BREEAM covers a range of building types including offices, homes, multipurpose developments, industrial units, retail units, courts, prisons and schools, and these are periodically updated.

BREEAM is a design and post construction stage assessment process. When a building is assessed, points are awarded for each criterion and a set of environmental weightings is then applied to each of the criteria. The weighted scores are then added to create a total score. The overall building performance is then awarded a "Pass", "Good", "Very Good", "Excellent" or "Outstanding" rating based on the score and a certificate is awarded to either the design or construction depending on which is being assessed. The categories of criteria for design and procurement include:

- Management (commissioning, monitoring, waste recycling, pollution minimisation, materials minimisation.)

- Health and Wellbeing (adequate ventilation, humidification, lighting, thermal comfort)

- Energy (sub-metering. efficiency and CO_2 impact of systems)

- Transport (emissions, alternate transport facilities)

- Water (consumption reduction, metering, leak detection)

- Materials (asbestos mitigation, recycling facilities, reuse of structures, façade or materials, use of crushed aggregate and sustainable timber)

- Land Use (previously used land, use of remediated contaminated land)

- Ecology (land with low ecological value or minimal change in value, maintain major ecological systems on the land, minimisation of biodiversity impacts)

- Pollution (leak detection systems, on-site treatment, local or renewable energy sources, light pollution design, avoid use of ozone depleting and global warming substances)

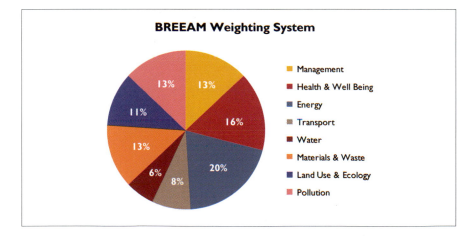

In addition to the BREEAM rating system, a self-assessment scheme for existing buildings called "BREEAM In-Use" has been developed to help building managers and owners reduce running costs and improve the environmental performance of existing buildings. The scheme consists of an on-line assessment tool which, when completed, is reviewed by an independent auditor before certification is awarded.

LEED v3 (LEADERSHIP IN ENERGY & ENVIRONMENTAL DESIGN, VERSION 3)

LEED is an international green building certification system developed by the US Green Building Council (USGBC). LEED provides third party verification that a building or community was designed and built using strategies aimed at improving performance in energy savings, water efficiency, CO_2 emissions reduction, improved indoor environmental quality, and resources management.

The LEED rating system addresses specific environmental building related impacts using a whole-building environmental performance approach. LEED covers a range of new and existing building types including: schools, retail, homes, neighbourhood developments, 'core-and-shell', commercial interiors. The rating system is arranged in five distinct environmental categories with bonus points being awarded for innovation in design and for regional priority:

Sustainable Sites
Construction related pollution prevention, site development impacts, transportation alternatives, storm water management, heat island effect and light pollution.

Water Efficiency
Landscaping water use reduction, indoor water use reduction and wastewater strategies.

Energy and Atmosphere
Commissioning, whole-building energy performance optimisation, refrigerant management, renewable energy use and measurement and verification.

Materials and Resources
Recycling collection locations, building reuse, construction waste management, purchase of regionally manufactured materials, materials with recycled content, rapidly renewable materials, salvaged materials and sustainably forested wood products.

Indoor Environmental Quality
Environmental tobacco-smoke control, outdoor air delivery monitoring, increased ventilation, indoor air quality, use of low emitting materials, source control and controllability of thermal and lighting systems.

Innovation and Design Process
LEED® accredited professional, and innovative strategies for sustainable design.

Realisation
Address regional specific environmental priorities.

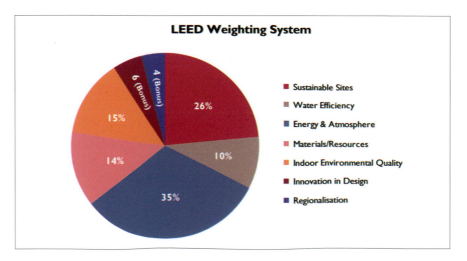

CASBEE (COMPREHENSIVE ASSESSMENT SYSTEM FOR BUILT ENVIRONMENT EFFICIENCY)

The Comprehensive Assessment System for Built Environment Efficiency was developed in Japan in 2001. CASBEE was based on the architectural design process, starting from pre-design stage and continuing through design and post design stages. CASBEE is composed of a suite of four assessment tools comprising pre-design, new construction, existing buildings, and renovation.

CASBEE uses an assessment concept that distinguishes environmental load (L) from quality of building performance (Q) to create an inclusive assessment indicator, the Building Environment Efficiency.

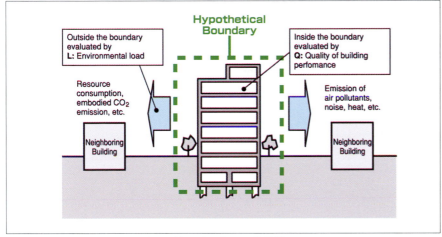

Definition of Q and L through hypothetical boundary. Source: CASBEE

Built Environment Efficiency (BEE) is defined as Environmental Load divided by Building Performance (BEE=L/Q). The results are plotted on a graph, with environmental load on one axis and quality on the other. The highest rated buildings will fall in the section representing the lowest environmental load and the highest quality. With increasing BEE value, total environmental performance is labelled as any of Class C (Poor), B-, B+, A, and S (Excellent).

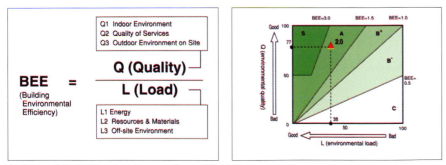

Definition of the BEES and results graph. Source: CASBEE

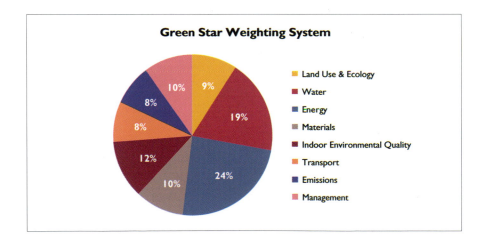

GREEN STAR (GREEN BUILDING COUNCIL OF AUSTRALIA)

Launched in 2003 by the Green Building Council of Australia (GBCA), Green Star is a voluntary environmental rating system for buildings located in Australia. The rating system covers a range of different new and existing building types including education, healthcare, multi-unit residential, industrial, office, office interiors, retail centre, office design, and office-as-built.

The rating system is arranged into nine distinct environmental impact categories: management; indoor environment quality; energy; transport; water; materials; land use and ecology; emissions; and innovation. These categories are divided into credits, each of which addresses an initiative that improves or has the potential to improve environmental performance. Points are awarded in each credit for documented actions that demonstrate that the project has meet the overall objectives of Green Star.

An environmental weighting is then applied to each category score (except innovation), which balances the inherent weighting that occurs through the number of credits available in any rating category. In addition, weightings also vary by geographical location, in order to reflect the important issues in each state or territory. The maximum possible score for the weighted categories is 100 with an additional five points available for innovation.

The Green Building Council of Australia only certifies buildings which achieve a rating of four star or above.

Evaluation
For a total weighted rating score of
- 10–19 pts   One Star
- 20–29 pts   Two Star
- 30–44 pts   Three Star
- 45–49 pts   Four Star (Best Practice)
- 60–74 pts   Five Star (Australian Excellence)
- 75+ pts   Six Star (World Leader)

Founded in 2007, the German Sustainable Building Council administers the awarding of the German Sustainability Certificate (GSC). The GSC certification process is based on the concept of integral planning that defines, at an early stage, the aims of sustainable construction.

The Certificate is based on a meritocratic rating system which examines the ecological, economic and socio-cultural elements of a development as well as the functional elements under the categories: techniques, processes, and location. The certificate is awarded for the building's quality based on five of the topics listed, with the quality of location presented separately as it is not defined as the building itself.

Each of the topics is divided into several criteria, for which a measurable target value is defined, and a maximum of 10 points can be assigned. The measurable targets for each criterion are clearly defined. At the same time, each criterion has a weighting factor which can impact threefold on the evaluation of its respective topic.

Each criterion then flows into the overall result in a clearly differentiated way and a software-supported computation displays the building's performance: by reaching a defined degree of performance, it is assigned the bronze, silver, or gold award. Grades are given for the total performance of the building as well as for the individual topics.

Evaluation

For a total degree of compliance of
- 50%, the bronze certificate is awarded
- 65% for silver
- 89% for gold.

Alternatively, the total degree of compliance is indicated by a grade: a total degree of compliance of
- 95% corresponds to grade 1.0
- 80% corresponds to 1.5
- 65% corresponds to 2.0

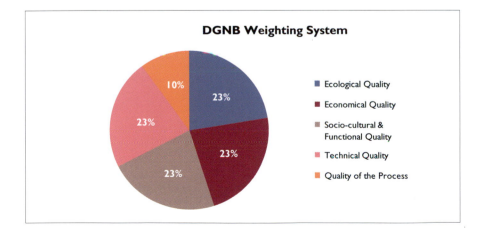

LIFE CYCLE COST

INTRODUCTION

At present, many building environmental costs (emissions of greenhouse gases; the consumption of finite resources such as hardwood and metals; and the creation of construction waste) are not reflected in either initial construction cost or in continuing building servicing costs. Water, waste and energy taxes are gradually changing this and will help make green building more economically attractive. To enable the client assess the financial return over a building's life of investments in energy saving or other resource-conserving measures, life cycle cost analysis is necessary. But life cycle cost analysis is also a valuable tool for rational decision-making in many building economic matters. Far too often, the entire focus is on initial cost, to the detriment of real value; as a result total costs (including maintenance and operation) over the building's or the component's life can be much higher than necessary.

LIFE CYCLE COST

The objective is to optimise the value of a construction project over its lifetime, having regard to all the project costs, both direct and indirect. This involves selecting an appropriate lifetime for the building. However, with maintenance, any building can last almost indefinitely, and it will be easier to assign a lifetime to replacement date for individual systems and components. For example, depending on specification, floor finishes might have a lifetime to replacement of from 10 years (inexpensive thin sheet flooring) to 30 years (hardwood strip). When annual operating and maintenance costs are added, this lifetime to replacement can help determine the life cycle cost. For a full environmental evaluation, it is necessary to ascribe costs to environmental factors such as pollution, resource depletion, etc.

The Green Guide to Specification: An Environmental Profiling System for Building Materials and Components, published by the UK Building Research Establishment, gives estimated replacement intervals for a wide range of building materials and components, over a 60-year building design life cycle, which take account of maintenance and refurbishment.

PAYBACK PERIOD

The simplest way to calculate the cost-effectiveness of an investment is to determine its payback period. The ultimate objective is to identify the value of a construction component or project over its lifetime, to enable selection based on life cycle cost. For commercial investment appraisal, future income and expenditure is discounted to a present value using an appropriate rate. The appropriate discount rate to use is the real rate of return required on the investment. For domestic consumers, this rate may be the difference between the after-tax interest rate on bank deposits and the rate of inflation. Rates vary with time and country, but with a 2% inflation rate and a 5% after-tax interest rate, the domestic discount rate is 3%. A higher rate of return is normally required in the commercial sector.

DISCOUNTING TO PRESENT VALUE

In the case of low energy or sustainable design, consideration of life cycle costs from the outset is essential. The balance between construction cost and cost-in-use is fundamental to the architecture of the building. For example, the design of a window will have implications for heating, cooling, ventilation and artificial lighting, pollutant emissions, plant size and maintenance costs.

The length of payback periods needs consideration. The payback periods used in different organisations and EU Member States vary considerably, from as short as three years to ten years or longer. Plainly, this one element has critical consequences for the evaluations of solar low energy strategies. Far-sighted clients, particularly those who will be owner/occupiers, may be willing to consider longer payback periods.

Direct and indirect: initial, life cycle, and environmental

Initial:
Design
Construction: supply and installation

Life Cycle:
Daily, weekly and annual maintenance including cleaning, repair, redecoration
Replacement, including removal, waste disposal, replacement
Running cost for energy consuming components

Environmental:
Resource depletion and environmental pollution
Extraction, manufacture, transport, use and disposal: to air, ground, water
Indoor environmental quality

The table above lists different cost types to be considered when evaluating life cycle and environmental cost. This does not deal with the issue of component quality. If, over say 50 years, the cost of a pvc tile floor finish is equal to the cost of a high quality hardwood strip floor, the architect might also ascribe an extra value given to the user by the visual and olfactory pleasure of the high-quality component over that associated with the cheap one.

COMPARISON OF INITIAL AND LIFE CYCLE COST: WORKED EXAMPLE

Incandescent lamp as against compact fluorescent; Discount rate 3%/yr; No cost included for - environmental cost of additional CO_2 and SO_2 emissions, estimated at 750kg and 8kg respectively over working life *(Browning and Romm, 1995)*; - labour involved in bulb replacement; - contribution to higher heat output (whether useful or surplus) of incandescent lamp.

			100W Incandescent	23W Compact Fluorescent
Initial cost, €			€1	€7
Supply and install			€14.00/yr	€3.22/yr
Running Cost: 1000 hr/yr, €0.14/kWh				
Life expectancy			1000 hours	8000 hours
Life cycle comparison for 8 year period:				
Initial capital cost				
Replacement cost, discounting at 3%/yr			€1	€7
Factors:	Year 1	0.971		
	Year 2	0.943		
	Year 3	0.915		
	Year 4	0.888		
	Year 5	0.862		
	Year 6	0.837		
	Year 7	0.813		
	Total	6.229 × €1	€6.229	€ 0.00
Running cost over 8 years				
Years 1-7, as above	6.229			
Year 8	0.789			
Total	7.018		X €14.00 = 98.25	X €3.22 = 22.60
Total life cycle cost over 8 years			€105.48	€29.60

Calculation of Payback Period for Investment

Total initial investment: €6
Return on investment over 8 years, discounted: €105.48-29.60 = €75.88 or €9.49/yr

Payback period: **8 Months**

REFERENCES

FOREWORD & GREEN BUILDING

Architects' Council of Europe (ACE). (1995). Europe and Architecture Tomorrow L'Europe et l'Architecture Demain. ISBN: 2.930164-00-x. ACE, Brussels.

Kerstein, K. (2004). Architecture and Quality of Life. Architects' Council of Europe (ACE), Brussels.

O'Cofaigh, E. et al. (1999). A Green Vitruvius - Principles and Practice of Sustainable Architectural Design. James and James (Science Publishers) for the EC DGXVII and the Architects' Council of Europe. London.

Union Internationale des Architectes (UIA). (1993). Declaration of Interdependence for a Sustainable Future. UIA/AIA World Congress of Architects, 18–21 June 1993, Chicago.

SECTION 2: ISSUES

Baker, N., Fanchiotti, A and Steemers, K. (1995). Daylighting in Architecture: a European Reference Book. James & James (Scientific Publishers) Ltd, London.

European Commission DG for Energy and Transport (EC). (2005). EC Green Paper on Energy Efficiency. [Internet] EC. Available at:
http://ec.europa.eu/energy/efficiency/doc/2005_06_green_paper_book_en.pdf

European Parliament and the Council of the European Union (EU). (2008a). Proposal for a Directive of the European Parliament and the Council on the Energy Performance of Buildings (Recast). [Internet]. EU. Available at:
http://eur-lex.europa.eu/LexUriServ/LexUriServ.do?uri=COM:2008:0780:FIN:EN:PDF

European Parliament and the Council; of the European Union (EU). (2008b). Directive 2008/98/EC of the European Parliament and of the Council on Waste and repealing certain Directives. [Internet] EU. Available at:
http://eur-lex.europa.eu/LexUriServ/LexUriServ.do?uri=CELEX:32008L0098:EN:NOT

European Parliament and the Council of the European Union (EU). (2010). Directive 2010/31/EU of the European Parliament and of the Council on the Energy Performance of Buildings Recast. [Internet] EU. Available at:
http://ec.europa.eu/energy/efficiency/buildings/buildings_en.htm

Heschong Mahone Group. (1999). Daylighting in Schools: An Investigation into the Relationship between Daylighting and Human Performance. Pacific Gas and Electric Company, USA.

Küller, R and Lindsten, C. (1992). Health and Behaviour of Children in Classrooms with and without Windows. Journal of Environmental Psychology, Vol. 12, Issue 4, Dec 1992: pg. 305-317.

Lockley, S.W. (2008). Influence of Light on Circadian Rhythmicity in Humans. In Squire. L. R. (Ed.), Encyclopaedia of Neuroscience, Oxford.

Roaf, S. and Hancock, M. (editors) (1992). Energy Efficient Building; a design guide. Blackwell Scientific Publishers, Oxford.

Sharon, J., Gochenour, S. and Andersen, M. (2009). Circadian Effects of Daylighting in a Residential Environment. In: Proceedings LuxEuropa, Sept 9-11 2009, Istanbul.

Ulrich, R.S. (1984). View through a Window may influence Recovery from Surgery. Science, Vol. 224, No. 4647: pg. 420-421.

World Health Organisation (WHO) (2010). Data and Statistics. [Internet] WHO. Available at: http://www.who.int/research/en/

SECTION 3: STRATEGIES

Barton, H., Davies, G., & Guise, R. (1995). Sustainable Settlements – A Guide for Planners, Designers, and Developers. University of the West England and Local Government Management Board, Luton.

Defra, (2010). [Internet] DEFRA. Available at: http://www.defra.gov.uk/

Eiker, U. (2010). Low Energy Cooling for Sustainable Buildings. (Stuttgart University of Applied Sciences). ISBN: 978-0-470-69744-3. John Wiley & Sons, Chichester.

European Alliance of Companies for Energy Efficiency in Buildings (EUROACE). (2010). Response to the European Commission Consultation on the Future "EU 2020" Strategy. Commission Working Document COM (2009)647. [Internet]. EU. http://ec.europa.eu/energy/efficiency/labelling/energy_labelling_en.htm (energy label)

Evans, Y. and Dwyer, T. (2010). Mini Combined Heat and Power Applications. CIBSE Journal, Aug 2010, (19): pg. 51-53.

Green Building Digest. (1995). ACTAC periodicals.

Harvey, L.D. (2006). A Handbook on Low-Energy Buildings and District-Energy Systems: Fundamentals, Techniques and Examples. Earthscan Publications Ltd., London. ISBN-13: 978-1844072439

Hegger, M., Fuchs, M., Stark, T., and Zeumer, M. (2008). Energy Manual – Sustainable Architecture. Birkhauser, Basle.

Hough, M. (1995). Cities and Natural Processes. Routledge, London.

International Energy Agency (IEA). (2010) Annex 45. Guidebook on Energy Efficient Electric Lighting for Buildings. ISBN 978-952-60-3229-0. Halonen, L., Tetri, E. and Bhusal, P. (eds). IEA, Espoo.

Karakatsani, A. et al. (2010). Ambient air pollution and respitory health effects in mail carriers. Environmental Research, April 2010, 110(3): pg. 278-85.

Martinez, N. et al. (1996). Architectural and Environmental Teaching. For EC DG XI.

O'Cofaigh, E., Olley, J. and Lewis, J.O. (1996). The Climatic Dwelling – An Introduction to Climate-responsive Residential Architecture. James & James (Science Publishers) Ltd, for the EC DG XII, London.

Welch, T. (2009). Heat Pump Technology. CIBSE Journal, May 2009. [Internet]. CIBSE. Available at: http://www.cibsejournal.com/

Woolley, T., Kimmins, S., Harrison, P. and Harrison, R. (1997). Green Building Handbook, Vol. 1. E&FN Spon, London.

Zimmermann, M. and Andersson, J. (1998). Annex 28 Low Energy Cooling – Case Study Buildings. EMPA ZEN for IEA, Duebendorf.

SECTION 4: ELEMENTS

Anink, D., Boonstra, C. and Mak, J. (1996). Handbook of Sustainable Building: An Environmental Preference Method for Selection of Materials for Use in Construction and Refurbishment. James & James (Science Publishers) Ltd, London.

Bloomsterberg, A. (2007). Best Practice for Double Skin Facades. EU Intelligent Energy Europe funded project BESTFACADE. [Internet]. Available at: http://www.bestfacade.com/

Chartered Institute of Building Services Engineers (CIBSE). (2006). Guide A: Environmental Design. Seventh Edition. CIBSE [Internet]. Available at: http://www.cibse.org/

Esbensen Consulting Engineers (1998). Windows - The Key to Low Energy Design. Energy Comfort 2000 Information Dossier No. 5 for EC. [Internet]. Available at: http://erg.ucd.ie/downloads

Hammond, G.P., and Jones, C.I. (2008). Embodied Energy and Carbon in Construction Materials - Inventory of Carbon and Energy (ICE), version 1.6a. University of Bath.

Howard, N. (1991). Energy in Balance. Building Services Journal, Vol 13: pg. 36-38.

Kendrick, C. and Walliman, N. (2006). Removing Unwanted Heat in Lightweight Buildings Using Phase Change Materials in Building Components: Simulation Modelling for PCM Plasterboard. Architectural Science Review, Vol. 50.

Lyons, A. (2007). Materials for Architects & Builders. 3rd Edition. Elsevier (BH), Oxford.

Minke, G. (2006). Building with Earth – Design and Technology of a Sustainable Architecture. Birkhauser, Basle.

Pennycook, K. (2008). The Illustrated Guide to Renewable Technologies. Building Services Research and Information Association (BSRIA), Berkshire.

Talbott, L. (1993). Simply Build Green: A Technical Guide to the Ecological Houses at the Findhorn Foundation. John Findhorn Foundation.

Whitelegg, J. (1993). Transport for a Sustainable Future: the Case for Europe. Belhaven Press, London.

SECTION 5: EVALUATION

Browning, W.D. and Romm, J.J. (1995). Greening the Building and the Bottom Line. Rocky Mountain Institute, Colorado.

Fowler, K.M. and Rauch, E.M. (2006). Sustainable Building Rating Systems – Summary. Pacific Northwest National Laboratory, Department of Energy, USA.

INDEX

absorption chillers 81

acrylic paint 119

active cooling 107

active façades 61

adaptation 1, 13, 82

adhesives 77, 119

adjustable shading devices 97

administration 12

adobe houses 114

aerated concrete 116

air conditioning 80, 81–82

air quality 45, 46, 74–77, 90, 119

airtightness 63, 64, 89

alkyd paints 119

alternative site development strategies 10

aluminium 117, 118

appointing consultants 6

aquifer thermal energy storage (ATES) 104

artificial lighting 68, 98

    see also lighting

ATES *see* aquifer thermal energy storage

atria 59, 71–72

audits 20

Australia 134

balanced ventilation systems 82–83

basalt cladding 114

BEE *see* Built Environment Efficiency

BEMS *see* Building Energy Management Systems

BIM *see* building information management

bioenergy 101

bitumen 121

black water 8, 10, 49, 56

boilers 79, 101, 105

boreholes 104

breathing walls 63

BREEAM *see* Building Research Establishment Environmental Assessment Method

brick 116–117

briefing stage 8–9

brownfield sites 8, 10, 47, 49

Building Energy Management Systems (BEMS) 85

building envelope

    components 92–97

    construction 17

    consultant inputs 7

    design stage 11, 12, 15

    issues 61–72

    renovation 87–89

building form 11, 12, 14, 58–60

building information management (BIM) 125

building-integrated photovoltaics 100

building regulations 13, 20

Building Research Establishment Environmental Assessment Method (BREEAM) 131

Built Environment Efficiency (BEE) 133

bulk materials 109

capillary systems 108

carbon 79, 86, 115, 116, 117, 121

    see also carbon dioxide; emissions

carbon dioxide 1, 78, 115, 116

    see also carbon; emissions

carbon monoxide 33

carpet 76–77

CASBEE *see* Comprehensive Assessment System for Built Environment Efficiency

cavity wall insulation 64, 87

ceiling fans 81

ceilings 75–76

cement 115–116

ceramics 75, 116–117

certification schemes 112–113, 119, 128, 130–135

Chicago Declaration, UIA 1

chipboard 76, 113

CHP *see* combined heat and power systems

chromic glazing 95

city block planning 43–44

clay 116–117

cleaning agents 120

client level 2, 5–6, 8

climatic data 125

coat method 88

cob houses 114

coefficient of performance (COP) 80

combined heat and power (CHP) systems 79, 80, 106

combustion 33, 101, 105, 106

comfort 19, 21, 22–31, 62, 82, 123

commercial buildings 53, 78, 83

commissioning 5, 18

compact fluorescent lamps 83, 84, 137

components 91–108, 128, 136, 137

composite insulating blocks 116

composting 50

Comprehensive Assessment System for Built Environment Efficiency (CASBEE) 133

computer aided design 125

concept design stage 11, 127–128

concrete 116

concrete core systems 108

condensing boilers 79, 105

conservatories 70, 71

constructed wetlands 50

construction

    evaluation 124, 127, 128, 131, 136

    materials manufacture 110

    processes 3, 4, 17–18

    renovation 90

    waste 17, 111

consultants 6–7, 9, 12, 14

contractors 9, 16, 18

control systems 78–85, 89, 98

cooling

    briefing state 9

building envelope 61, 62

building form 58

components 103–108

consultant inputs 7

finishes 73

glazed areas 66–69

renovation 90

services, equipment and controls 80–82

simulations 128

site planning 57

sunspaces 70–71

COP *see* coefficient of performance

copper 117, 118

core systems 108

cork flooring 77

costs

    briefing state 9

    building envelope 61

    consultants 6, 7

    life cycle 8, 136–137

    phase change cooling 107

    photovoltaics 100

    preliminary design stage 12

    reductions 1

    renovation 86

    vegetation 54

    see also economics

cross ventilation 58, 68, 71, 72

cycle routes 54

daylight 52, 57, 97

daylighting 65, 66, 68–69, 72, 74, 94

daylight linking controls 85

demolition waste 111

dense materials 45

density 47, 54

dependency on oil 1

detailed design stage 15, 127

developed design stage 13, 127, 128

DGNB *see* German Sustainable Building Council

diffusion open construction 63

dimmer controls 98

discount rates 136–137

disposal of waste 111, 116

documents and services 11, 12, 13, 16, 17

doors 89

double glazing 66, 96

double skin façades 80, 94

drainage systems 55–56, 92

draught stripping 89

Dublin transport systems 48

durability 2

earth 114–115

Earth berms 54

eco labels 119, 120

economics
    building envelope 92, 93, 94, 95, 96, 97
    heating and cooling 103, 104, 105, 106, 107, 108
    lighting controls 98
    renewable energy 99, 100, 102
    see also costs
Eicker, U. 78
electrical resistance heating 79
electricity 7, 78, 99, 100, 101
electric lighting 83–85
    see also lighting
electrochromic glazing 95
elements 91–121
elephant grass 101
embodied energy 110, 115, 116, 117, 121
emissions
    CHP 80
    energy efficiency 1, 36
    formaldehyde 74, 75
    fuel 78
    health 32, 33–34
    indoor air quality 32, 76
    materials 109, 116, 117, 119, 120, 121
    renovation 86
    transport 48, 110
    ventilation 82
    see also carbon; carbon dioxide
energy
    building envelope 70
    certification 132
    evaluation 124, 125, 127–128
    finishes 73
    green design 1
    heating 59, 78
    management systems 18, 85
    materials 117, 121
    operational performance 19
    refurbishment 20
    renewable 50, 99–102
    site planning 56–57
    urban density 47
energy efficiency
    finishes 74
    heating and cooling systems 105, 106
    renewable energy 99
    services, equipment and controls 78–85
    sunspaces 71
    urban areas 43, 50
energy performance 73
envelope *see* building envelope
environmental impacts
    buildings 21
    evaluation 123, 124
    finishes 73, 75–77
    green design 1
    materials 109–112, 119–120, 121
    operational performance 19
    rating systems 130–135
EPBD *see* European Directive on the Energy Performance of Buildings
EPDM *see* Ethylene-Propylene-Diene Monomer
EPS *see* expanded polystyrene
equipment strategies 78–85
Ethylene-Propylene-Diene Monomer (EPDM) 121
EU Ecolabel 119
European Directive on the Energy Performance of Buildings (EPBD) 38, 86
European Union, evaluation 123
evacuated tube solar collectors 102
evaluation 123–137
expanded polystyrene (EPS) 121
exposed slabs 62
external insulation 64, 87–88
external shading devices 67, 97
extraction of materials 110, 117
extract ventilation systems 82
extruded polystyrene 121

façades 61, 80, 86, 94, 116
fees 5–6
fibre-board 113
finishes 73–77, 136, 137
fixed shading devices 67, 97
fixtures and fittings 2, 74
flat plate solar collectors 102
flat roofs 64, 88
floors 62, 64, 73, 76–77, 88
fluorescent lighting 83, 84, 85
forests 112
Forest Stewardship Council (FSC) 112–113
formaldehyde emissions 74, 75
foul water 50, 56
frame materials 96
FSC *see* Forest Stewardship Council
fuel 78
functionality issues 14, 125

gas-filled multiple glazing 96
gasification wood boilers 105
geltaftan buildings 114
geometry 125, 127
German Sustainable Building Council (DGNB) 135
GGBS *see* Ground Granulation Blastfurnace Slag
glass 117
glazing
    building envelope 61, 65–69
    developed design stage 13
    electrochromic 95
    façades 116
    high performance 96
    prismatic 95
    renovation 89
    site planning 56–57
    solar stairs 80
granolithic floors 76
gravel 116
Green Guide to Specification: An Environmental Profiling System for Building Materials and Components 136
green roofs 92

green spaces 49, 54–55
Green Star, Green Building Council of Australia 134
grey water 50, 56
grid-connected photovoltaics 100
ground coupled air systems 103
Ground Granulation Blastfurnace Slag (GGBS) 115–116
groundwater 104

hazards of renovation 90
health 21
heating
    briefing state 9
    building envelope 61, 62, 65–66
    building form 58
    components 103–108
    consultant inputs 7
    electrical resistance 79
    energy 59, 78
    finishes 73
    HVAC systems 81
    renovation 90
    site planning 56–57
    solar thermal systems 102
    sunspaces 70–71
Heating, Ventilating and Air Conditioning (HVAC) systems 81
heat island effect 45
heat loss
    building envelope 61, 62
    comfort 22–23, 29
    floors 64, 88
    glazing 96
    house type 58
    insulation 63
    renovation 87
    roofs 88
    windows and doors 89
heat pumps 79–80
heat recovery 15, 82–83
heat recovery ventilation control units 81
heat waste 106
high performance windows 96
high pressure sodium lighting 84, 85
holographic film 95
HVAC *see* Heating, Ventilating and Air Conditioning systems
hybrid cooling systems 80
hydrocarbon-based paints 119

illuminance 74
impervious surfaces 55, 56
incandescent lighting 85, 137
inception 3, 4, 5–10
indigenous planting 54
indoor environment
    air quality 74–77, 90, 119
    certification 132
    operational performance 19
    temperatures 59, 81, 82
induction lamp lighting 84
initial costs 8, 137

initial studies 10

innovation 132

insulation
    building envelope 63–64, 65
    concrete 116
    earth 115
    glazing 69
    green roofs 92
    renovation 87–88
    ventilation 82

integrated approaches
    design 3, 43, 44
    passive systems 78
    photovoltaic systems 70, 100
    renovation 86

interior shading devices 97

internal insulation 63–64, 87

internal temperatures 59, 82

International Organization for Standardization (ISO) 111–112

investment 136, 137

ISO see International Organization for Standardization

labelling systems 86, 112, 119, 120

landscaping 7, 12, 87

land use 47, 48

LCA see life cycle analysis

lead 118

Leadership in Energy & Environmental Design, Version 3 (LEED v3) 132

LED lighting 84, 85

LEED v3 see Leadership in Energy & Environmental Design, Version 3

life cycle analysis (LCA) 109–112

life cycle costs 1, 8, 136–137

lighting
    briefing state 9
    consultant inputs 7
    control systems 98
    design 15
    incandescent 85, 137
    renovation 90
    services, equipment and controls 83–85

light re-directing systems 69, 95

light shelves 69, 74, 97

linear green links 49

linoleum 77

living roofs 92

load-bearing capacity 14

localised lighting 85

local site analysis 51

louvres 67

low-emissivity coatings/glazing 96

low-energy glazing 66

low energy transport 48

LT Method 126

luminous flux 85

macro-scale site analysis 51

maintenance 5, 18, 19, 136

management 2, 3, 17, 18, 85, 90

manual evaluation tools 126

manufacturing 110, 119

masonry 15, 63, 64

masterplanning 43, 44

materials
    briefing state 9
    certification 132
    dense 45
    design stage 11, 12, 15
    finishes 73
    indoor air quality 74–75
    life cycle costs 136
    overview 109–121
    renovation 89
    thermal mass 62

matt paint finishes 74

mechanical services 15, 78

mechanical ventilation systems 80, 81, 82–83

mercury vapour lighting 84, 85

metal halide lighting 84, 85

metals 117–118

metering systems 89

microclimate 45–46, 49, 51, 53, 87

micro-scale site analysis 52

micro-turbines 99

Minergie Eco Label 120

Miscanthus giganteus 101

mixed-mode cooling systems 80

moveable shading devices 67, 69

natural cooling 80

natural floor coverings 77

natural paints 76, 119

natural ventilation 68, 81, 82

neighbourhood strategies 43–50

night ventilation 68, 72

non-toxic finishes 75, 76

Nordic Swan Eco Label 120

northern latitudes 27, 52, 56, 59, 62, 70, 102

nylon 76

occupancy sensors 98

occupant comfort 19, 21

occupant comfort see comfort

off-grid photovoltaics 100

oil dependency 1

Okalux glass 65

opaque elements 61–64

openings 59
    see also doors; windows

open loop systems 103

operational level 3, 4, 5, 18, 19, 127, 128

organic materials 50, 110

orientation 56–57, 128

outdoor lighting 98

overhangs 67, 69, 97

owner-occupiers 2, 8

paint 74, 75, 76, 119

pale surfaces 57

panel systems 108

paper 75, 113

part-load conditions 82

passive systems 6, 43, 73, 78, 82, 107

payback periods 8, 136–137

PCMs see phase change materials

pedestrian routes 54

performance
    building envelope 17, 61
    design 14
    evaluation 123, 124, 125, 127–129, 130–135
    finishes 73
    heat pumps 80
    operational 19
    refurbishment 20, 86–87

phase change materials (PCMs) 107

photocells 98

photovoltaics (PVs) 70, 100

pitched roofs 64, 88, 100

planning
    city block 43–44
    design 11, 12, 14, 15
    initial stages 10
    site planning 11, 53–57
    tender stage 16

plant fibres 113–114

plaster 75

plywood 76, 113

pollutants 46, 74–75, 82

polystyrene 121

Portland cement 115

post occupancy user surveys 19

pre-finished modules 88

preliminary design stage 12–13, 127, 128

preservatives 120

prismatic glazing 95

processes 3–20

PVC 77

PVs see photovoltaics

quality 2

radiant heating/cooling systems 108

rainwater run-off 55–56

rammed earth constructions 114

rating systems 79, 130–135

recycling 111, 117, 118

redirecting light 69, 95

reflectance 74

reflective finishes 73

refurbishment 3, 4, 5, 20
    see also renovation

renewable energy 50, 99–102

renovation 86–90
    see also refurbishment

residential area site strategies 53

resistance storage heaters 79

resources certification 132

retrofit strategies 86–90

reuse of waste 111

reversible heat pumps 79

roof gardens 54

rooflighting 69

roofs 64, 70, 88, 92, 100, 102
roof/wall junctions 64
row houses 58

sand 116
sanitary fittings 15
sealants 120
seasonal efficiency 79
secondary glazing 89
self-assessment systems 131
services
    briefing state 8
    client-architect contract 5
    construction stage 17
    design stage 11, 12, 13, 15
    evaluation 125
    initial studies 10
    life cycle cost analysis 136
    operation and maintenance 19
    quality of 2
    refurbishment 20, 89
    strategies 78–85
    tender stage 16
shading devices 46, 59, 67, 69, 94, 97
shelter belts 55, 56
short rotation 101
shutters 67, 69
simulation tools 123, 127–129
sinusoidal floor slabs 62, 63
site level
    briefing state 9
    certification 132
    construction procedures 17
    planning 11, 53–57
    selection 43, 51–52
    waste 111
    working space 16
small-scale wind turbines 99
softwood timber 76
solar
    access 46, 52, 55
    air temperatures 62
    availability evaluation 126
    collectors 102
    gain 66, 128
    glazing transmittance 66
    renewable energy 102
    shading 67
    stairs 80
    thermal panels 70
southern latitudes 57, 59, 60, 62
spatial organization 58
specialists 6–7
    see also consultants
stack ventilation 71, 72, 81
stains 75
standards 17, 111–112, 125
steady state efficiency 79
steel 118
stereographic sun charts 126
stone 76, 115
stormwater 92

strategies 43–90
straw 113–114
structure 7, 13
sub-contractors 16
SUDS see sustainable urban drainage systems
sunlight 45, 52
sunspaces 58, 70–71
supervision 17–18
supply-only ventilation systems 82
surface cover 55
suspended ceiling panel systems 108
suspended floors 88
sustainable building rating systems 130–135
sustainable urban drainage systems (SUDS) 92
synthetic materials 120–121

temperature
    atria 72
    building envelope 62
    condensing boilers 105
    green spaces 49
    ground coupled air systems 103
    heat island effect 45
    indoor 59, 81, 82
    radiant heating/cooling systems 108
    trees 55
tenants 8
tender 3, 4, 5, 16
terrace houses 58
thermal bridging 63, 64
thermal comfort see comfort
thermal mass 59, 61, 62, 63, 68, 73
thermostatic radiator valves 89
thin-layer insulation 88
tile 116–117
TIM see transparent insulation material
timber 63, 64, 66, 76, 77, 110, 112–113
time control 85
timescales 9
timing devices 98
topography 52, 57
translucent elements 65–69
transparent elements 68
transparent insulation materials (TIM) 65, 89
transpired solar collectors (TSC) 93
transportation 48, 54, 110, 114, 115, 116
travel times 48
treatment application methods 77
treatment of water 50, 56
trees and shrubs 55, 57
    see also vegetation
tri-generation 106
triple glazing 66, 96
trombe walls 93
TSC see transpired solar collectors
tungsten halogen lighting 84, 85
turbulence 45, 46

UIA see Union Internationale des Architectes
ultra-sonic sensors 98
unglazed solar collectors 102
Union Internationale des Architectes (UIA) 1

urban strategies 43–50
U-values 64, 66, 67, 92, 96
validation of simulations 128–129
varnishes 76
vegetation 49, 54, 55, 57, 87
venetian blinds 69
ventilated façade insulation 87, 88
ventilation
    atria 71–72
    briefing state 9
    consultant inputs 7
    cross 58, 68, 71, 72
    design 15
    glazing 69
    mechanical systems 80, 81, 82–83
    renovation 90
    site planning 57
vinyl flooring 77
visual delight 2
VOCs see volatile organic components
volatile organic components (VOCs) 76, 119

walls 62, 63–64, 75–76, 87–88, 93
waste
    briefing state 9
    building materials 116, 117
    construction 17, 111
    heat 106
    operational performance 19
    renewable energy 101
    site planning 55–56
    water conservation 50
water
    briefing state 9
    certification 132
    consultant inputs 7
    operational performance 19
    renovation 90
    site planning 55–56
    waste linkages 50
water-based paints 119
weather gaskets 66
weighting systems 131, 132, 134, 135
wetlands 50
whole-building approaches 130, 132
whole-of-system approaches 3
wind 45, 46, 52, 56, 57, 99
windbreaks 56
wind driven ventilation 81
wind energy 99
windows 68–69, 89, 96
    see also glazing
wood 75–76, 112–113
wood flooring 76
woodpellets 101
wood preservatives 120

zero energy transport 48
zinc 118
zoning regulations 47, 48